Jacqueline du Pré

A BIOGRAPHY

CAROL EASTON

Hodder & Stoughton

LONDON SYDNEY AUCKLAND TORONTO

The excerpt from "Sub Contra" is from *The Blue Estuaries* by Louise Bogan.
Copyright © 1968 by Louise Bogan. Reprinted by permission of Farrar,
Straus and Giroux, Inc.
The poem "Give us this night" is reproduced from D. J. Enright, *Paradise
Illustrated*, Chatto & Windus 1978, by permission of Watson, Little Ltd.

British Library Cataloguing in Publication Data

Easton, Carol
   Jacqueline du Pré: a biography.
   1. Cello-playing. du Pré, Jacqueline, 1945–1987
   I. Title
787'.3'0924

ISBN 0-340-42534-2

Published by Hodder and Stoughton,
a division of Hodder and Stoughton Ltd,
Mill Road, Dunton Green, Sevenoaks, Kent TN13 2YA
Editorial Office: 47 Bedford Square, London WC1B 3DP

Photoset by Rowland Phototypesetting Ltd,
Bury St Edmunds, Suffolk

Printed in Great Britain by St Edmundsbury Press Ltd,
Bury St Edmunds, Suffolk

Jacqueline du Pré

This book is for Alice Sommer

Illustrations

Between pages 128 and 129

Jackie at the London Cello School
Jackie accompanied by her mother (Rex Features)
William Pleeth's pupil (Erich Auerbach; by permission of William Pleeth)
With Stephen Bishop (Erich Auerbach)
With William Pleeth (David Farrell)
The Barenboim quintet (Reg Wilson: Camera Press)
Jackie and Daniel at the time of their marriage (*The Times*)
Charcoal drawing by Zsuzsi Roboz (by permission of the artist)
Rehearsing for a Prom (G. Macdomnic)
With Sir John Barbirolli and Suvi Raj Grubb (G. Macdomnic)
With Daniel Barenboim in 1976 (Clive Barda)
The public face (Universal Pictorial Press)
The ecstasy of music (Clive Barda)

Acknowledgments

Although Jacqueline's husband, brother and sister declined invitations to contribute to this biography, other sources did so, in the interests of a fair and complete picture of Jacqueline, with extraordinary generosity. Some of them spoke off the record, for background and to confirm information that originated elsewhere; they know who they are, and they have my gratitude. On the record, I wish to thank John Amis, Lady Evelyn Barbirolli, Clive and Rosie Barda, Kate Beare, Martin Bernheimer, Stephen Bishop-Kovacevich, Harry Blech, Alison Brown, Jennifer Ward Clarke, Patrick Casement, Jill Severs, Trevor Connah, Sonia Corderay, George and Jane Debenham, Norman Del Mar, Madeleine Dinkel, Basil Douglas, Sybil Eaton, Jean Fonda, Rabbi Albert Friedlander, Alexander Goehr, Robin Golding, Dawn Goodwin, Jane Goodwin, Miss Greenslade of Queen's College, Rabbi Hugo Gryn, Mira Henderson, Anthea Hogan, Antony Hopkins, H. E. Humphrey, William Ingrey, Nan Jamieson, Erica Goddard Klien, Hugh Maguire, Suzie Maguire, Sylvia Makower, George Malcolm, Mary May, Zamira Menuhin, Anatole Mines, Anne-Marie Morin, Lucretia Mrosovsky, Christine Newland, Christopher Nupen, Margo Pacey, Jill Pullen, Rosemary Rapaport, Denis Richards, Zsuzsi Roboz, Jack and Linn Rothstein, Aniela Rubinstein, Jeremy Siepmann, Ursula Strebi, Noel Taylor, Peter Thomas (and his mother, Mrs. Mona Thomas), Elizabeth Vanderspar (and her son, Christopher), Julia Wheatley, Ian White and Elizabeth Wilson.

For information about Iris du Pré's early years in Plymouth, thanks to Megan Flemington, Miss L. R. Martin, and John Mitchell.

For details of Jacqueline's early years in Croydon, thanks to Ms. Ashdown, Doris Austin, Sheila Bannister, Ms. M. Bolwell, Barbara Chaput de Saintonge, Anne Conchie, Sister Jean Daniel, Ms. Flinn, Cynthia Isserlis, Joan Johnston, Rebecca Jones, Cindy Kennett, Mary Knight, Ms. Lawrence, Andrea Rivers, Geraldine Roberts, Jessica Saraga, Phyllis Short, Dr. Parthenope Bion Talamo, Leslie Turner, Sara Whitehead and Mary Whorlow.

For providing details of musical events, thanks to archivists David Browner, of the *Jerusalem Post,* and Heinz Berger, of the Israel Philharmonic Orchestra; and to researcher Roberta Smith, of the Faculty of Music, University of Toronto.

For their insights into the physiological and psychological effects of multiple sclerosis, I am grateful to psychologist Shevy Healey, Ph.D., and to neurologists Harry Powell, MD, of the University of California at San

Diego, and George Ellison, MD, of the University of California at Los Angeles. They all stressed the importance of reiterating a point made in the text: that the vast majority of people with multiple sclerosis – an estimated eighty-five per cent – have a mild form of the illness, and are able to continue their lives with only occasional and/or minor disruptions.

My deepest gratitude goes to William Pleeth, his son Anthony and his daughter, Jan Theo; to Dr. Adam Limentani, who agreed to see me because Jacqueline had spoken so freely to so many people about her analysis with him; and to Olga Rejman, Gerard Leclerc and Marcia Zeavin.

For their encouragement during dark days, thanks to Nancy Gayer, Fenella Greenfield, Carol Lee and Frances Ring.

For their fine eyes and sensibilities, thanks to editor Jane Osborn and copy editor Claire Trocmé.

This book would not have been started without the prodding of my agent, Mike Hamilburg; the steady and empathetic support of Ion Trewin, Hodder & Stoughton's editorial director, ensured its completion.

. . . Lest the brain forget the thunder
The roused heart once made it hear, −
Rising as that clamor fell, −
Let there sound from music's root
One note rage can understand,
A fine noise of riven things.
Build there some thick chord of wonder;
Then, for every passion's sake,
Beat upon it till it break.

Louise Bogan, "Sub Contra"

Introduction

Playing lifts you out of yourself, into a delirious plane where you feel abandoned and very happy.

When Jacqueline du Pré played the cello, she knew exactly who she was. From the time she was five years old, she had found in her cello a friend, confidante, playmate, refuge – an unfailing source of solace and a channel through which she could express her deepest feelings. In its music, she was able to simultaneously lose and find herself. It gave her affirmation and was, in the literal meaning of the word – *means of living, sustenance* – her livelihood. But at the age of about seventeen she began to wonder, *Who am I when I'm not playing the cello?* She put the instrument away for a time and wrestled with the question. Then she put the question, unanswered, away, and got on with her phenomenal career.

Ten years later, when her fingers began to lose their feeling, her doctors, unable to find an organic cause, referred her to a psycho-analyst. Two years after that, when it became evident that the problem was indeed physiological – that it was the diabolically unpredictable and incurable multiple sclerosis – she continued in analysis, and the question *Who am I?* became crucial. But although the analysis continued until her death, albeit as little more than a token exercise for the last years, Jacqueline never did resolve the question of her identity apart from the instrument that had defined her. It was as though the double shock of the illness and the loss of the cello had jammed some essential channel, blocking out answers.

Tragedy cannot be quantified, and Jacqueline's loss was incalculable. When I met her, in the summer of 1982, it seemed that she had little left to lose. In the nine years since her final, disastrous public performance, she had lost control of her legs, then her arms, then the rest of her body. She suffered from double vision and tremors of the head so severe that they made reading, or even watching television, impossible. Attended by a live-in nurse, a cook and an as-needed chauffeur, she lived in her bed and her wheelchair. Her marriage had become little more than a financial arrangement. She was unable to dial a telephone, to feed herself, to speak without considerable difficulty, to change her position or to do anything at all for herself – except think. Yet she clung to her landlocked life with a baffling and humbling tenacity.

As a child, Jacqueline had been isolated by her talent. As an adult, however wide her travels, she was confined to the rarefied, insular concert world. Now she lived in the inexorably shrinking world of the invalid. The media had long since enfolded her in a shimmering cocoon of myth; over the original image of the one-time "golden girl" with the fairy-tale career and story-book romance had been superimposed that of the courageous tragic heroine who never complained, who accepted her fate so gracefully that some friends, taking her most frequent expression at face value, called her "Smiley" – a nickname that horrified her analyst. It would be a terrible disservice to her and to other victims of disabling diseases to perpetuate the fiction that she set some impossible standard of saintliness, and it detracts not at all from her indisputable courage to say that in her last years she did complain – that she was, in short, human. She was grateful for the talent she'd been given and the opportunities she'd had to use it – but she could also recite a litany of grievances to which there was simply no reply. Her parents hadn't loved her, she said; her siblings had resented her, and her music had precluded the friendships and accoutrements of a normal childhood. She had received admiration when what she'd craved, and continued to crave, was affection. She was generous, even profligate, with her own affections; she never merely liked people, she *loved* them, and frequently told them so. She wished, she said, that she could love her parents.

In the years after 1982, the only constant relationships in her life were with her analyst, Dr. Adam Limentani, and Ruth Ann Canning, the nurse who cared for her with double-edged devotion. Old friends remained faithful, but few of them had the time and emotional stamina to visit her often. Her parents visited infrequently, her brother and sister scarcely at all until the final weeks.

During the course of researching this book, dozens of people who knew Jacqueline from childhood onward but who at various stages of her life had lost touch told me of their regret at not having re-established contact when they heard of her illness. They spoke of not having wanted to intrude, of feeling that she had moved into a world they assumed was filled with people with whom she had infinitely more in common than with their comparatively ordinary selves.

The consequences of that assumption was that Jacqueline, dreading the prospect of an empty evening, sometimes desperately phoned everyone she could think of, virtually begging them to visit her.

Into the vacuum drifted a motley collection of people drawn to her by curiosity, or by her fame, or by hidden agendas of their own. When offered any diversion, she always accepted. Thus did a noted Scottish psychoanalyst invite himself to her house one evening, drink a large quantity of her brandy, rant melodramatically about the pain her condition was causing him and then, with neither encouragement nor permission, kiss her goodbye on the lips. I saw a titled Englishman, also quite drunk, tell her that her illness was caused by events in a past life, and that a faith healer he knew could make it possible for her to walk. I saw people who obviously cared for her enormously pet and patronise her like a beloved puppy. Perhaps worst of all, I saw people deny her her feelings, scold her for using language that made them uncomfortable, and bombard her with cheery small talk at times when what she wanted to talk about was despair.

I met Jacqueline du Pré on a sunny summer afternoon, when a student of hers invited me to go along to a lesson. She took me to a mews in Knightsbridge, near Harrods – to Jacqueline, "the corner drugstore". The white house was set in a courtyard filled with blooming plants; inside, the spacious sitting-cum-dining room was panelled with dark mahogany and brightened by chintzy fabrics, fresh flowers and sunshine. A closed cello case leaned in eloquent silence against a wall, beside a gleaming grand piano and below a framed photograph of a pensive Edward Elgar. Jacqueline herself dominated the room, sitting very straight in a wheelchair upholstered in green velvet. Her fine blond hair hung, shining and straight, to well below her shoulders. She had a large-boned, squarish face, coarse skin and a rosy, glowing complexion. Her teeth were discoloured and crooked, but her smile was luminous. At thirty-seven, she looked more girl than woman. Her pellucid blue eyes, fringed by pale yellow lashes, drifted independent of each other. They turned in my direction and I asked nervously where she wanted me to sit. She said "Down", and the lesson began.

The student, Marcia Zeavin, was on leave from the San Diego Symphony; she had told me that Jacqueline was an inspired and inspiring teacher, particularly helpful with interpretation. Jacqueline formed her words with great effort and spoke in a strained, low-pitched voice; she cleared her throat with ticlike frequency. Her comments were invariably constructive – try this, try that, more bowing, make it more of a statement – and delivered with patience and great good humour. Violent tremors occasionally forced her right hand rapidly back and forth, beating a tattoo on her stomach. When Marcia played certain slow passages, Jacqueline's hand sawed the air in a grotesque parody of bowing. Disapproval was expressed with mock horror, as "Mein Gott! Sounds like muck sweat!" or "Do you know the word, *coy?*"

There was a good deal of nervous laughter during the lesson. Afterwards, Jacqueline asked if we'd like to hear her "new" record. It was a collection of short pieces she'd recorded in her teens; she was thrilled that EMI had re-released it. It was a rather sombre programme. Of Bruch's *Kol Nidrei* she said, "So virginal. I made that before I became a Jew. I didn't know what a Jew was then. It was just a word in the Bible." She had recorded it, she told us, because her teacher was Jewish. "He called it a *goyische* version." We heard "The Swan", from Saint-Saëns' *The Carnival of the Animals*, a *Fantasie* by Schumann, and Fauré's *Elégie.*★ "It's sad," Marcia whispered. Jacqueline said, "It's an *elegy*. It's *supposed* to be sad. He wrote it after his friend died. He was lucky he could get his feelings out that way."

After each piece she asked, "Was that good? Was that any good?" Assured that it was far better than good, she then asked if we'd like to hear her recording of the Elgar Cello Concerto, recorded in 1970 with her husband, Daniel Barenboim, conducting. "It was my swan song," she said pensively, "but I didn't know it." To listen with her to music that even under ordinary circumstances wrenches the heart was to share her profound and endless mourning. She said that the tone of the cello goes "straight to the crying zone", and that the return to the slow passage in the Elgar "tears me to bits every time I hear it . . . It's like the distillation of a tear." Since 1975, she had not been able to cry.

Jacqueline was in fine form that day. She asked Marcia to retrieve a letter from her handbag; "Would you read it, my love?" The writer was Prince Charles, once a cellist himself and a great admirer of Jacqueline's. "Please excuse this being typed," it began, and went on to thank her affectionately for her congratulations on the birth of Prince William. She said it was for her collection – her fourth letter from Charles. He had come to the house once for dinner, and she had been to the palace to accept her OBE. As she spoke, the chasm between us, already vast, widened in my mind. Finally, she asked

★ Recorded seven years after the other pieces, in 1969.

Marcia to read a poem by D. J. Enright – one I subsequently read to her so many times that I know it by heart. This is the poem:

GIVE US THIS NIGHT

Our Freud which art in heaven
Give us this night our nightly symbol
Give us to dream of serpents and cups
Not of you know what.

Almighty Freud, ruler of night and day,
Give us dreams that are unmistakably dreams
Lead us not into reality.

Deliver us from the conscious,
That we waken bewitched by the workings
Of the Unconscious. Grant us to wake
In pleasure and pride, not terror and sweat.

Give dreams in our time, O Merciful Freud,
That are worthy of thy name
Lest the night be no better than the day.

Before we left, I impulsively asked Jacqueline if she'd like me to come and read to her some time. To my great surprise, she accepted. Thinking that she'd want to hear some old favourites, I asked for requests. "I never read," she said. "I'm a virgin. You decide." I told her I'd try. But after a couple of sessions it became evident that being read to was not what she wanted. She wanted someone to pass the time with. And although my experience, by virtue of birth, history and geography, was light years away from hers, I did have the time. I'd had a brief relationship with a cello long ago, when it was taller than I was, but I knew as little about classical music as Jacqueline knew about writing, the major theme in my life. I didn't know the difference between a fugue and an étude; she claimed never to have heard of *Gone With the Wind*, or Paul Newman, or Charlie Parker. But we discovered that we shared a curiosity about language, an appreciation of the absurd, an impatience with hypocrisy and preten- sion and a prejudice against prejudice, which she called the disease of tiny minds. She was inordinately proud of having converted to Judaism at the time of her marriage, and of the fact that her doctors and most of her friends were Jews. Her mother, she said, was an anti-Semitic Christian. Mine was an anti-Semitic Jew.

Multiple sclerosis has, in some cases, one benign symptom: clinical euphoria, which Jackie called giggleitis. To make her laugh was easy, and tremendously rewarding. She loved dirty jokes, the cruder the better. She loved to play. A favourite playmate was the actor Edward Fox, who arrived breathless one evening, apologising for being late "because our 91-year-old neighbour, Lady Diana Cooper, had a crisis." Without missing a beat, Jackie said, "Her father died?" Her sense of humour was an effective line of defence, and a release as well; if she couldn't cry, at least she could giggle. But there were times when it failed her, when the hopelessness of her predicament overwhelmed her and she would ask, "How can I bear it?" In such moments, the bonds that formed our improbable friendship were formed.

When I met Jacqueline I knew scarcely a soul in London, and it was inconceivable to me that I would stay longer than a few months. Season followed season, and work came my way – but the novelty of England wore thin. I told Jackie that I missed my children more every year. She said, "I'll be your child." With no illusions about my indispensability, I searched for *simpatico* people who might fill the gap in her schedule when I left. I found some, but postponed my departure. I lived in my suitcase, poised for flight – but I stayed.

When I told Jackie about whatever I happened to be working on, she always asked, "Why don't you write about me?" I told her, truthfully, that it would be too damned hard. At the end of 1986 I did leave London, for good, I thought; but in California, I could not get Jackie out of my mind. With that distance between us, my perspective shifted. I returned to London and told her I would write her biography. She was immensely pleased. When she died in October 1987, this book was well under way.

Biographers pick the bones of other people's memories. More than a hundred people generously contributed to this book, speaking candidly of Jacqueline's significance to them and, in some cases, of their own guilt and regrets. Others declined to co-operate on the grounds that she was "no longer herself", and should be remembered only for her music. If the Jacqueline I knew was not herself, who was she? And to say that only her active music-making mattered is to discount more than a third of her life, during which she profoundly influenced a great many strangers, students and friends.

The essential Jacqueline – generous, bright, gifted, with an inordinate capacity for giving and receiving love – never changed. Taught early on that some of her deepest feelings were unacceptable, she learned to camouflage them with a smiling mask. Behind it lay a complex, private and paradoxical personality, parts of which would remain an impenetrable mystery even to its owner. Much of it, however, was revealed to me bit by bit, by Jackie herself, and through the insights and observations of people who played a variety of roles in her life. Gradually, like a photo in solution, this picture emerged.

Part One

1

At the age of three, Jacqueline du Pré set off on her tricycle one morning and was not seen again until nightfall, when the police returned her, quite unperturbed, to her frantic mother. Asked where she had been, she replied, "to see the sea". The sea was fifty miles away. The next morning, she set out again, certain of her destination and determined to get there.

Jacqueline never lived by the sea, but her affinity for it was natural. Her father's family had lived on the windswept Channel Island of Jersey for generations, and her mother's father, William Greep, came from a long line of fishermen who had worked fishing trawlers out of Plymouth Sound.

William and his wife, Maud, lived on the ground floor of a terrace house in Peverell, a quiet, lower-middle-class district of Plymouth. He was a joiner in Devonport dockyard near by; tall, easygoing and personable, he had a good singing voice, although he never displayed it beyond the local church choir and social gatherings. His tiny wife was physically and temperamentally his opposite. From the day of their daughter Iris's birth – June 6th, 1914 – Maud was fiercely ambitious for her only child. When Iris was seven Maud provided her with a piano and, according to her cousin John Mitchell, who lived upstairs, "virtually tied her to it to make her practise".

Iris attended Devonport Secondary School for Girls; schoolmates remember her remarkably upright posture, her sparkling cleanliness and her superior skill at hockey, swimming and everything else she attempted. She had a sunny disposition and great strength and enthusiasm. When a geography mistress once asked her to assist in moving an upright piano, she did so with such gusto that it fell, with much clanging, onto the floor. Physically, she resembled her father – tall, with naturally curly dark hair, greyish-green eyes and a square, dimpled chin. In her teens she was a prefect, and very popular. She performed in all the school concerts, sometimes playing her own compositions. Eventually she attracted the attention of Walter Weekes, Hon. Conductor of the Plymouth Orchestral Society, who took her on as his student. She competed in Plymouth music festivals, gave a series of recitals with a woman cellist at a local mental hospital, and had acquired a reputation as quite a gifted pianist when, at the age of eighteen, she won a scholarship to the London School of Dalcroze Eurhythmics.

Émile Jaques-Dalcroze, a Swiss musician and educationist born in 1865, had devised a system of co-ordinating stylised floating, walking and running movements with certain musical works, for the most part Bach's. Students worked with a pianist, their movements determined by the length of each note; there was much discussion of crotchets, quavers and semiquavers. The purpose of these rhythmic gymnastics was to promote children's posture, physical grace and listening skills.

Iris lived with four other women in a big four-storey house near the school, in Brompton Road. The women, all of them older than Iris, used the house not only as a home but also as a Children's Music Studio, where they taught classes. There were five grand pianos in the house, and two uprights. Iris shared the fourth floor with Mary May, who had studied with Jaques-Dalcroze at his original school in Geneva. Mary assumed a sort of big sister role in Iris's life; she found the younger woman to be "very intelligent, but ignorant of everything in the world except music. She was wide-eyed, natural and totally unsophisticated. She was almost a danger to live with. If she wanted to boil the kettle, she forgot to put the water in. Or you'd meet the bath water coming down the stairs. Her room was a disaster. Her mother spoiled her terribly; she'd never even learned to hang up her clothes. But we all loved her dearly. We enjoyed each other's company hugely and always had a lot to chat about. We discussed the world upside down and sideways."

Iris completed the three-year Dalcroze course in two years, obtained her teacher's certificate and won another scholarship, this time to the Royal Academy of Music. In a letter that appeared in the 1934 Devonport school magazine, she wrote that London was "the most thrilling place to live in, provided one can escape from it at least three times a year". In addition to studying at the Academy, she said, she was teaching eurhythmics in three schools, to children aged three to fifteen years, and enjoyed teaching the youngest most of all.

Academy students led an exclusive life, oblivious of the outside world and bored or baffled by anyone who failed to share their preoccupation with music. Margo Pacey, who knew Iris at the Academy, remembers her "very strong, almost Rossetti face and big, honest eyes. She was an open-air sort of person, with a tremendous laugh." Like Iris, Margo studied piano with Eric Grant and composition with Theodore Holland, whom she describes as "an English aristocrat, not the sort of person you generally meet in the musical world. He was a very rich man – civilised, broad-minded, avuncular, a great friend to many young musicians. He used to invite students and friends of his who were interested in music and all the arts to big parties in a wonderful music room at the top of his fabulous house in Kensington. At the end of the evening he'd send us home in taxis. He was a big, slow-moving man, about sixty at that time, but he seemed terribly old to us. He had a young wife, half German, just a little older than Iris and me. She used to copy his scores in a most beautiful copperplate."

During her five years at the Academy, Iris shone. She won awards and prizes for piano, composition, harmony, aural training and musicianship. In 1934 she competed at the Plymouth Music Festival and won first prize: a piano. She composed ballets, one of which was given an amateur performance in London. To support herself, she taught piano and eurhythmics at schools in Kensington, Letchworth and East Grinstead, and also at the Children's Music Studio in Brompton Road, where she remained happily ensconced. She also taught – for a pittance, but some prestige – as a deputy professor at the Academy, substituting for regular instructors who were away. It was a hectic schedule that left little time for social life, but Iris didn't seem to mind. Mary May sometimes took her to her family's home in Earls Court, where Mary's mother unofficially adopted her. Mary recalls that a lodger in her parents' home developed a considerable crush on Iris. "His name was Joseph Luns; he was a young Dutchman with a face like an elongated egg and so tall, about six foot four inches, that he had to bend over to talk to you. He later became Foreign Secretary for Holland."★ But Iris was interested only in music and in her musical friends; Luns never stood a chance with her.

Through Mrs. May, Iris also met Violet Becker, who would become a pivotal person in her life. Mrs. Becker was extremely wealthy, childless, and patron to a number of young musicians. Mrs. May knew that Iris's finances were strained, and suggested that Mrs. Becker invite the young woman to play at one of her glittering parties. When she did, it was such a success that Mrs. Becker arranged a recital for Iris at the Wigmore Hall – another success. But Violet Becker's fateful influence on Iris's life was her offer to subsidise a course of study with Egon Petri.

★ In 1971, Joseph Luns became Secretary-General of NATO.

Petri was a widely-acclaimed German-Dutch pianist who had studied with Busoni and taught at the Manchester College of Music. He was admired for his profound, powerful style, particularly when he played Bach and Liszt, the big pieces that were in fashion at the time. Iris had big hands, loved big pieces and admired Petri greatly; she said as much to Violet Becker one day at lunch. Violet said, "Would you like to go to the summer course that he's giving in Poland?" Iris, who had never been anywhere other than Devon and London, was thrilled. The year was 1938 – politically, an historic summer – but politics would have nothing to do with the events that would irrevocably change the tone, texture and direction of Iris's life.

In an odd little book called *When Poland Smiled*, Derek du Pré wrote obliquely of his courtship of Iris Greep. He had recently become the first du Pré permanently to leave the island on which his ancestors had lived since the Norman invasion of William the Conqueror in 1066. Derek had attended Victoria College in Jersey and then, instead of joining the family's prosperous perfume business, gone to work in a bank in St. Helier, the island's capital. In 1936 he had travelled modestly in France and in Czechoslovakia, where a young violinist he met on a train casually invited him to visit the Polish Ukraine. Two years later, despite reports of German troops massing on the Czechoslovakian frontier, du Pré accepted the invitation.

When Poland Smiled is a young man's enthusiastic and, considering the times, strangely apolitical account of an idyllic holiday. Du Pré was charmed by everything he saw – people, customs, scenery. In Cracow he saw the first Jews of his life, and found them to be an exotic novelty. He wrote of walking through the Polish countryside playing his small accordion, encountering other travellers with whom he sang Bavarian yodelling songs. At a villa near Zakopane, a climbing centre in the Carpathian mountains, he met the "nice girl full of youthful verve" who was studying with Egon Petri.

Du Pré wrote of climbing with Iris through August snow past tiny shepherd huts, accompanied by the tinkling of sheep bells far below. In a hut at the summit they joined about forty-five climbers of various nationalities who slept in rows on the floor of one large room. "Full moon flooding down the valley; great black shadows on the mountainside seemed to stand out, and patches of snow appeared to be great white holes while far, far away we could see the moonlight reflected from tiny lakes. The only sounds were those of a distant waterfall and an occasional fall of snow." On another day, exploring a valley, "Iris and I played mouth organ and tin whistle for peasants

. . . It was by no means unusual to meet musicians walking in the fields and valleys with violins and cellos which they strapped to their persons. The peasants would gather round and dance mazurkas and polkas until they dropped with fatigue."

In this romantic setting, it would have been difficult for a young couple *not* to fall in love. The book contains a photo of them in peasant costumes, gazing into each other's eyes. Du Pré was thirty, six years older than Iris, and strikingly handsome – tall and fair, with pale blue eyes. By the time he left Zakopane, they had agreed that Iris would contribute a chapter on Polish and Ukrainian folk music to his book. And when Iris returned to London some weeks later, it was clear to Mary May that although du Pré had not declared his intentions, it was Iris's intention to marry him.

Derek was a frequent visitor at the Brompton Road house, but he remained firmly uncommitted; the fact that his cultivated, well-to-do family would think the daughter of a joiner an unsuitable wife would probably have been a consideration. Nevertheless, once England entered the war, time was a luxury no one could afford. On July 25th, 1940, without notifying either of the families, the couple were married in the Kensington Register Office. It was a quiet affair; the only witnesses were a court clerk and Mary May, who carried a large bunch of anemones. According to their marriage licence, they were already living together at 35 Nevern Place, SW5, in Earls Court.

Derek joined the Grenadier Guards, trained at Caterham and Sandhurst, and received his officer's commission. Iris kept up her musical activities. No longer a student herself, she continued to teach. With Winnie Copperwheat, a viola player she knew from the Academy, she gave recitals at music clubs. She played solo piano on wireless broadcasts from London and from the west of England. Some of the musicians who knew her at that time believe that she was extremely ambitious but that despite her talent and dedication, she lacked the necessary presence for a successful concert career. Mary May believes that from the time Iris met Derek, her only ambition was to be his wife and have his children. At any rate, in the autumn of 1941, while Derek was still in training, she became pregnant. The baby, a girl, was called Hilary.

Two years later, Iris told Mary May's mother that she'd been trying unsuccessfully for another pregnancy and was getting injections from a pregnant mare to help things along. The outcome, not necessarily of the injections but of her attempts to conceive, was a second daughter, Jacqueline Mary, born in Oxford on January 26th, 1945. Her godparents included Mrs. Theodore Holland, wife of Iris's former composition professor at the Academy, and Lord Lascelles (now Lord Harewood), whom Derek had met at an Officer Cadets Training Unit course in 1942.

After the war the family lived for a while in Camberley, in Surrey. In the spring of 1948 a son, Piers, was born. Derek took a job in the City, editing an accounting journal, and the family settled in Purley, a suburb south of London. Purley was a desirable upper-middle-class area, originally a planned community of tree-lined streets and substantial turn-of-the-century houses with large gardens. The du Prés lived in a big rambling house at 14 Bridle Way, convenient to schools. With three small children, Iris, whose own mother had taught her nothing whatever about keeping house, learned to cook and to make clothes for the children – but music was never far from her mind. It is not surprising that she should look for signs of musical talent in her offspring. What *was* somewhat surprising was that all three of them showed a definite aptitude for music. Hilary learned the piano easily, and played with great flair. Piers eventually took up the clarinet and had a fine singing voice, although he was never motivated to develop either talent. But it was Jackie in whom Iris saw the most exciting promise. Years later she would tell interviewers that at nine months the baby had repeated rhythms tapped out on her high chair, and that at eighteen months she had sung the tune – not the words – of "Baa, Baa, Black Sheep" all by herself. Just before Jackie's fourth Christmas she sang "Away in a Manger" to her mother so perfectly and with such feeling that "I was very conscious that there was a great deal more to it than just a little girl singing. [It was] quite devoid of the slightest precociousness . . . a perfectly rounded little performance."

When Jackie was four, she was able to pick out pieces on the piano simply from having overheard her sister's lessons. But the crucial musical event in her childhood, which she later recalled with perfect clarity, occurred just before her fifth birthday. "I remember being in the kitchen at home, looking up at the old-fashioned wireless. I climbed onto the ironing board, switched it on, and heard an introduction to the instruments of the orchestra. It must have been a BBC *Children's Hour*. It didn't make much of an impression on me until they got to the cello, and then . . . I fell in love with it straightaway. Something within the instrument spoke to me, and it's been my friend ever since." She told her mother, "I want to make that sound."

Naturally, Iris looked at once for a teacher. She had heard about Mrs. Garfield Howe, whose son-in-law, the pianist Denis Mathews, she knew from her Academy days. Anna Howe was a Russian-born

Jewess – stocky, with dark hair and eyes and beautiful, well-kept hands. Her daughter, now Mrs. Mira Henderson, describes her as "a good musician in a totally mad way. She wasn't a particularly good pianist or composer, but she had an extraordinary ability to make people play. She believed she could teach any instrument – and she did! When Iris brought Jackie to my mother and said she wanted to learn the cello, my mother, who knew *nothing* about the cello, said, 'Oh, of course I'll teach her!'"

Mrs. Howe appeared at the du Pré house for Jackie's first lesson bearing what Jackie called "this whopping creature" – a full-sized cello, far too big for the child. Jackie played it standing up, like a double bass. Mira had a daughter, Rachel, who was about Jackie's age and was studying the cello at the London Violoncello School. Mira was herself a cellist, and had written out "a little book with pictures and rhymes to go with little tunes to play with one finger for my Rachel. My mother said, 'Just lend me your book.' She gave it to Jackie's mother. I'm not saying she copied it, but she made a tremendous success of writing similar tunes with poems and illustrations from my idea. She eventually published them in a book, *Songs for my Cello and Me.*★ It's been the basic book for starting many a child on the cello."

The book was comprised of tunes and drawings Iris wrote at night, when the children were asleep. Jackie was thrilled when she woke to find a new piece, with words and pictures, beside her bed. When she had mastered it and was ready to produce a new sound, Iris would write a song that introduced that sound. In the morning, Jackie would leap out of bed and rush downstairs to play the new tune with her mother. The words might be as simple as "C, G, D, A, We'll have lots of fun today," but each one was a new, and achievable, challenge. "Jackie's First 'Cello Book" is dated March 1950, and contains fourteen songs. Two months later she was ready for a second book.

The cello is a difficult instrument to play, particularly for a child. It requires all the delicacy of control and perfection of ear that a violin does, and greater muscular control, as well. The strings are thicker and harder to press down than a violin's, and the distances to reach between the notes are longer. On Jackie's oversized (for her) instrument it was an especially long reach to the high notes, but she managed everything with astonishing speed. Mary May visited Iris just after Jackie began learning the cello. "Iris asked her to play for me, and I've never forgotten it. Jackie sat in her little chair with her

★ Followed by *Songs for my Fiddle and Me* and *Hilary's Songs*.

music in front of her, and the moment she got hold of the instrument she was kind of transfixed, as if she was mesmerised! She was no longer a child of five!" Indeed, her affinity for the instrument and her instinctive feeling for phrasing verged on the preternatural. She knew even then, she said many years later, that she was "pretty good" just by seeing the surprise on people's faces when she played. "I had a great sense of pitch, so I knew how to find my note and was determined to play it. Playing the cello was the most natural thing in the world for me to do. I loved the actual physical feeling of making the notes, and the feeling of the hair on the string. I marvelled that these two things could bring about a sound so absolutely fantastic." Like a bird thrown into the air, she had found her element.

After three months of Mrs. Howe's idiosyncratic instruction, Iris decided, much to the teacher's irritation, that the child needed "proper" cello lessons. An audition was arranged with Herbert Walenn, who ran the London Violoncello School. Many distinguished cellists had studied with Walenn as children. He was a small, white-haired Edwardian, always impeccably dressed; a short leg caused him to limp. His school was in Nottingham Place, near the Academy. Like Walenn, it was a nineteenth-century anachronism – dimly lit and formal, with a few withered palms in pots, green lino on the floors and signed photographs of past pupils on the panelled walls. One of Walenn's assistants, Alison Dalrymple, was considered to be the finest children's cello teacher in London. Walenn decided that Jackie would study with her.

In her own inimitable fashion, "Dally" was every bit as eccentric as Anna Howe. She was a large South African woman, remembered vividly by Mira Henderson as "rather bulldoggish, with an extraordinary hairstyle – little dyed blond sausages all over her head, as though they'd been put in rollers and never brushed out. She was terribly illogical in the way she showed a child how to hold a bow or play a tune, but she was a born musician when it came to teaching children. She had a lovely voice and an absurd, exaggerated sort of manner. She made a lot of jokes, which both she and the children found extremely funny. Every child who was learning the cello seemed to be learning it from her, and all of them adored her."

If a child is to have a professional career playing a stringed instrument, five is considered the optimum age to begin. A five-year-old's hands and muscles are still very small and delicate, however, and it is important that lessons take place in an informal, relaxed way, so the child learns to play without unnecessary tension. At five, a gifted child is very serious in wanting to learn – but if the teacher is too exacting, the child may never express his or her own ideas and may merely try to copy the teacher. Alison Dalrymple seemed to know all this instinctively, although she lacked formal training and had never been a player herself. She told Iris to replace Jackie's grown-up cello with a smaller instrument that conformed to those of the other children – a great blow to Jackie's pride. Lessons took place once a week. At the end of each term, Miss Dalrymple organised a little concert; the children would dress up and play their little pieces to each other, and then have a party. Mira Henderson remembers "all those little things sitting there, a whole crew of musicians' children: Sidney Griller's son, Watson Forbes's son, Vivien Joseph's. The tiny cellos were very difficult to tune because the pegs were so close together.

"Little girls at the London Violoncello School were the first to be taught to sit in the 'masculine' way. Until the Second World War, the cello had been very much a man's instrument; it was considered rather immodest to play the cello. Girls were taught to sit with one leg discreetly tucked under the instrument; the right knee dipped down in a sort of side-saddle position. It was awkward and illogical, and terrible for the back. But the first women who played with their knees sticking out and the cello between them were considered hussies."

The programme of a school recital given on July 5th, 1952, has Jacqueline du Pré performing Schumann's *Andante*, Schubert's *Moment Musical*, a "traditional" piece with a quartet, and three "short trios". Another student, Winifred Beeston, played "Singing and Swinging" from Iris Greep's *Songs for my Cello and Me*. It was obvious to Mira Henderson even then that Jackie was the star "by a long, long way. She was a plump little girl with fairly pale blue eyes. She didn't say much; it was mother who did the speaking up, and I think that other little girls found it difficult to relate to her. But everyone was impressed by her extraordinary ear and her ability to listen with intense concentration, aware of the sounds she produced."

2

I n *Nature's Gambit*, a ten-year study of six child prodigies, psychologist David Henry Feldman writes that there have always
been child prodigies, and that they have always been perceived
as somehow unnatural, and treated with a mixture of fear, contempt,
jealousy and awe; the very word *prodigy* originally meant something
abnormal or monstrous. Dr. Feldman describes the shock to a family
when the extreme talent that presages a prodigy appears: "It demands
nothing less than the willingness of one or both parents to give up
almost everything else to make sure that the talent is developed. This
may be at the expense of the other children; even if a sibling is equally
talented, it may simply not be possible to do what must be done for
both children."

If Hilary had been gifted in anything other than music, her life
would have been immensely easier. Unfortunately for the entire
family, her musical talent rivalled her sister's. Iris's friends were all
aware of it. Violinist Rosemary Rapaport, who knew Iris at the
Academy, remembers a mutual friend telling her that Iris Greep had
two fantastic children – both geniuses. They were five and seven at
the time. According to pianist Doris Austin, "When Hilary was
seven, it was she who seemed to be the shining star." After Jackie
took up the cello, Hilary turned from the piano to the violin and then
to the flute, which remained her primary instrument. Rosemary
Rapaport considered her to be amazingly good at the piano and "as
glittering as a flautist can be. But the flute isn't a glamorous instrument. It can't compete with the cello. And Iris put all her eggs into
Jackie's basket."

Both girls performed on BBC children's television programmes,
but not together. In her only public statement about her sister – on
a radio tribute to Jacqueline on her fortieth birthday – Hilary said,
"We never practised together and rarely played together. We irritated
each other. We did some trios with my mother, but it was more of
a fight than a joy. Perhaps we were jealous of each other. When
people came to the house to listen to her, I remember hiding in the
kitchen. I don't remember feeling jealous, but perhaps I had felt it

for so long that it seemed normal. She didn't talk much; she talked through her cello. She was better with adults than with children. People used to ask me, 'How is your wonderful sister?' "

At five, Jackie entered the kindergarten at Commonweal Lodge, a private, genteel, old-fashioned school in Purley. Hilary was already a student there; teachers remember both children as sparkling, full of life and perfectly normal, fond of sport and games. Junior School teacher Cynthia Gosnell found Jackie to be "a very nice little girl, with nothing at all unusual about her. We had a concert once and she brought her cello and looked absolutely lost sitting behind it on the platform. If you had said, That girl is going to be one of the most outstanding cellists of our day, I'd never have believed it. It was Hilary who was thought to be the musical one. She was really good at the piano!" Miss Ashdown, then secretary of the school, says, "We weren't aware that Jackie was musical until Mrs. du Pré told us she wouldn't have so much school time because of her music work. The school didn't approve; it believed that children should get general education before they specialised."

Perhaps because the school took that attitude – or because it seemed a good idea to separate the two sisters, or because Jackie met Croydon High School's stiff entry requirements and Hilary did not – Iris transferred Jackie to Croydon High School for Girls when she was eight. The school, founded in 1874, is one of the oldest in Britain dedicated to girls' education. The standards were higher than those of Commonweal Lodge, the staff better qualified, the equipment superior. Students were not accepted unless their IQs exceeded 120. Miss Bolwell, the headmistress, tested Jackie and assessed her as "nothing extraordinary, but with a good IQ. Her father brought her for the interview and test. He told us that her gift was musical."

Croydon High School consisted of a row of red brick Victorian buildings which had been built as private homes in what is now central Croydon, adjacent to Purley. The girls wore navy blue jerseys with green-and-white stripes round the cuffs and the V-neck; navy-blue tunics; bottle-green ties; white shirts, and navy-blue velour hats with white bands, on which were pinned green metal badges in the shape of the school symbol, an ivy leaf. Jackie's first teacher was Miss Welton, now Mrs. Flinn. "There were only about twenty girls in my form, so I knew them all well. We met in a small house called The Elms; it had six classrooms. I taught geography, art, needlework, history, nature studies, English and maths. Miss Bolwell taught Scripture, and Miss Morgan, music. Jackie played the triangle in the percussion band. She used to show me her mother's little drawings on her cello exercises. They were very professional, bright and lively; she was thrilled with them.

"On wet days, or while they waited for second sitting for lunch, Jackie would entertain the other girls in the hall, playing songs from *Hans Christian Andersen* on the piano. The children sat cross-legged on the floor and sang along; we were her first audience. The Elms had a very relaxed atmosphere. At the end of the school day the parents waited at the bottom of the stairs, so when we came down with the children we got to know and chat with them. Jackie and her mother laughed a lot together; they seemed almost like sisters, quite devoted to each other and happy. I remember children going to Jackie's house for parties."

Schoolmate Parthenope Bion, who attended the parties, recalls that unlike other children's parties, all the games were musical. "During tea, someone started to tinkle a spoon or a fork against their cup or glass and soon, under Mr. du Pré's direction, we were all drinking tiny amounts, or having them added, to make the right notes to play 'Happy Birthday' on our tea cups. All good, healthy fun – but was Jackie ever allowed to do things which weren't musical? Or was she in the same sort of position that pipe smokers find themselves in, that of *always* being given gifts which have to do with smoking, as though they never did anything else?" Mary Knight, also a guest at the parties, remembers, "Her cello was hanging on the wall. It was pointed out to us as Jackie's cello. We knew she was good at it – I played my recorder with her, and somebody said she had perfect pitch – but that didn't mean anything to us, really. To us, she was an ordinary girl who played the cello. She was a very big girl with short, straight, fair hair. I remember teachers rebuking her for her big handwriting, and for signing herself Jackie instead of Jacqueline. Up until she won the Suggia prize, she had a very normal sort of life."

In 1953, Herbert Walenn died. It was discovered that although he had kept up all the concerts and other traditions at the school, it had been insolvent for some time. He had told no one, not even his staff, and had kept up appearances even as he saw it all slipping away. Within a year of his death, the London Violoncello School closed. Alison Dalrymple continued her teaching elsewhere, but Iris felt that Jackie had gone as far as she could go with "Dally" and needed someone who played, as well as taught, the cello. She consulted her musical friends and as a result of their suggestions and some degree of serendipity, decided on William Pleeth.

★

William Pleeth was then thirty-eight – two years younger than Iris – and had already achieved a distinguished career. Born a Londoner into a musical family of Polish Jews, he had been, like Jackie, a prodigy. His natural talent for the cello was obvious by the time he was seven, and he had studied with Herbert Walenn at the London Violoncello School at the age of ten. He hated "ordinary" school and was allowed to leave it at thirteen, when he won a scholarship to study in Leipzig with Julius Klengel, one of the most respected cellists of his generation, whose students had included Feuermann and Piatigorsky. Pleeth received rave reviews for his début at the Leipzig Conservatory. The following year he left Klengel and Germany, and never had another lesson.

Pleeth's London début in 1933 led to a successful career as a soloist but he says, "I never had the bug for that lonely, peripatetic life. You spend hours alone working out your concerto – Elgar, Dvořák, Schumann, whatever. You formulate this great work of art in your mind and you are ready to give *your* interpretation of what you want it to be – and what happens? You arrive, you play it with a so-called great conductor, and all you have is a bash through."

Despite his disdain for solo work, music was written especially for him and also for him and his wife, pianist Margaret Good – with whom he began playing sonatas in 1938 – by Edmund Rubbra and a number of other composers. In the early Fifties, with Eli Goren, he formed the Allegri Quartet. Chamber music, "the working out of a piece of music with three other human beings whom you have affection for", became and remains his passion. He had done a bit of teaching while in the Army, and continued to do so after the war. Gradually he accepted fewer solo engagements and took on more students. When Iris phoned him in 1954 to ask if he would listen to her daughter play, he had been professor of cello and chamber music at the Guildhall School of Music for seven years.

Even today, in his seventies, Pleeth overwhelms students at his master classes with his energy, his flamboyant gestures and his rhetoric, rife with *sweethearts* and *darlings*. The ten-year-old Jackie had never met anyone remotely like the dynamic, dramatic character who greeted her for the first time at the front door of his north London home. Pleeth was of medium height with a chunky body, thin legs and muscular arms. He had dark hair, a ruddy complexion, prominent nose, hooded brown eyes and the large, capable hands of a carpenter. He spoke in a deep, powerful voice, with a thoroughly un-English lack of inhibition; his warmth and vitality charged the air. To the child from proper Purley, in whose home voices were never raised and emotions hidden like shameful secrets, Pleeth was more than a breath of fresh air, he was the whole outdoors. He would become her "cello daddy", dearer to her than her own father and the most enduring love of her life.

In the light, airy music room, Iris sat at the Steinway grand and accompanied her daughter in some small pieces. Pleeth, who had never before taught a young child, was touched and excited by the "simple little lass with blond hair. She played with a calm confidence and a degree of concentration that would be extraordinary in an adult. There was nothing precocious about her; she came uncorrupted. Alison Dalrymple had given her a wonderful grounding, but she hadn't yet been given enough musical food for her whole little tiny being to get involved in." It was agreed that he would give her hour-long lessons on Wednesdays and Saturdays. From the beginning, "It was like hitting a ball across to a wall; the more you hit, the more it would return. I could see the potential quite strongly on the first day. As the next few lessons went on it just sort of unfolded itself like a flower, so that you knew that everything was possible. The speed with which she tackled every assignment was like letting a horse off the reins."

Within a few months, Pleeth recommended Jackie for the prestigious Suggia Gift. The Portuguese Guilhermina Suggia, born in 1888 and acknowledged as the greatest woman cellist of her time, had taken up the cello at a time when few women in her country sought careers of any kind, let alone playing what was then considered a masculine instrument. She began playing publicly at the age of seven, led the cello section of the Porto City Symphony at twelve, and went to study with Klengel in Leipzig at thirteen. At seventeen she made her solo début and met Pablo Casals, who became her teacher and with whom she had a turbulent and ultimately disastrous love affair. Casals was older by twelve years and had a highly developed sense of propriety; the young woman's volatile, sometimes violent, temperament both attracted and repelled him. Although Suggia lived and worked with Casals in Spain for seven years and was even billed on some programmes as Mme. Casals-Suggia, she never accepted his proposals of marriage.

In 1912 Suggia ended her relationship with Casals and moved to England, where she had an impressive concert career. Ironically, she is probably better-known today as the fiercely beautiful subject of Augustus John's portrait of her than for her music. John painted her in profile in a long, low-cut crimson velvet gown that set off her jet-black hair and creamy skin, holding, but not playing, her cello in

34

the side-saddle position. In 1923 she returned to Portugal, married a doctor and remained there until she died in 1950, at the age of sixty-two. *The Times* obituary read, "For a time, she and Casals were the world's leading cellists . . . Her technique and control were of a classical purity, but her interpretations were animated by a warmth of temperament and latent passion that belonged to her by birth and nationality. Something of the beauty and power of her phrasing is conveyed in the well-known portrait of her by Augustus John, since they were derived not only from her bow arm, but by her total absorption in what she was playing."

Suggia specified in her will that her Stradivarius cello be sold to finance a private trust fund, called the Suggia Gift, to be administered by the Arts Council of Great Britain and awarded to exceptionally talented cello students of any nationality under the age of twenty-one who possessed the potential of first-class performers. Under the chairmanship of conductor Sir John Barbirolli, himself a one-time cellist and student of Herbert Walenn's, a panel of illustrious musicians was formed.

The first audition took place at the Royal Academy of Music on July 25th, 1956. Jackie, aged eleven, was the youngest of the five applicants. The event was an administrator's nightmare, for despite the carefully timed schedules, throngs of applicants, accompanists, parents and teachers milled around backstage. Theoretically, each applicant was to perform for twelve minutes and leave the stage before the next one emerged from the Green Room – but timetables meant nothing to Barbirolli, who was frequently moved to interrupt with comments and advice from the back of the hall.

Although pre-performance nerves are common to most soloists, whatever their age and calibre, it would not be until years later – and then with good reason – that Jacqueline would anticipate performing with anything but joy. At a previous competition – a music festival at Central Hall, Westminster, when she was eight and some competitors more than twice her age – she had skipped down the hall outside the room where the judging was taking place so lightheartedly that someone said, "It's easy to see you've just had your turn." Excited but not at all anxious, she said, "Oh, no! I'm just *going* to play!" She had performed a composition of her mother's, and won first prize.

Barbirolli read Pleeth's letter of recommendation to the panel: "She is the most outstanding cellistic and musical talent I have met so far, to which she adds incredible maturity of mind. I am of the opinion that she will have a great career and deserves every help to this end." The conductor regarded the child with interest. He helped her to tune her instrument and then took a seat at the back of the hall next to another panellist, instrumentalist Lionel Tertis. Accompanied by her mother, Jackie played a piece by Vivaldi. She was no more than two minutes into the piece when Barbirolli turned to Tertis and said, "This is it!"

Jackie went on to play pieces by Saint-Saëns and Boccherini. Pianist Gerald Moore, who was present although not on the panel, and who had often partnered Suggia, would later write, "A little girl with flaxen hair played to us, nay attacked us. She stood hardly as tall as her cello. Her auditors were electrified." Barbirolli's notes read:

> Vivaldi: certainly talented. Nice tone. Good intonation.
> 'Swan': very immature musically. Not very imaginative.
> Boccherini: more advanced technically than musically. Feel that she should now really get down to her cello.

The panel recommended an Award of £175 to cover the cost of two lessons a week with Pleeth, under the auspices of the Guildhall School – on condition that Jackie devote at least four hours a day to practice while still continuing her general education. The headmistress of Croydon High School agreed to this proviso. Iris later told a *Guardian* reporter, "It was enlightened of Croydon High School to let Jackie drop such studies as needlework. The usual attitude to music in British schools is that one may take it as a hobby until one has passed school certificate – and by that age it's too late for most children to make a career."

The Suggia put Jackie irrevocably out of sync with her peers and ended any semblance of a normal childhood. To children, especially as they approach puberty, all differences are damning. The award propelled Jackie out of her classmates' orbit into a world where there was no time for the shared rituals of adolescence. Miss Margaret Adams, the obliging headmistress, arranged a special timetable for her. Iris would drive her to school after her early morning practice (in deference to the neighbours she waited till 7.30 to begin), drive her home at lunchtime for more practice and return her to school for an hour or two before collecting her and then, twice a week, drive into London for her lessons with Pleeth. Instead of learning science with the other girls she was given instruction in German, which she hated, but which Miss Adams and Iris agreed was more appropriate for a potential international soloist. Even had there been time for gym or games, possible damage to her hands would have ruled that out.

Throughout her adult life, Jacqueline maintained to friends and interviewers that school had been a misery for her. She told of children dancing in a circle round her chanting "We hate Jackie" and said; "When I left, at the age of ten, it was a golden day." So it was surprising to discover that she was remembered by a number of classmates and teachers and listed in school records as a student, albeit a part-time one, at Croydon High School until she was fourteen – and after that for a year at Queen's College in Harley Street in central London. The girls who were considered to be closest to her – although only one of them saw herself in that way – are thoughtful, not insensitive women – a journalist, an editor, a psychoanalyst, a social worker. None can recall ever witnessing or hearing of Jackie being treated badly, let alone tormented – although Miss Welton concedes that "Children are very much in a pack, and students in Senior School won't accept anyone different. Partly it's their jealousy of success, partly their fear of the unknown." If the chanting incident did occur, it would have been traumatic for any child – immeasurably so for one of Jackie's sensibility. If she imagined or even invented it, the feelings of rejection it represented were achingly real.

Gifted children need friendship just as other children do; they need acceptance for the individuals that they are, and are becoming. Instead of acceptance, Jacqueline got admiration. After her award was announced at prayers, Miss Hunt, the music teacher, told the class, "You are all going to say when you're older that you went to school with Jacqueline du Pré." She was right, of course; even as Jacqueline came to disclaim her connection with the school, the school clung to its connection with her.

Her demeanour at school remained cheerful, friendly and self-sufficient. At nine she had moved out of The Elms into Homestead, a different and much more formal house. Her teacher there, Jean Daniel, found her to be "a lovely child, very peaceful and friendly, full of fun. Gentle, and slowish in her manner. She seemed happy enough." It appeared to classmate Andrea Barron that "Everybody liked her, nobody ever thought to be jealous. She never showed off or behaved as though she thought she was special. She was the star at some of our school concerts; she played 'The Swan' once. Everyone said, 'Isn't she wonderful!' But I can't remember her having any special close friend. She seemed not to need anybody. We really never knew her. There was no bonding; we never took her into our lives. We left her alone on her pedestal."

Anne Conchie, who was two years behind Jackie, says, "I was always surprised when she said she'd had virtually no schooling. It was a traditional school, stuffy by modern standards, but they went out of their way to help her, to arrange for her to put her cello studies first and to fit her other studies around that. The school acknowledged that she was not exactly one of us but that there was a connection, and that we were to be proud of her. And we *were* proud of her."

Leslie Turner, another classmate, agrees: "We all thought she was a pretty good thing. But I can't remember anyone being closer to her than I was, and I wasn't what you'd call close. I used to play recorder with her at her house. The family seemed close, but I didn't know them intimately. I have a strong sense of Jackie's never seeing herself as outrageously talented or special. I remember the music teacher asking if she had perfect pitch, and playing notes behind her back for her to identify. But looking back, I can see distance between her and other people. She was so busy with practice, she never had time to hang about with the other kids."

Parthenope Bion recalls, "We passed as friends and I think that we thought of ourselves as such. I was invited to one of Jackie's very first – if not *the* first, apart from the school things – public concerts. I think that her parents were anxious not to push her as a 'child prodigy', so this concert, which she gave at about twelve, was not very much publicised. She played part of the programme and the rest was a women's choir. But I don't remember ever playing with her during break. I don't know what games she liked. I think she was always 'elsewhere', unconsciously occupied with music, and this cut her off from other children. I suspect that she was extremely lonely, that she found it extremely hard to make friends with, or even simply to meet, people who could get into touch with her, and that her contemporary schoolmates were simply not up to understanding her most important aspect. I suspect also that her family may have contributed to her isolation by pushing the music side too much. It was as though they said, 'You speak only Icelandic? Good, we are going to give you the best teachers in the world of that language, all your books will be in that tongue, the instructions on your toys, your prayers, your diet.' Forgetting that their daughter was actually living in Purley and going to school in Croydon, where only a very few people even knew where Iceland was, let alone that one could actually get there."

Another classmate, Jessica Saraga, says, "I don't suppose she ever worked out who we all were. We all knew she was a great musician. I felt that she wasn't really there in spirit. Watching her play you could tell *why* she wasn't really there and where she really was. She came alive when she played."

The extraordinary change that occurred when Jacqueline entered a world that was entirely her own intimidated adults and children alike. Rebecca de Saintonge, the only person who considers herself to have been a close friend of Jackie's at Croydon High School, says, "She frightened us. She was so ordinary in her everyday life but when she played her cello, she was transformed. The violence of her personality was difficult for a young person to understand."

Between the ages of seven and thirteen, Jacqueline spent a good deal of time with Rebecca. When Jackie stayed overnight at the de Saintonges', she would improvise on the piano and Rebecca would dance. To Mrs. de Saintonge, Jackie seemed entirely without strain in those years. "She was one of the nicest children I ever met – well-mannered, amiable, not at all temperamental. She was probably the dullest of all Rebecca's friends – I suppose because she was all music. It was rather frightening to see her playing, she was so fierce and dramatic. I remember her coming to a party of Rebecca's when she was about nine. She looked interested, but she just sat and watched. Her mother rang up the next day to thank me; she said Jackie didn't have many opportunities like that."

Rebecca often stayed overnight at the du Pré house. "I felt that they hadn't much money. A desk in the centre of a large playroom at the top of the house seemed to be a prize possession. Jackie was allowed to do her homework on it. I wasn't an achiever in school, and Jackie was always very sweet and tender with me. Once when we were doing exams she said, 'Don't worry Becky, my father was never good at anything at school except drawing straight lines.'

"We were very close until we were about thirteen. Jackie was the first person who told me about periods; her mother had told her. We were both horrified and amazed. Then when I got interested in boys, Jackie got more and more involved in her music. We never shared our feelings. Parthenope and Andrea and I were all used to communicating, but not with Jackie. We couldn't communicate with her through music, and she couldn't communicate with words. Our interests – boys, mostly – didn't seem to be part of her life. She was so serious about her music, she made me feel rather silly.

"After she moved to London I know she was lonely. Her mother rang up and told us so. But I was nervous about seeing her. She was becoming famous and I didn't want to appear to be friendly just for that reason. I was already so far removed from her world, I thought she'd find me boring. Eventually, I lost touch.

"I had so much love for Jackie, but I was afraid of her. She was such a strange creature. When I heard about her illness I hadn't seen her for years, but I used to wake up in the night thinking about her. I prayed for her every night for two years. But to this day, I have no idea who she was."

3

N o one can explain exactly what drives a prodigy's engine – what motivates a child to excel at an adult's work. It may be as uncomplicated as the sheer joy of doing something extraordinarily well. Studies of gifted children do show that they typically share certain traits that Jacqueline displayed when quite young. They have prodigious memories, and seem able to call upon vast resources of energy to create and sustain their momentum. Their curiosity is often so demanding that parents and teachers can easily feel battered by their questions. Michal Hambourg, concert pianist, teacher and adviser for the National Association for Gifted Children (USA) writes in *If You Think Your Child is Gifted*, "Musical people hear music all the time when doing other things. In musical children this preoccupation is often misunderstood as a lack of attention; but it is really a creative process." Rosamund Shuter-Dyson, editor of the (UK) *Journal of the Society for Research in Psychology of Music and Musical Education*, has written (in "Musical Giftedness", her contribution to *The Psychology of Gifted Children*), "What may strike the observer [of musical prodigies] is what an 'ordinary' child the gifted youngster is, as soon as he is away from his instrument" – an observation made by virtually everyone who knew the young Jacqueline.

In *The Psychology of Music*, A. E. Kemp published the results of his 1981 study of the personality structure of the musician, identifying a profile of traits for the performer. He found that instrumentalists, especially string and woodwind players, tend to be introverts with exceptional inner strength, independence and a strong need to break away from conventional modes of thinking. He concluded, "All musicians agree that the outstandingly gifted child is immediately recognisable, unmistakable, and very rare."

Iris must have known that four hours of practice a day is mentally, if not physically, exhausting for an eleven-year-old child, but felt there was no alternative if Jackie was to realise her potential in these crucial development years. She worried about the imbalance in her younger daughter's life, particularly on such occasions as the family holiday in Dartmoor when Jackie, during a walk on the moors in fine weather, suddenly burst into tears, explaining between sobs that she missed her cello. The responsibility of cultivating and protecting Jackie's talent both thrilled and troubled Iris, and took such a disproportionate amount of her time that it would have been surprising if her other children hadn't been jealous. To Iris's great credit, she enthused and encouraged, guarded vigilantly against exploitation, and did her best to keep the household on an even keel by emphasising "normal" family activities. Perhaps in deference to Derek's taste, they went to pantomimes but not concerts. She did take Jackie to hear William Pleeth play the Schubert C major Cello Quintet, which caused the child to "nearly drown out the music with my tears, I loved it so," but she never took her to hear a soloist play with an orchestra. It was probably just as well; Michal Hambourg has warned of the dangers of exposing musical children to concerts when young. "The quality and concentration is different from that of the average listener, and they become either exhausted or overstimulated by too much listening. For them music is not a drug, and it must remain full of meaning. To young people who are musically sensitive the powerful sounds of an orchestra can be unbearably painful; also, music is the point of immense feeling in their lives and sometimes they find that they cannot endure the things that music says to them."

Two months before Jackie's fourteenth birthday, the family moved from Purley to central London. Derek had a new job: Secretary of the Institute of Cost and Works Accounting. The Institute occupied a three-storey house at 63 Portland Place, between Regent's Park and Oxford Circus. The du Prés were allowed to live in a small flat at the top of the building, on condition that no noise would disturb the employees below.

To reach the flat, one had to walk through the formal reception and corridors of the Institute, past people working at their desks and into an iron cage of a lift barely big enough for two people – or one person and a cello. The flat was modest and homely – chintz, prints and a plain carpet. The kitchen doubled as sitting-room, and the family congregated around the huge dining table. Jackie's bedroom was soundproofed with double doors and windows, acoustic tiles on the ceiling and two layers of carpeting on the floor. The soundproofing was so effective that she found it impossible to produce a big or a beautiful sound on her cello, only dead ones. Outside the window was a tiny balcony, but the window had to be kept shut when she practised during business hours, even on the hottest summer days. She loathed practising in this purgatory of a room. To escape it she tried to practise early, late and at weekends, when the Institute was shut and she could use other parts of the building.

In January 1959, Iris enrolled Jackie in Queen's College, in nearby Harley Street. Jackie was by then quite big for her age, and painfully self-conscious about her appearance. Queen's girls were for the most part aspiring débutantes; instead of uniforms they wore fashionable clothes. In her plain blouses and pleated skirts, the unsophisticated, socially awkward Jackie must have been an easy target for snubs, at the very least. Her January enrolment, five months after the other girls had formed friendships and cliques, hermetically sealed her isolation.

The correspondence between Iris, the headmistress of Queen's College, and the administrator of the Suggia Trust documents the most miserable year in Jackie's young life. Miss Kynaston, the headmistress, made special allowances for Jackie, requiring her to take only three subjects – English, German and French – on the condition that her work be on a level with that of her class. But she was well behind the rest of her class from the outset; although she had had two years of French in Croydon, the French teacher found her work "shocking". She was only expected to attend a minimal eight hours of classes a week, but when lessons with Pleeth (which had to be arranged to suit his busy schedule) or special rehearsals (as of the Lalo Cello Concerto for a Saturday morning children's concert with the Royal Philharmonic Orchestra, at the Festival Hall) conflicted with classes, she skipped the classes.

In April, she slid farther behind during two successive bouts of flu, from which she did not fully recover until after a ten-day family holiday spent walking on Dartmoor. In May, Iris wrote to the headmistress that her daughter had little time for homework because she was studying, "among other things", three concertos and a Bach unaccompanied suite, and that "obviously, music must come first for her". She intended, she said, to withdraw Jackie from school at the end of the year and to put her in the hands of a private tutor.

Miss Kynaston liked Jackie, admired her ability, and believed this to be a critical time in the girl's life; she wrote to the Suggia Trust that Jackie's general education was being neglected. The Trust replied that its interest was in Jackie's musical progress, and that her parents were responsible for her general education.

Dismayed, the headmistress asked friend and fellow educator Philip Wayne to intercede. Wayne met both Jackie and her mother; he was impressed by the girl's intelligence and sense of humour, and by the

maturity with which she told him that she didn't want to be "a horse
in blinkers". Wayne then wrote his own letter to the Trust, reiterating
Miss Kynaston's concern; Jackie needed the company of girls her
own age, he said, and besides, good tutors were hard to find. "She
will be the smaller musician if she misses the chance of a larger
education," he wrote, adding that he believed her to be well worth
all the trouble taken.

Iris continued to write excuses for Jackie's absences from class, and
for her failure to turn in homework assignments. When she missed
exams, Iris wrote that as she would not be taking GCE, perhaps the
exams were not so important.

Pleeth was aware of his pupil's distress; there were tears during
lessons, but no explanations. He shrugged it off as "problems at
school or the usual adolescent mummy-hate, nothing serious. It only
lasted a few months." Leaving school at an early age had never caused
him any problems – but he had not had Jackie's cloistered childhood.
As he watched her talent unfold, he quite naturally felt that nothing,
certainly not school lessons, should interfere with her music.

Initially shy and reserved with her teacher, Jackie-had gradually
relaxed and become deeply attached to the emotionally generous
Pleeth, whom she called Uncle Bill. They worked together for an
hour or more twice a week, his schedule permitting. He found
her progress phenomenal. At thirteen she had memorised, in one
astonishing week, the first movement of the Elgar Cello Concerto
and the extremely difficult first Piatti Caprice, very fast and two
pages long, and performed them almost impeccably. When she was
fifteen, Pleeth says, "There was this volcano in her, waiting to erupt.
Once it started, it was an endless, tremendous force. There are so
many aspects of such a talent: her musical memory, the speed of her
development, the dynamic of her personality, the sort of inner
burning lyricism, the drama."

Pleeth combined a thoroughly pragmatic approach to technique
with an almost mystical approach to the music that ideally en-
compasses it. To teach spiccato (a "bouncing bow" technique), for
example, he enfolded Jackie's hand in his own while she held the
bow, "as though I were the glove. We were one hand. I had her
absolutely relax, then I did the spiccato. She tasted physically what
it meant. Gradually I withdrew my hand and she was doing it. After
that I would go into the theory."

He was emphatic about the importance of understanding the cultural context of the music in order to interpret it properly; "otherwise," he says, "everything sounds alike. It entails a lot of discussion

about our art, our past, all the connecting up of the whole thing – the whole as opposed to separate parts. For example: introducing the *Kol Nidrei* I'd say, 'Do you know what this is about?' 'No,' is the answer. Then you discuss the Jewish religion a bit, you talk about the Day of Atonement, the most tragic day, and how it is sung by the cantor in a wonderful primitive voicing. You try to convey the smell, the flavour of the two-thousand-year-old culture. One thing leads to another; *Nothing is separated from anything else. This whole scene is an unwrapping of an endless universe.* A lot of my teaching is done through talking about that. But I talked about it less with Jackie than with other students because her progress was so rapid, there wasn't time."

In his book *Cello*, Pleeth wrote, "In the end one's playing should sound as unscientific and as uninhibited as the singing of a child's nanny who has not studied music but who will sit by the cradle and sing to the child with the most beautifully natural freedom." To achieve this illusion of effortlessness, the cellist devotes thousands of hours to the consideration and practice of countless possible fingerings, bowings and nuances that make up the tremendous potential for variety in any single phrase. Unlike the piano and many other instruments, the cello requires entirely different functions of the right and left hands – a bit like rubbing one's head while patting one's stomach, but with infinite intricate variations. The right hand produces the sound, the left produces the colour. "When you play," Pleeth wrote, "try to imagine that your right hand and fingertips are moving over the contours of the music in the same way that a blind person feels an object with his hands and fingertips." The *left* hand, in contrast, "needs complete freedom to go wherever the music directs it – like the weathervane on top of the church that's so well oiled that it moves with the slightest breeze." The point is well made, but the freedom is restricted by the necessity to pinpoint, without benefit of frets or any other guide on the fingerboard, the precise bit of the string to depress. Miss it by a fraction of a fraction, and the note goes wrong.

Pleeth considers four hours enough to practise every day, "provided the person is also spending time *thinking* about the right things, practising in their head. You can sit in an armchair and study the score, learn counterpoint, visualise strokes, go over what you learned yesterday, ask yourself questions like Why do I always play in one spot on the fingerboard, consider how what you play relates to what the keyboard instrument plays. It's no good just practising the cello. All the technique in the world can't make music; it makes *technique*.

Only when the technique is unconscious can the student become creative.

"There is a difference between being a cellist and being a musician. To become a musician takes courage; it means implanting the music in our mind and heart. Our heart has the most wonderful partner in our hands; their gestures are the outward expression of what we feel inside. All our movements when we are playing should come as a spontaneous reflection of the emotions evoked by the music. No matter how powerful a player you are, even if you are able to take the sound of the cello to its physical limits, there will always come a point where the little cello has its end. Only something spiritual can carry on beyond that. You, with your drama, make the rocket carry on."

He brought Jackie along with enthusiasm, confidence and delight. There were problems, but they were surmountable. Her first finger was nearly as long as her second; it made it difficult to get her hand into position until Pleeth, after considerable trial and error, discovered the angle that suited her perfectly. A continuing problem for Pleeth was "balancing her physical power with spiritual power. This young-ster was already starting to get this tremendous sense of drama. It was hard to get her to hold back just a fraction so she wouldn't strangle the instrument with too much temperament and a big sound. You have to learn that what you *don't* do counts for a lot."

When Jacqueline was working on a sonata or a concert, "Once the piece got ripe, Iris would come along and accompany her. She was an excellent pianist – a little mechanical and cool, but there was a sense of honesty in her playing. Jackie learned from what I said to Iris about the piano; it expanded her musical mind."

In October, Iris wrote to Miss Kynaston to apologise for Jackie's absence from school the next day, explaining that she would be at the Mansion House to receive three prizes at the Guildhall School of Music's annual award ceremony. The headmistress's reply was congratulatory, and expressed the hope that Jackie had at last adjusted to Queen's, and was happier there. Two months later, however, Iris wrote that she and her husband had decided to withdraw their daughter from the school at the end of term.

Miss Kynaston could hardly have been surprised but the music teacher, Miss Greenslade, was. She says, "We'd been told not to encourage Jackie with music, that she had come to Queen's because she wasn't interested in anything except her cello. When I heard she was leaving I was very surprised. I told her I would have loved her to come and play to us – and at the end of term, she came! Her

46

mother and sister played with her. None of the girls had realised what was in their midst."

Today there are specialised schools – the best known is Yehudi Menuhin's, in Surrey – that give musically gifted children a sense of connections and community. Charges of élitism notwithstanding, such schools allow students to receive general as well as musical educations, geared to their special needs. William Pleeth doubts that even the Menuhin School, where he has taught, could have accommodated Jacqueline's unique talent and personality. In any event, in 1956, as Jacqueline herself was to say years later, "It was a question of either/or. If you waited until schooling was finished to concentrate on music, it was about ten years too late."

Jacqueline often expressed regrets about having been "under-educated", but never about the time she spent with the cello. It was her "best friend", she said, "until I was seventeen. No one who has not experienced it can know just what it means to have a private world of your own to go into, to be quite by yourself whenever you need it. It was my gorgeous secret – an inanimate object, but I would tell it all my sadness and my problems. It gave me everything I needed and wanted. Playing was the cream. When I played, it never bothered me what happened. But I realised later that it didn't necessarily equip one to deal with one's fellow humans."

In 1978, talking with a *Sunday Telegraph* reporter about her child-hood, she said, "Other children didn't like me. I was very introverted and desperately shy. Children are so quick to spot this. They knew of the existence of the cello and taunted me with it. That's when I went and talked to it, saying, 'never mind; they have no idea how to play it.' I loved the fact that one could be very private with the cello and communicate one's innermost thoughts to it. It became a person, you could even say a love. *Everything* went into that instrument. So it began to assume rather human qualities. I'm not sure that is a good thing. It was the saving grace of my childhood, but in a sense it is a pity now, that one had to put all one's eggs in that basket."

Music had dominated the first fourteen years of Jacqueline's life; now it took over completely. Iris's attempts to find someone to coach her daughter in academic subjects led nowhere, and eventually, other priorities prevailed. In the confines of Portland Place Jackie practised, practised, practised. To Iris's great relief, she finally acquired a friend: violinist Peter Thomas, a year and a half older than herself, who had appeared with her on children's television when she was about twelve. With the musician's extraordinary memory for programmes,

Thomas, now leader of the Philharmonia Orchestra, recalls, "I played the first movement of the Bach Double with Diana Cummings and Jackie played the first movement of the Saint-Saëns [Cello Concerto]. She invited me to play with her at her house, and I went often during the next four or five years. I never saw any other friends of hers there; I don't think she had any. She must have felt lonely. She was very keen on being friendly with me, and both her parents really liked me going there. Iris was very keen to have a bloke come into Jackie's life, someone not as talented, a normal kid who played football. I was studying at the Academy, very near Portland Place, and I saw a lot of her. We became close friends. We used to take walks; we talked a lot. She was a very lovable girl with an open face, a calm exterior and a nice naïveté. Lots of musicians are very intense, they have a big engine. Jackie was laid back in a funny way. Placid. It made her musical passion surprising. As much as the music absorbed her, I never thought of her as ambitious.

"Sometimes I went with her to Bill Pleeth's and we'd play duos. I often went to her house on Saturday afternoon, stayed overnight and went home absolutely knackered. I wasn't used to Jackie's type of playing. She played *everything* from memory, even her studies, the dull exercises that everyone does. Once she said, 'Why don't we learn the Brahms Double?' I said that'd be nice. We got the music. I went home and learned the first page. I went back a week later and she'd learned the whole thing by memory! I just wanted to get back to my football pitch!

"I don't think Jackie overpractised, but she missed out on her childhood. She would have been just as good if she hadn't been so much with the cello – but I can't criticise Iris, she did everything she could to make a nice home. She didn't work until Jackie moved away; she was just a mum at home.

"Hilary was fantastically talented, an excellent pianist; I remember playing a trio with her. She only switched from piano to flute when she was fifteen or sixteen, and she became a very good flautist very quickly. The family seemed absolutely normal to me, but of course I was just a kid. They were all very unworldly, they led a simple life. Their holidays were walking holidays."

Iris drove a Dormobile, a small minibus equipped with seats and a stove, big enough to carry the cello. They took it on camping holidays in Dartmoor and Devon. Once, purely by coincidence, the Pleeth family, holidaying at a hotel in Kingsbridge, spotted the du Pré family on the beach, where all the children proceeded to play together in and out of the sea.

Anthony Pleeth, three years younger than Jackie, was Piers's contemporary and playmate. He was learning the cello and when his father was away on tour, "he entrusted Jackie with my progress on the cello. I remember her putting a cork from a wine bottle between my thumb and first finger, trying to teach me to play in thumb position when I was eleven. We knew even then she was a force quite out of the ordinary. She was an outgoing, jolly, happy kid, always a lot of fun. At fifteen, she was about twelve stone. That power is a big advantage on the cello. The women who sound like men tend to be built more like a man.

"Her family appeared to be very happy and conventional, with an upper-middle-class British confidence and children they were very proud of. Derek was an imposing English businessman type. Iris was one of a breed of successful proud English mums, but exceptional in that she'd been very gifted herself. She had a hockeysticks kind of optimism; I can still see her enormous smile, her genuine delight in how the kids were growing up, how exciting life was."

Anthony's sister, Jan, was Jackie's age and sometimes stayed over-night with her at Portland Place. "We did terribly ordinary things, and had terribly ordinary conversations. We used to lie in bed at night and talk about boys and periods. Jackie was a great giggler. We made up a language and spoke it, and wrote each other letters in it. We never talked about music." The family seemed to Jan almost too good to be real – "idealised, just like in the Peter and Jane books. That was my perception as a child. There were no scenes or tantrums like in my house. I don't remember anyone ever quarrelling or shouting or the kids ever crying. Hilary and Jackie were always doing things for one another, helping one another out. Iris was always smiling; she never looked disapproving or cross. She was friendly and warm and mumsy, always cooking lovely casseroles and cakes. She never wore make-up, nor did Hilary. None of them was interested in clothes or that sort of thing. Iris wore tweeds a lot; even when she didn't, you'd think of her in tweeds. Derek was a rather remote businessman, but really nice.

"Either her parents were very caring people, or they were great actors."

4

In September 1960, the fifteen-year-old Jacqueline attended Pablo
Casals's master class at the Summer Academy of Music in
Zermatt, Switzerland. Her tuition and expenses were covered
by the Suggia Award.★ Casals had not spoken Suggia's name in
public since the end of their affair, except in the context of her career.

Although summer music courses proliferated in Europe at the
time, Casals's was by far the best known and most in demand. A
number of distinguished musicians taught at Zermatt – Sándor Végh,
Carl Engel, Will Hauslein, Emil Hauser – but Casals, who had
revolutionised the technique and repertoire of the cello, was very
much a legend at eighty-four, and his class was the main attraction.
At the end of the three-week course, teachers and selected students
would perform. Sometimes Casals himself, who had not played
publicly in any country that recognised the Franco regime since 1957,
performed.

Zermatt was a slightly touristy town in a stunningly beautiful
setting – high in the Alps with a view of the Matterhorn, rushing
streams of melted snow and a tranquil atmosphere. An international
assortment of students who were considered "most promising" by
the musical hierarchy in their respective countries were quartered
all over the town in chalets and hotel rooms. They carried their
instruments to and from classes, through narrow streets that bustled
with tourists, hikers and horsedrawn carts with tinkling bells; auto-
mobiles were banned. Every evening, goats were brought down
from their pastures and herded up the road. Classes were held in one
of the big hotels.

Out of a total of fifty or sixty students, including violinists and
singers, perhaps a dozen were cellists, who attended Casals's classes
along with about fifty paying listeners. Casals's students met with
him as a group for three hours several times a week, and spent most
of the rest of their time practising. Cellist Jennifer Ward Clarke, who

★ Each year from 1956 to 1962, Jacqueline formally auditioned for the Suggia
committee and was granted a renewal of the award.

attended the class that year, recalls, "You'd turn up at the hotel and wait for Casals to walk in with his lovely young Puerto Rican wife. It was an extraordinary moment for us; we were very young and he was very old, a legendary figure. You knew all his old records and had read books about him and then, there he was!"

Casals's wife, Martita, was a former student, sixty years younger than the master. She sat near him, taking notes. "She had a great plastic bag full of pipes, maybe a hundred different ones, and every once in a while he'd turn around and she always seemed to know which pipe to hand him. Perhaps different shapes for different times of day." Ms. Clarke thought Casals "a wonderful teacher. What he wanted from everybody was simply that the music should *live*. He would say just a few things about accentuations and phrasing and shaping the music. He never went into questions of technique. That wasn't what the classes were for – unless, for instance, you were using your bow in a very unmusical way. I remember a young pink-faced Englishman who looked terribly middle-aged and played in a very middle-aged sort of way. Quite correctly and nicely, but boringly. When he finished, Casals beamed at him and said, 'But music is LIFE! Where is yours?' Here was this old, old man, absolutely brimming with life. He would demonstrate all the time – he would pick up his cello and play a phrase and then you'd hear it, that tremendous vitality and enthusiasm."

She remembers that Jacqueline looked "like a very shy schoolgirl, and *very much* with her mother. I don't think her mother ever left her side. She played two or three times and then, at the end of the course, the Saint-Saëns Cello Concerto – we were doing concertos that year – with her mother accompanying her. It took everyone's breath away. Here was this very lumpy schoolgirl with frightfully short straight hair and completely unglamorous clothes – but when she sat at the cello, there was this amazing spirit, energy, life! She *threw* herself into it unlike anyone else in the class.

"She was by far the youngest, but she didn't play as a student at all. She performed! Most of us felt very much in the position of the student sitting there at the feet of the master Casals, waiting for his opinions and advice. No one played with a sense of performance; it was a lesson situation. Whereas with Jackie, she got up there and we were her audience! And she simply performed to us! She presented herself *completely* as she was. I don't remember Casals saying a great deal to her. He sort of sat back and accepted it, as though here was something that would develop anyway. There were little things, the kind of things he would usually have picked up, but she was so completely compelling, he just left her alone, as though he didn't want to interfere."

After hearing Jacqueline play for the first time, Casals had asked where she came from. "England," she told him. He replied, "With such temperament? Impossible." Such musical extravagance couldn't possibly be English. "What is your name?"

"Jacqueline du Pré."

"A-ha!" said Casals triumphantly.

According to William Pleeth, another observer remarked to Casals after Jacqueline played, "Doesn't she *move* an awful lot?" Casals said, "Oh, I *like* it – she moves *with* the music!"

Jacqueline loved the magnificent setting, loved being abroad for the first time and hearing other languages spoken; but she was not impressed by Casals, and was disappointed at having so little private time with him. She later said, "It gave me pleasure to talk with him about the music and to play for him, but I didn't find him daunting. He was surrounded by all these old ladies who just wanted to lie at his feet. He listened but he was dogmatic. He wanted everything to be played his way and I could see what he wanted and did it without being told, but I was a bolshie fifteen-year-old, very proud of my own teacher, and I didn't want to accept too easily what Casals said to me, even though he was Casals." She was aware of her gift, and anxious that it not be interfered with, either by Casals or by subsequent teachers with whom she studied. Only Pleeth had her complete trust.

Back in London, Iris and Pleeth agreed that the time was right to begin planning Jacqueline's official début recital. It would take place just after her sixteenth birthday, in the Wigmore Hall.

Her performances had been carefully limited thus far to children's and young musicians' concerts. In March 1959, she had played the Lalo Cello Concerto, first with fellow pupils at the Guildhall end-of-term concert and then (the first movement only) on BBC Television, with Norman Del Mar conducting. In May of that year she played the Lalo (with the BBC Welsh Orchestra) in Cardiff; the last movement of the Haydn Cello Concerto in D major (with sections of the Royal Philharmonic Orchestra) at the BBC's Lime Grove studios; and finally, as a member of the Artemis String Quartet, a three-minute piece by Purcell on *Focus*, a *Blue Peter*-type BBC programme, again from Lime Grove. In June 1959, Pleeth had arranged a recital of chamber music for the Horsham Music Circle. With Hilary playing flute, Christina Mason piano and Peter Thomas violin, Jacqueline had played music by Bach, Rolla and Beethoven.

In 1960, Jacqueline won the Guildhall School's Gold Medal for outstanding instrumental student and four subordinate cello prizes, including a silver challenge cup. Like the Suggia, these were, strictly speaking, awards, not competitions. Pleeth, wary of the dangers of competition for all students, realised that "for Jackie, there *was* no competition", and discouraged such activities. The one exception was the Queen's Prize for the outstanding British instrumentalist under thirty. A panel of four judges, chaired by Yehudi Menuhin, unanimously voted to award it to Jacqueline. Menuhin was dazzled by her talent and invited her to play some trios with himself and his pianist sister, Hephzibah. In November 1960, she gave what she considered to be her first "real" recital at the Kensington studio of violinist Sybil Eaton for an audience of about eighty people.

A London début is a launching pad for an artist, the only way to get the necessary national reviews that lead to other engagements. The Wigmore Hall was and remains the traditional trial-by-fire platform for young musicians making their London débuts. Carefully designed in 1901 for acoustical quality, it is to this day the oldest and most beautiful small concert hall in London, and is regarded by musicians with great affection. In 1961 the cost of the hall, accompanist, printing and publicity was about £300, and was normally borne by the performer. It was also customary to hire an organisation to handle all the details of producing the concert. An arrangement was made with Ibbs & Tillett, impresarios and agents, to perform that function for Jacqueline. To accompany her at the piano, Ernest Lush was a natural choice. He was agreeable and reliable, the most popular partner for such occasions. It would be the first time Jacqueline had performed with any pianist other than her mother and, although inevitable, must have caused Iris mixed feelings.

Pleeth helped plan a rather long and demanding programme, with contrast a major consideration: an unaccompanied Bach suite, sonatas by Handel and Brahms and Debussy, and a group of Spanish songs by de Falla. A few weeks before the recital, Jacqueline acquired a cello to suit the occasion. Her previous instruments had been a 7/8 Guarnerius, a Ruggieri and a full-sized 1696 Tecchler, all gifts from her godmother. Mrs. Holland had remained a patron of the arts after her husband's death. Now, she arranged for Jacqueline to choose between two fine old cellos. With her selection of a nut-brown Stradivarius, made in 1673 (twelve years before Bach and Handel were born, as Jacqueline liked to point out) and then valued at £35,000, everything was in place for the evening of March 1st, 1961.

★

Jacqueline appeared happy and calm before the concert, with no perceptible pre-performance nerves; she ate a hearty meal and walked onto the Wigmore platform with the assurance of a veteran performer. The hall's 550 seats were filled with the élite of the tight little music world; word was out that this promised to be a special evening. It was, in fact, historic. The first selection was Handel's G minor Sonata. During the first movement, to Jacqueline's dismay, her A string began very, very slowly to unwind. As it got looser she compensated with fingerings higher and higher up on the string until finally it lost all its tension. With complete aplomb, she excused herself, went backstage and restrung it. When she returned to the platform, the audience was more than ever on her side. As the programme progressed, the atmosphere became electric as people realised that they were witnessing magic – a quality of playing that William Pleeth called "the perfect marriage between real passion and an innocent reverence. It was a spiritual, not just a physical thing. She let each piece *live* so completely. People were practically crying."

Of the reviews that appeared the following day, *The Times* was typical:

Over the past few weeks London musical audiences have heard several promising and more or less young recitalists. Of these Miss Jacqueline du Pré, who played the cello at Wigmore Hall last night, is but sixteen years old, and yet to speak of promise when reviewing her performance would seem almost insulting, for she has attained a mastery of her instrument that is astonishing in one so young.

The long programme seemed to tax her not one whit. Even a recalcitrant A string which forced her to make a second beginning to Handel's G minor Sonata at the start of her recital could neither unseat the conviction of her interpretations nor disturb her technical control for an instant. After Handel she tackled the E minor Sonata of Brahms and gave it warmth and breadth in the first movement, an enchanting grace in the second and a vivacious intensity in the last that entirely dispelled the workaday gruffness of much of its counterpoint. Debussy's mercurial Sonata was equally well done, and after the interval Miss du Pré presented an account of Bach's C minor unaccompanied Suite that thrilled the blood with its depth and intuitive eloquence. She ended her programme to good effect by displaying her technique and the complete range of tone colours that she and her Stradivarius can command in a transcription of Falla's *Suite Populaire Espagnole*.

Other reviewers rhapsodised similarly. Percy Cater wrote in the *Daily Mail*, "Jacqueline was born to play the cello. She thoroughly understands its genius, and so instinctive is her reaction to the music that one feels the subtlest ideas of the composer to be embraced. She is in love with the cello. She sways it with her in each work. Her feelings – serious, stern, proud, triumphant – are shown in her movements and in her face." The *Guardian*'s Colin Mason wrote, ". . . she is already well on the way to a place in the top flight of cellists." In the *Daily Telegraph*, Martin Cooper wrote, "We are accustomed to British artists who seem instinctively to divorce themselves from their music, but here is a young player whose technical accomplishments have not prevented her from being wholly committed to whatever she plays – and this is one of the first essentials of a great player."

The following morning, offers for recitals and orchestral engagements began flooding in. Pleeth, who had come to love Jacqueline like an adopted daughter, advised caution. "Jackie started to get overwhelmed by people who *wanted* her. She needed time to grow naturally, on the platform and off. To work a bit, release a bit. I told Iris I thought twelve concerts that season would be enough, while she continued her lessons. I tried to put the brakes on, but it wasn't in my hands to say, 'No, you can't do that.' Ibbs & Tillett were in that position, I suppose. And Iris, up to a point. Jackie accepted that she could do whatever she was called upon to do."

5

I bbs & Tillett meant Emmie Tillett, the *grande dame* of agents. Few people today can remember Ibbs, but no one who came into contact with Emmie Tillett will ever forget her. She began her career as a secretary and then married the boss, John Tillett; after his death in the Forties she built the organisation into the most powerful music agency in Britain. In 1961 she was slightly older than the century – tall, with a grey Eton crop and a formal manner, majestic as Queen Mary. Despite her considerable wealth she eschewed taxis and took buses to work; her only extravagance was the Jaguar automobile she drove at terrifying speed. She could be a charmer or a dragon as the situation dictated, and intimidated her artists as well as the young men who worked for her. Her integrity was beyond question, her word her bond. She was above all a shrewd business-woman with a product to sell – a product she knew had an unpredictable market value and shelf life.

Ibbs & Tillett was plugged into hundreds of small music clubs in England. Every major town had one, and many small towns as well. Funded by Arts Council grants and relatively inexpensive subscriptions, the clubs put on about six concerts a season, providing bread and butter for scores of young musicians. To supplement that basic diet, the agency booked its artists into similar dates with chamber music societies in Europe.

In the early Sixties, Ibbs & Tillett seemed to represent everyone in the concert world; those at or on their way to the top got Mrs. Tillett's personal attention. They included Andrés Segovia, Heather Harper, Janet Baker, John Williams, John Ogdon and Jacqueline du Pré.

Of the assortment of offers that followed Jacqueline's début, by far the most prestigious was an engagement with the BBC Symphony Orchestra at the Royal Festival Hall on the first available date, exactly a year away. In the meantime, Ibbs & Tillett accepted dates for Jacqueline, accompanied by her mother, in Amsterdam, Rotterdam, London and the provinces. In April, Jacqueline performed Bach's unaccompanied Suite No. 1 in G for an audience of about three hundred people at a concert sponsored by the National Trust at Osterley Park, a stately home west of London. That summer she played the Bach again, on BBC Radio. With pianist Antony Hopkins she played three Schumann *Fantasies* at Goldsmiths' Hall; Hopkins was "thrilled by her formidable talent. She flung herself about a bit, but the glorious tone, the intuitive phrasing, the total involvement that we all came to associate with her playing were already there." After the concert Iris asked Hopkins, who was more educator than performer, if he would give Jackie some lessons in general music appreciation, to widen her musical horizon. Hopkins agreed. "She came to my home at Brook Green, rather scared, very quiet. I talked to her about modulation, key relationships and form, about which she knew next to nothing; but she had such an amazing ability to completely identify with the music and the composer that I soon realised she needed no help from me. For example, I played a bit of a Beethoven sonata to her, a piece she didn't know. It was the recapitulation in the Opus 10 C minor Sonata. Where there is a pause, I stopped and said, 'What do you reckon the next note should be?' It was a surprise note, completely unexpected. She immediately said, 'D flat.' Her intuition was uncanny."

At a music club in Upminster on November 15th, Jacqueline played chamber music with violinist Peter Thomas, his pianist sister Judith, and young Anthony Pleeth. Also on the programme was Piers du Pré, playing a short solo piece by Gerald Finzi on clarinet. Finzi's son, Christopher, had married Hilary two months earlier.

In January 1962, Jacqueline played a Delius Cello Sonata at the composer's centenary celebration in Bradford, where he was born. Her accompanist was Ernest Lush. *The Times* reviewer wrote, "It has been said, with some truth, that one either loves or hates Delius on first hearing and remains either friend or foe for life . . . But it would be a singularly implacable foe who might not have been won over by Miss Jacqueline du Pré's persuasive account of the 1917 cello sonata."

For her Festival Hall début on March 21st, 1962, Jacqueline performed with a full orchestra for the first time, playing the work with which she would be most closely identified for the rest of her life. Percy Cater wrote in the *Daily Mail*:

Jacqueline du Pré, a brilliant cellist now, at 17, and regarded as on the threshold of a distinguished career, made her "adult" début at the Royal Festival Hall last night in the Elgar Concerto.

Her playing united technical command with a maturity of feeling remarkable for her age.

At the close Rudolf Schwarz, the conductor, and the BBC Symphony Orchestra, her colleagues in the work, enthusiastically applauded her. The big and cordial audience recalled her three times.

The Elgar Concerto, with its serious beauties, its frequent changes of mood and tempo, poses some formidable interpretative problems. The tall, fair girl in evening dress of pale blue, hair bobbed, and with fringe, was a picture of self-possession throughout its 29-minute course.

She reacted instinctively to its emotions, profound and serene. The tone of her walnut-coloured 1673 Strad, which might have been larger had the player been more familiar with the hall's acoustics, was heartfelt.

The soloist gave us smooth and sympathetic phrasing, a moving range of nuance. She swayed to the rhythm, in fast figuration her head tossed, her fingers raced confidently bridgewards and down.

An occasional fault of intonation, unusual with her, I attribute to the tension of the occasion. But a calmer platform figure could hardly be imagined.

To me it was affecting that this later Elgar work, with its hints of autumn, should be presented to us by a girl in her springtime.

The tension was the reviewer's fantasy; Peter Thomas had gone to Portland Place at teatime to wish Jackie good luck and found her perfectly calm, "no nerves whatsoever. 'Oh, let me make you some tea,' she said." On the following day she told a *Daily Express* reporter, "I wasn't really nervous playing the Elgar, but terribly excited. In fact it's difficult to tell sometimes what state one's in. It seemed to pass in a dream. It was terrific when the audience called me back again and again." Much later in her life, Jacqueline spoke of how she had loved the whole concert process. "Walking on stage – the recognition, the applause, the rumble of interest from the audience when I appeared. It never occurred to me to be nervous. I thought of the audience as a group of friends who had come to hear me play, and I found that very moving. I just *played*, and enjoyed it. Thinking about the notes would have spoiled the enjoyment. The work was all done beforehand."

Even before the Festival Hall concert, the media had sniffed the perfume of incipient myth: the prodigious talent, the youthful innocence, the golden hair and radiant smile. Press accounts of the day describe a charmed life lived under a cloudless sky: "Although she insists she is very single minded, music is not her only interest. She has a refreshing enthusiasm for a wide variety of things and is currently taking lessons in fencing, French literature, dramatic art with a teacher from RADA, and is taking up mathematics – 'because it helps to develop a logical, lucid mind.' Not content with that, she also paints when she has time. She works in oils and doesn't hold with abstracts but likes the picture to resemble something." There were references to talks and walks in the park with her "wide circle of friends . . . although she lives and works to a strict time-table in which there is no room for the usual social frivolities which fill the minds and lives of most girls of her age." A *Guardian* reporter called her "the first cellist of potential greatness to be born in Britain" and compared her with Christine Truman: "both seem the epitome of the nice English tennis girl . . . When she plays seriously, though . . . the tennis girl disappears and is replaced by a musician, lips tight, eyes on some far focus. Her hair is thrown back; her bow sears the strings." The *Daily Express* pictured her listening to records (but never popular music) and enjoying the theatre and concerts, and noted that the money from her own concerts went directly into the bank. "Her happiest times," said the *Evening Standard*, "are the holidays at Dartmoor, 'stone-hunting' with her family, all keen amateur geologists." The *Evening News* had her "studying the Old Dutch School of paintings and reading poetry, biography and the 'classic' authors: the Brontës, Austen and Trollope."

All the stories contained bits of truth, but the larger truth was that although the performing Jacqueline was confident, fulfilled, often ecstatic, off the platform she was confused, unhappy and immature, struggling with the chemical and emotional changes of adolescence, and with a growing discontent with the claustrophobic confines of Portland Place. The flat was in the centre of London, but inside it was entirely family-oriented, just as in Purley. Although Iris was a musician, she had not been part of any musical scene since her teaching days. As reported, holidays were primarily confined to collecting rocks – Derek's passion – and also to visiting relatives, in Dartmoor or Jersey. Jan Pleeth (now Jan Theo) recalls that the atmosphere was almost abnormally normal. "If a stranger had walked in, he'd never suspect that in that house lived anyone at all special. The household didn't revolve around her or her career. There was absolutely no sign of fussing over her health or anything else. There had to have been *some* pushing, but they never let it show. Looking back, it does seem a bit too good to be true."

Professionally, Jacqueline was naturally moving out of her mother's orbit. At home, she rebelled against bonds that remained symbiotic and tangled. With the same determination with which she had set out at three "to see the sea", she fought to break out of the bubble that had both protected and restrained her from everything except music and family.

At seventeen, she ventured onto the tube for the first time in her life; until then, Iris had driven her everywhere. She developed a ravenous curiosity and began asking what life outside music was about. With Peter Thomas she signed up for a course in philosophy at the School of Economic Science that they'd seen advertised in the tube. It turned out to be more about self-improvement than philosophy and they dropped out after a term. Peter was a life-saver. When Jacqueline was invited to play in private homes, which was becoming a frequent occurrence, she was embarrassed by her ignorance of conversational topics, and took Peter along to talk for her. Iris told Peter's mother, "Their friendship is so good for Jackie because she's a bit shy."

Through the violinist Sybil Eaton, in whose studio Jackie had given her first recital, Iris at last found a coach to expand her daughter's non-musical horizon. Lady Clwyd was a sixth-form teacher at Queensgate School in South Kensington. She also gave unofficial seminars on practically every subject, coached students for exams, and counselled teenage girls with their academic and personal problems. She was a high-powered Scot with a great love for music and a radiant warmth, to which Jackie immediately responded.

Jacqueline was sixteen when she first went to Joan Clwyd's Holland Park home, ostensibly for coaching in English and history. In practice, the teacher simply pursued any subject in which Jackie expressed an interest. The relationship quickly became close. Alison Brown, daughter of the late Joan Clwyd, recalls, "My mother saw that Jackie's problem was a great lack of confidence in the real world, in practical things like bus routes and tube trains and just how to get around as a competent sixteen-year-old.

"My parents kind of adopted Jackie. My father [Lord Clwyd] was a great amateur musician, very direct; he accepted her completely for what she was. I think Jackie felt very much at ease with him. She came to the house a lot and she loved going along with us to visit our friends, sometimes for relaxed, chamber music-making weekends. We had one family of friends who lived in south London, Sir Noel Hutton and his wife. He just loved Jackie, and Jackie loved his red racing car. She would go up to him and whisper, 'Do you think I could have a ride in your red car?' And he would take her out and drive all around. It was such a change from that cello duty, it just gave her a feeling of delight and fun."

The Clwyds held open house for a wide circle of literary, artistic and musical friends who tried to put Jacqueline at her ease. It was a step towards independence, but not the real thing, for Iris and Derek became friends of the Clwyds as well. In the summer of 1962, Jacqueline went a bit farther afield. Joan Clwyd sent her for additional informal coaching to her friend Lucretia Mrosovsky, who recalls, "Joan asked could Jackie come for lessons; I said, 'In what?' She said, 'In anything!' She said Jackie only knew about the cello and needed to be put in touch with the big world. Joan was a terrifically affectionate person and she really minded what happened to Jackie as a *person* – she could see that the music was all right. She wanted to widen her and protect her at the same time. Genius is a burden. To have that gift, and all the people wanting you. Surely even if you are a genius, you have to have an adolescence.

"My husband had just retired. We had a nice big house in Wimbledon, the children were there, it was a normal kind of life. Jackie came once a week for a very short period of time. I remember her being sort of comfortable in shape, her hair quite natural, very much not 'done'. She had a rather soft voice and wonderful open smile. Everything seemed to be absolutely shining for her.

"The only sort of solid thing I can remember that we talked about was the Bible. She had never read it! I read bits from the Book of Genesis, and then we just started talking. Another time I took out a lovely big globe that my son had been given and said, 'Let's look at this.' She had never touched a globe. She was absolutely fascinated! We would talk for a while and then she'd go off downstairs with the children and stay for some kind of rough supper.

"Of course everybody in the house loved her straightaway. My prickly son, who was twenty-four, a postgraduate; and my daughter, who was at the Guildhall studying music. Two things stick in my mind. One was when the grown-ups were in one room and the young in the room next door. I heard Jackie sort of fooling around on the piano and then suddenly I heard the most unearthly, beautiful sounds coming out of my daughter's rather ordinary violin. My daughter told me later that she'd been practising and had left her violin out, and Jackie had picked it up and held it like a cello and played it, and got this lovely tone!

"The other thing was, I was in the kitchen getting the dinner and the children all came trooping in to sort of get in the way, the way children do. I was chopping parsley on a board, chopping it with a knife – and Jackie said, 'What a lovely sound!' And ever since, whenever I chop parsley, I think of Jackie. And it *is* a lovely sound. But no one would ever think to stop and hear it.

"Not long after that Jackie went off to Paris to study with Tortelier and I never saw her personally again."

6

The dynamics of families often defy explanation, particularly by the family members themselves. From the outside, observers saw nothing unusual in Jacqueline's family. Certainly there is no doubt that Iris du Pré did everything she could to create a "normal" atmosphere in a house where the presence of a most extraordinary child precluded any possibility of normality.

Families of highly gifted children deserve sympathy, not envy, for the prodigy's gift is both a blessing and a curse. It affects the family's activities and priorities, straining its resources of time, energy, finances and emotional support. Educators and psychologists agree that the impact of a prodigy on a family's equilibrium can be as great as that of a mentally or physically disabled child. Explicitly or as subtext, everyone in the family gets the message: the prodigy will fulfil her destiny, whatever the cost.

In *Nature's Gambit*, Dr. Feldman refers to historical cases of families with several highly gifted siblings "in which one emerged as the premier talent. Mozart toured Europe with his sister, Nannerl, until he was about fifteen, at which point her career as a piano prodigy declined. Menuhin had two younger sisters, Hephzibah and Yaltah, highly accomplished musicians, but their careers never took off." The mother of a musical prodigy in Dr. Feldman's study confided that "while she suspected that the prodigy's younger brother was just as talented as his big brother she had neither the time, resources nor energy to try to develop and encourage his talent as well." The general consensus about Jacqueline's sister's talent is that she had great potential which was never realised. During Hilary's adolescence Iris told Mona Thomas, Peter's mother, "It is difficult for an older child to find that her younger sister is cleverer than she is." To onlookers, the sisters appeared friendly enough; their relationship seemed to improve, if anything, after Hilary's early marriage. At nineteen she went to live with her husband near Newbury in Berkshire, about fifty miles northwest of London, where she emulated her mother by turning her creative energies to producing children – four of them – and teaching.

Jacqueline later spoke of having been jealous of her sister's GCE success, which came at a time when Jackie herself was increasingly distressed about having only one string to her bow. Her musical progress had been so natural and in most respects so enjoyable that she'd had no chance to develop resources for coping with the larger world. Although lack of interaction with her peers had stunted her emotional and intellectual growth, she was beginning to meet people who assumed that her brilliance and maturity as a musician must naturally be reflected in every other aspect of her personality. At seventeen, she was treated like a child at home and an adult elsewhere; she was comfortable in neither world, but only in the private one she shared with her cello.

She did, as the newspapers reported, make sporadic attempts to develop new interests: painting, fencing, drama and even, at Yehudi Menuhin's suggestion, yoga. At the same time, she was having her busiest professional year to date. In 1962 she gave her first television recital, accompanied by Iris; performed Bloch's *Schelomo* with Terence Lovett at the Royal Academy of Music; and performed Boccherini's B flat Cello Concerto with Gordon Thorne and the Philomusica Orchestra at the Merchant Taylors' Hall. Of the latter concert, Charles Reid wrote in the *Daily Mail*, "She gave to every phrase and phrase sequence the darting life of a trout in a stream." Accompanied by her mother, she appeared at festivals in Bath, Cheltenham, Chester and the City of London. A review of the Cheltenham concert noted, "Her performance of music by Beethoven, Debussy and Edmund Rubbra varied somewhat in style – chiefly because the piano accompaniment was often inadequate." From that date, Iris found herself more often in the audience than on the stage when Jacqueline performed. After twelve years of accompanying her daughter, she had become expendable.

In August, Jacqueline played the Elgar at her first Promenade concert at the Royal Albert Hall, with Sir Malcolm Sargent conducting the BBC Symphony Orchestra. Sir Malcolm took the opening slightly faster than Jackie wanted it, but when she came in with the haunting, lyrical nine-eight theme she gently but quite firmly slowed it down, leaving the conductor no alternative but to follow her. After the concert Sir Malcolm told her, "I've conducted all the great cellists, but I've never enjoyed a performance as much as tonight's. That concerto belongs to you." The next day *The Times* critic called her "the first of the postwar generation to emerge from prodigyhood. Miss du Pré is a remarkable interpreter and cellist . . . her attitude to

Elgar's Cello Concerto was that of a thinking adult and not of an intuitively musical child."

One of Iris's earliest successors as Jacqueline's accompanist was Jill Severs, who first played with Jackie in 1960 at the beautiful seventeenth-century Fenton House, in Hampstead, north London. Jill, then twenty-six, lived with her husband and small child in the garden cottage behind Fenton House. "Jackie's mother brought her over to meet me. Iris was a very nice lady and this child was obviously the apple of her eye. She dressed her like a little schoolgirl. She was gauche and gangly, with long legs and arms – very, *very* enthusiastic, completely unspoiled and unsophisticated. Her hair was very short; she seemed more like thirteen than seventeen. She would say very abruptly, 'I must go for a run!' and she'd go galumphing off round Fenton House gardens like a great big colt. Then she'd come back and we'd play Bach. And with the first stroke of the bow across the strings, she was sort of possessed. You almost had the feeling of, *'My God, who's in there?'* And then she'd be her natural Jackie self again.

"I had a good time introducing her to playing chamber music with a harpsichord. I don't think she'd ever *met* a harpsichord before. She was already quite a *big* player, and she had to tone herself down quite a bit. We had an instant rapport. We had lots of rehearsals, and we chose the programme together. Jackie played the unaccompanied Bach Suite that she'd played at her début. We also both wanted to play Bach together, so we did: the D major Gamba Sonata. We played a Vivaldi sonata and I played a group of harpsichord solos, so it balanced out nicely. I remember Bill Pleeth coming along to a couple of rehearsals and being very delighted and pleased.

"We did the programme on two consecutive evenings – once for a lot of friends, as a sort of try-out, and then for a packed house, a National Trust-type audience. Jackie was an absolute natural; it was as if she'd been born with a cello in her hands. She wasn't at all an intellectual player, she was completely instinctive, incredibly responsive. Her sensitivity to the actual sound of a note was remarkable. She was very much a soloist, so she asserted herself. She just gave it out and there it was, take it or leave it. It was extraordinary to hear, from such a little girl, this passionate, fiery playing. Landowska's playing had the same quality.

"Iris was very conventional, and she must have thought we were a little bit Bohemian. I was very much aware that Jackie had been shut off from life, overprotected; she hadn't had the wear and tear, the hurly burly of an ordinary kind of school. We introduced her to all sorts of things. I don't think she'd ever been to the cinema! She had a roaring ride in our MG, whizzing round the park in this little sports car with the roof down. I remember her delight. I think we even gave her the first glass of sherry she ever had. Her background was so completely different from the sort of jet set life she had later on."

Jan Theo was aware that the seventeen-year-old Jacqueline was desperately lonely. "I took her along to parties at the Guildhall School a few times and introduced her to my friends there but it was a disaster, because by that time she was well-known enough that music students were very self-conscious about having her around." Jacqueline's own self-consciousness compounded the awkwardness. "She was gawky, with no sense of style or presentation. Her clothes were rather dowdy. I tried to persuade her to wear make-up, at least on the concert platform, but she didn't want it. Only lipstick. Of course she didn't need it with that smile, especially when her wonderful hair got longer."

In the summer of 1962, Jan went with Jacqueline to the Dartington Summer School of Music in the bucolic Devon countryside. "It was ostensibly for Tortelier's master class, but it was really a social thing. It was one of the few places Jackie could go as a famous musician and not feel self-conscious but just have fun, meet people. Meet *men*. There were classes, there was tennis, and swimming; we'd sit around and talk, go to concerts in the evening." John Amis, Secretary of the school from its founding in 1948, had created an atmosphere dramatically different from the intense discipline of Zermatt. The biggest musical names – Copland, Hindemith, Hess, Schnabel, Virgil Thomson, the Amadeus Quartet – taught at Dartington, not for the minuscule remuneration they received, but because it was such a pleasant place to be. About 350 students attended each of the four week-long sessions. Meals were communal, and the pub was the hub of the social scene. People might go to Dartmouth for dinner, or visit the moors or the sea. There was a party every Friday night, and a steady stream of visitors – friends or pupils of the artists, boyfriends or girlfriends of the students. They were welcome to stay for a meal, or overnight. Dartington was hardly a hotbed of fornication but, as Amis points out, "nobody did bed checks".

Jacqueline had spent the odd day at Dartington in previous years, either with her family or with Peter Thomas's family; now she was there for a week. She was glad to be there, but still so shy that some people found it contagious. John Amis admired her playing but when he was with her, "I became shy and gauche as well. Only once was I ever able to get on her wavelength. It was at a party, around midnight, and Jackie was looking rather miserable and unhappy. I asked if she'd like to play some music, and her face lit up; she said, 'Oh, yes!' I said, 'I've got Bloch's *Schelomo*, the piano part. Would you like to play that?' She said, 'Oh yes, I would love to!' So we went to a room. I'm not a good pianist, but I knew the piece well. It's a very orgiastic, orgasmic piece, and she adored it. She gave it the works. It was marvellous, absolutely *charged*. It remains one of the outstanding memories of my life! When it was over she said goodnight, and that was it."

On another evening, Jacqueline asked Paul Tortelier if he would help her with *Schelomo*. Subtitled "A Hebrew Rhapsody", the piece is filled with romantic melancholy and bittersweet harmonies; Jacqueline loved it, played it many times, but never recorded it. On a radio broadcast twenty-three years later, Tortelier recalled the Jacqueline he met at Dartington that summer: "With her short blond hair and clear blue eyes, she was a Wagner heroine. She was Siegfried. When we played together, she knew what I would do before I did it. One night, after a recital I had given, she asked me if I would help her with *Schelomo*. 'Why not?' I replied, 'but when?'

" 'Why not now?' she asked.

"As there had been a dinner after the concert, it was already past midnight. I protested that people were sleeping. 'We needn't worry about that,' she persisted. 'There's a room where we can work without disturbing anyone.' I thought it strange to give a lesson in the dead of night, but when she begged you like that, you couldn't resist. She began to play and I began to explain, and in our enthusiasm the lesson lasted a good two hours. At two thirty we were still playing and discussing *Schelomo*."

Jacqueline found Tortelier's style of teaching more exciting than that of the venerable and dignified Casals, and it was decided that in the autumn she would go to Paris and study with him at the Conservatoire. The tuition would be paid by the Suggia Trust, during her seventh and final year as its recipient. She told Jan Theo she would rather stay in London and continue studying with Pleeth but that her mother insisted, claiming it would be good for her career to spend time with Tortelier. Later, when a newspaper referred to her as a pupil of Tortelier's, she wanted to write and complain that her teacher was William Pleeth; her mother discouraged her, for the same reason.

★

Jacqueline made her first recording for EMI that summer (it was released the following year), and found the exacting technical process discouraging – "the very opposite of what music-making is all about," she told Alan Blyth of *The Gramophone*. Unlike the concert hall, where she could send the sound out boldly to the very last row, the studio microphone picked up the slightest unpleasant friction of her bow. She was accompanied on the various short pieces by Gerald Moore (piano), Kinloch Anderson (harpsichord), Roy Jesson (organ) and John Williams (guitar). She played the Adagio and Allegro from Bach's D major Gamba Sonata; Saint-Saëns' "The Swan"; Falla's "Jota" from his *Suite Populaire Espagnole*; and Bruch's variations on the Hebrew melody "Kol Nidrei", the most substantial piece in the group.* Although Jacqueline never liked her recording of Bruch's *Kol Nidrei*, William Pleeth considers it to be "much nicer than some superficially dressed-up ones".

In September she made her Edinburgh Festival début, playing Brahms's Second Cello Sonata with Ernest Lush. The *Daily Express* praised her "sturdy, robust and healthy ardour, like a rider at a point-to-point to whom purpose means more than niceties of style . . . her talents are unquestionably those of a great soloist of the future." Three weeks later she flew to Stavanger, Norway, to play the Elgar in a "Gateway to Britain" series. The following month she played the Schumann Cello Concerto in Berlin (with the Berlin Philharmonic) and in Paris, where she remained for her lessons with Tortelier.

It was Jacqueline's first trip abroad by herself, with no Iris to chaperone or chauffeur her. Classes were held at the Conservatoire, to which she carried her cello on the Métro from the several *quartiers* in which she lived. She relished the independence, but the unfamiliar territory and her old difficulties with French only deepened her loneliness. To make matters worse, she discovered that instead of the private lessons she had expected, she was merely a member of a class. It was at the Conservatoire that Jacqueline had the only two harmony lessons of her life. At the first one, the class was tested for pitch by single notes being played. Jacqueline felt very proud of her ability to recognise each one correctly until she realised that in the French system, the entire class is *taught* perfect pitch, and they were all able to identify the notes.

* She also recorded *Sicilienne* by Maria Theresia von Paradis (a blind concert pianist for whom Mozart wrote a piano concerto), Mendelssohn's *Song Without Words*, and three *Fantasie* pieces by Schumann, which were not released until 1982.

Great performers rarely make great teachers; the gifts come from different sources, and are perhaps incompatible. At Dartington, Jacqueline had been captivated by Tortelier's playing and by his *élan*. In Paris, disenchantment quickly set in. William Pleeth had encouraged Jackie, with great kindness and patience, to let her talent unfold in its own unique way. Pleeth knew there was more than one good fingering or bowing for any passage, and many ways of performing any given work. Tortelier was more arbitrary and analytical; Jacqueline felt that he tried to impose his own theories of technique, such as the use of his long peg, on her, and resisted mightily. Also, although she may simply have resented the fact that Tortelier wasn't Pleeth, to whom she was intensely loyal, she found the 48-year-old Frenchman's celebrated charm a bit calculated.

Jacqueline's time in Paris was interrupted twice by prior commitments with the BBC Symphony Orchestra in London: a UN Day concert at which she played the Elgar, with Norman Del Mar conducting, and a concert at the Royal Festival Hall, where she played the Schumann Cello Concerto. Of the Festival Hall performance, *The Times* reviewer wrote, "All customary strictures on youthful prodigies and premature concert-giving go by the board in the way of this young player, for she is already an artist in her own right, with as instinctive a feeling for the true significance of every phrase as had she had a lifetime of experience behind her." In December, the *Daily Express* named her Soloist of the Year. Sydney Edwards, its music critic, wrote: "There was a huge array of talent to choose from, ranging from the 78-year-old Artur Rubinstein jumping about on the piano stool and throwing off two concerts in one evening, and John Ogdon, back from Moscow bestrewn with honour. But Jacqueline du Pré has exceptional qualities for her age, and she is such a *nice* girl. I think we have a world class winner here."

The recognition was gratifying but confusing. Publicly Jacqueline was a world class soloist; privately she was one of many students in the class at the Conservatoire, and increasingly lonely and depressed. In February she decided to cut short her stay in Paris by a month and fly home. After her final lesson, Tortelier told her, with eerie prescience, "You will be the Ginette Neveu of the cello." Ginette Neveu was a brilliant young French violinist whose career ended tragically in an air crash just after the war.

When Jacqueline returned to London, just after her eighteenth birthday, she was seriously questioning whether she ever wanted to play the cello again.

Part Two

7

Late adolescence is a dangerous time for musical prodigies; they are prone to crises, burn-out and even full-blown breakdowns when they leave their childhood, or the lack of a childhood, behind. Casals wrote in his autobiography of his "'epoch of distress' at fifteen, after years of working harder than a child should . . . It made me physically ill . . . It was terrible." Although Casals relished his rare communication with audiences and had already tasted success, he was overwhelmed by doubts and suffered from severe depression for three long years. Pianist Lorin Hollander lost his confidence at seventeen and then, terrifyingly, control (eventually regained) of the right side of his body. In his late teens, Yehudi Menuhin began questioning how and why he played as he had done instinctively almost from babyhood – and found himself almost incapable of playing at all. His predicament was analogous to that of the cyclist who tries to analyse intellectually the process that has always come easily, and promptly falls off his bike. Adolescence is the time, said Menuhin, when the goose may lose its ability to produce golden eggs.

In 1967, after Jacqueline had become one of the most admired and sought-after soloists in the world, her mother told an interviewer, "Just when she'd had tremendous success, she began to have serious doubts as to whether she was good enough. She just wondered if she had the ability to carry on with this tremendous career. She became very depressed and was completely lost for a time – she didn't touch the cello at all." Jacqueline herself said, "I was changing from a child into an adult, and work took on a different kind of aspect. I didn't have that many engagements. I felt a little bit lost."

In the spring of 1963 Jacqueline gave a recital with Jill Severs; they played Bach by candlelight in a beautiful old hall in Cambridge. When they next played together, something curious and unprecedented took place. The venue was Corsham Court, a beautiful old stately home. The programme included the Vivaldi E minor Sonata; Jacqueline didn't have the music, but she knew the piece well. Near the beginning of the fast movement, she simply dried up. Jill was astonished;

73

she stopped, and they began again. At the same spot in the music, Jacqueline dried up a second time, and then a third. After a fourth start she played straight through, flawlessly. She offered no explanation, but it was clear that something was disturbing her normally indestructible concentration.

She discontinued her lessons with Pleeth and refused most engagements.* She slept a great deal – perhaps a symptom of depression – but sporadically continued her extracellistic activities. In 1963 she mentioned to Joan Clwyd's daughter, now Alison Brown, that she thought she would like to study maths, a subject closely allied to music. Alison, seven years Jackie's senior, introduced her to her friend and contemporary, George Debenham, a maths teacher who lived quite near Portland Place. Debenham says: "She would come once a week to my place in Regent's Park. In the beginning, the lessons lasted about an hour. She was playing occasionally at that time, but not much, after having actually stopped altogether for a while. She was going through quite a crisis and was very much of two minds as to whether she wanted to go on with her music. My main recollection is of someone who had been pushed too hard and was finding it very difficult to bear up against the strain. She desperately needed a break, time to gather herself up.

"She felt torn between her need to fulfil her tremendous musical gift and her desire for what she saw as a 'normal' life, with a husband and children. She didn't want to fail herself, or other people. A lot of money had been invested in her, apart from everything else. People's lives were geared around her, all expecting things of her. But there were also things inside herself that she wanted to fulfil. She was very young; she didn't want the pressure of *having* to perform. It was an enormous burden – a very tense, difficult situation. Inside Jackie, the conflict was pretty stormy. I think she was tussling with it all the time."

For more than half of her life, Jacqueline had focused on a single goal, imposed to some extent, if only through osmosis, by her mother. She had lived entirely in the present, with no thought of what an adult career would entail. Now she contemplated the solitary, peripatetic life of an international soloist – the pressures, the frustrations, the times when she would be expected to perform whether she felt like it or not. What she played, and where she played it, would be controlled to a great extent by agents, impresarios and

---

* She did honour a previous commitment to repeat her 1962 Prom concert – the Elgar, with Sir Malcolm Sargent conducting.

record companies. Her best friend, the cello, had become a relentless taskmaster that could never be satisfied. Dedication, intuition and her natural gifts had brought her a long way; to go farther would seem to require a conscious choice, perfection of the work over that of the life. To deepen her musical insight she would need to bring to it the weight of experience, of living; but if she continued to work as single-mindedly as she had in the past, when could she live? The dilemma made her feel more isolated than ever. Joan Clwyd offered understanding, but Jacqueline needed the support of someone of her own generation. She turned to George Debenham, who was only too happy to provide it.

Debenham found her to be "a very intelligent person and immensely curious about all sorts of things. She was very conscious of having missed out on a lot of life, having concentrated her whole being on the cello. She was particularly conscious of the fact that other people were different. She wanted to learn the things that other people had learned.

"I started by teaching her about the basics of mathematics. It was very basic; she hadn't got far in her school learning. I would give her homework and she'd bring it back the next week, sometimes having succeeded, sometimes not. But the lessons strayed from mathematics. She was really asking about all sorts of things: the physical world, how things are made up – physics and astronomy and chemistry. I got to know her quite well. She was very shy to begin with, after having been cocooned by her family for so long. She seemed very young for her age, innocent of the world. She'd been so isolated. I suspect she was at home all the time, practising, practising, practising, then getting wheeled out onto the concert platform and performing. I think it was a very tight, close existence. It must have been hell. During the time when I saw a lot of her, she became much more outgoing and bouncy. She had her low periods, but she wasn't depressed as such. She had a tremendous sense of humour. She was a tremendous tease and a great mimic. My main impression of her was really her joy of life."

The bubbling, infectious *joie de vivre* that characterised the essential Jackie caused the vast majority of men, women and children who came into contact with Jacqueline to fall quickly and happily under her spell. Those who fell quickest and hardest tended to be introverted characters who found her emotional generosity irresistible. If Jackie was "bouncy", Debenham was the opposite: tall, dark and dour, he perceived life as a thoroughly serious enterprise. Even though he has since moved out of teaching and into computer marketing, he retains an academic aura. He was a solid, stable young man – the sympathetic rock that Jackie needed at the time. He was also an amateur pianist, and knew a good deal about music. Quite naturally, they soon became more than friends.

In January 1964, three weeks before Jacqueline's nineteenth birthday, the *Evening Standard* ran a story by Sydney Edwards about "this golden-haired, pink-cheeked, happy girl . . . the first cellist of potential greatness to be born in Britain." She was preparing for a recital in Westminster Abbey and a Festival Hall concert in April, at which she would play the Elgar – not, she told Edwards, because she had a particular fondness for the work, but because "this is the work I'm always asked to do. I like all the concertos – Dvořák, Schumann, Haydn, Saint-Saëns. They all reflect different moods." Edwards asked whether she ever got moody. Yes, she said, occasionally – and music was not always a release. "One can always associate oneself with the expression of the music, but one should not use the music for self-expression only. It's important to give what the music itself wants to say." She went on to say that she no longer had "torments of conscience" about not practising four hours a day, and that she'd dropped her yoga class at London University because "it requires a tremendous amount of self-discipline and I've been rather lazy." Edwards was captivated; he said she made him feel ten years younger. In the accompanying photo her smile was dazzling, her hair shoulder length – it would never be short again. She told Edwards that she didn't cook, or do much else at home except look after her room. She did not tell him that Portland Place, and the role she was expected to play within it, had become intolerable to her. To grow up, she would have to get out.

George Debenham knew of her problems at home. "Her father wasn't a strong personality. Her mother was an extremely strong personality. I suspect Piers found it quite difficult having a celebrity for an older sister; she was so highly directed, and he didn't know what he wanted to do." In 1964, Derek du Pré left his job with the Institute of Cost and Works Accounting and went to work for the Chartered Accountants Society of London. It meant leaving the Portland Place flat. Iris and Derek and Piers moved to Gerrards Cross in Buckinghamshire, west of London. Jacqueline moved into a top flat in Kensington Park Road owned by Christopher Finzi's younger brother, Nigel, but found it disappointingly dreary and lonely. She was delighted when Alison Brown, just back from Cambridge and beginning her training as a silversmith, invited Jackie to share her basement flat in Ladbroke Grove.

Outside the confines of Portland Place, Jacqueline began to play again. William Pleeth says, "She'd had a hunger to explore other interests, other parts of herself, but she wasn't sure what she was hungry *for*. She never really came to terms with the conflict; she just sort of went on with her career."

Her return to the concert platform in April, playing Elgar at the Festival Hall, was not auspicious. Perhaps because of her time away from the cello or because critics were for the first time applying adult standards to her playing, reviews were less than glowing. The *Daily Express* called her performance "stiff and square, lacking the conviction to give character to her outstanding talent". *The Times* questioned the choice of the Elgar for "so young if highly gifted an artist . . . It is music cast over with a dark, pessimistic shadow, and this would demand an interpretation of a degree of maturity which is beyond Miss du Pré's present achievement. True, she played in a technically almost impeccable style, producing rounded and resonant tone throughout and demonstrating her left-handed agility in the finale. But . . . her performance failed to capture the intrinsic spirit of the concerto, remaining on the surface a good deal of the time. Nor was the collaboration between soloist and conductor [John Pritchard] ideal."

Jackie never minded what the critics wrote; she said, "One has to be one's own thermometer," and was the best – and harshest – judge of her playing. If she was unhappy with her performance, she knew that she could improve it – if she made the commitment that she continued to resist.

In Ladbroke Grove, the offstage Jackie began to come into her own. Alison Brown had adored Jacqueline from their first meeting at the Clwyd home, some four years earlier. "She struck me just by the clarity of her eyeball, really – the direct gaze that she had. I *instantly* loved her. We spent a year basementing together in 35 Ladbroke Grove, and a year in another basement flat at 15 Addison Avenue. That was a very formative time. I really believe that that was the time when the disease began to hit her. Even then she complained of numb fingertips, and having to warm up for considerable periods before a concert. And I remember her quite often being confused about her eyesight, that it would get blurred.

"She was like a jaunty tomboy, really. But once you started to interact with her, she was ageless. That was the extraordinary thing about her. Once you'd start to converse with the mind behind the silly jolly schoolgirl, you knew you were dealing with a very mature soul. Conversations with Jackie were always highlighted by the unexpected. She had a very quirky tongue, a wicked sense of humour. If you were having a serious conversation about something she'd suddenly tip the scales completely with a certain delicate drawl in her vocal cords, and you'd be tumbling on the floor with the joke of it."

Jacqueline had a slightly breathless, enthusiastic manner of speaking, and during her time in Paris she had picked up a faint shadow of an accent – not identifiably French, but definitely foreign. It was probably unconscious – a trick of her hypersensitive ear – and she never acknowledged it or the various other accents she subsequently acquired, depending on the people and places she encountered. Alison vividly remembers "her clipped, foreign-sounding way of talking. She used her voice the way a great actress would use it. It had a lot of hoarse breaks in it and was capable of vast ranges of innuendo. She could be devastating when she offered some sharp criticism or jokey comment in her most *prim* voice.

"Jackie had the most unusual set of eyes I ever saw. She could melt people instantly with her eyes. She looked at you and spoke to you as though you were very important and precious, and her words would go right into you; she completely meant what she said. She gave to the most humdrum dialogue the same intensity that she gave to her solo passages. She had a Rabelaisian sense of humour. She could break the bubble of any pompous situation, but there was a wonderful tenderness in her as well.

"The moments I spent with her were like gold. Her life was rarefied and hothousey, and she lived intensely in the present. She was very busy, always in demand – rushing in and out, snatching hurried meals, always in motion. I was also busy, doing an art history thesis and silversmithing; I had my study groups and esoteric dancing, and I spent one evening a week in a choir. Our hours were quite different, so we led very separate lives – and loved each other all the more because we met so rarely. We seldom had a meal together. Jackie cooked some bready things, but she was in no way a homemaker. She used her time very well. I never saw her sit back and relax and loll, or read a book. She did love going for walks, sometimes at night, to clear her head.

"Both flats had two bedrooms; Jackie had the larger one because of her cello, but I hardly remember her practising at all. I do remember that she was extremely fussy about her hair. She was constantly washing and doing things to it. While she was living with me, one of my mother's friends advised that she get her hair cut by a posh Italian haircutter in Knightsbridge – because Jackie's hair was getting

a bit long, even for her. It was down to her coccyx. This was before
an important concert, one of the Elgar ones. Jackie came back from
the haircut and wept for about two days. It was only shoulder length,
but for somebody who's used to having hair right down her spine,
this was a great shock. She felt shorn and weak – like Samson. Her
hair was a part of her concert personality. Playing didn't feel so good
without it swinging around.

"If you think about beauty in conventional terms, Jackie should
have been a boy. She had this big rawboned body, obviously the
correct body for the cello. Her appearance veiled the most piercing
intellect I have confronted during my life. She could slash aside
the fuzzy or the superficial and home in instantly on the matter in
hand – an extraordinary quality in someone who still looked just like
a schoolgirl. Though I was seven years her senior, I had a real awe
and reverence for this deeply loving, mature and compassionate
intellect. I was honoured to have her in my flat.

"She had this really brash clothes sense, very *sportif*. She liked to
wear outrageous navy-and-white sailor suits – short, because that
was the style at the time – and bright, eye-catching colour combi-
nations which were not at all flattering. She loved stripes and jolly,
zingy T-shirts – all in such marked contrast to the very sophisticated
dresses she later wore when she performed."

Those sophisticated gowns were the creations of Alison's friend,
Madeleine Dinkel. "Jackie met Madeleine when I took her to an
esoteric group called the Study Society, of which Madeleine and I
were both members. Madeleine had no official rating as a dress
designer but she was an artist, brilliant in all that she touched, and
she was responsible for some magnificent dresses. Jackie was very
pleased with those dresses."

In the sitting-room of the same Hammersmith flat to which Jacqueline went in the Sixties for fittings and chats, Madeleine Dinkel
mused, "If I were to tell anyone who knows me now that I used to
make dresses for Jacqueline du Pré, they wouldn't believe me." She
first met Jackie in 1962: "She was an adolescent; she still had a lot of
puppy fat. She was totally uninhibited, with a most colossal laugh
and a lot of excess energy. Her voice was quite powerful and loud –
you'd imagine she could sing jolly well. The sheer generosity of her
personality seemed to sweep everyone into her heart. I myself am a
rather restrained sort of person, but that didn't seem to stop her
making a friend of me.

"Jackie's world was entirely different from mine. I'm a graphics
designer; I was working as a freelance artist for publishers, doing

book jackets and calligraphy and teaching at art school. Although I wasn't a dressmaker, I could turn my hand to anything. I'd always made things for myself, and I'd designed and made wedding dresses for quite a number of people. I cut my own patterns and designed around their personality. It was always a great success, but there was nothing commercial about it; they were all people I knew. Jackie was a big girl and she couldn't just go into a shop and buy herself a dress to fit, to play the cello in. Anyway, she had no dress sense at all. Who does, at that age? She was far too busy doing music. And musicians generally don't have much visual sense, anyway. So she just got clothes to cover her! I couldn't bear to see this marvellous person, full of genius and vitality, wearing these dreary, awful clothes! I saw her play at the Albert Hall wearing just a sort of circular skirt and blouse and afterwards I said, 'Jackie, you can't wear these awful clothes. I'll make you a proper dress!'

"'Oh, *will* you?' said Jackie. 'Oh, *do*!' And she hugged me. She was a great hugger and I, a very thin, inhibited person, was totally crushed by all this vitality. So I did.

"The first and grandest dress I made was of gold silk. It was the first of many. It was very beautiful; I made some bloody good dresses, if I say it myself. The dresses worked because I didn't have any preconceived notions about the sort of thing she should wear. I just built them around her, so that she could sit in this most ungainly way with her cello between her legs. The constructional problem was a challenge to me. I got beautiful fabrics, and built the dresses so they would take the strain. My goodness, the way she played that cello, it was like an athletic performance. The sweat poured down her, so she'd have to wear a woolly vest underneath to take the sweat. The dresses were all lined and backed so that they wouldn't split, with a close-fitting bodice but room for movement under the arm.

"Jackie was so generous and warm, she'd tell you things to cheer you up or to make life richer for you. She told me once she'd gone to play a concert in Berkshire or someplace at an historic home of the Quakers. It was an afternoon concert, and lots of children came. She said, 'There were children that had a real childhood, like in a story book,' which was very touching. She said one little girl was much more enchanted by the fact that she was a princess in a golden dress than by the music.

"We became quite intimate; you do, if you're making clothes for people. She'd ring me up sometimes from outlandish places, just for a chat. France, Italy, America. I was a sort of therapist – not part of the musical world, from a totally different milieu. She used to tell me all sorts of things about her life. She wasn't a flirt exactly, but she had lots of little flirtations. She was very warm, and had lots of sexuality. She'd fall into relationships very easily, and men would fall under her spell. It seemed to me that the right sort of life for her would have been to have lots of men, and I'm sure they'd have all benefited tremendously! She was just sort of a big force of nature!

"Jackie wore my dresses all over the world – Carnegie Hall, the Albert Hall, you name it. I made nine or ten, each different. I used jewel colours of very good material, so that they showed in the artificial light on the stage: deep purply blue, blue-green. I made one out of a colossal quantity of flame chiffon. And a white crêpe one, to wear at an outdoor concert in Siena. A very fine one of black velvet. But most of them were wild silk, because in artificial light, it's the only thing that holds the light. I'm afraid to say that in my cupboard is a big roll of eight yards of beautiful green silk which I bought to make her a dress with when she was past playing. It was never cut." Dreamily, in a tone that belied her words, Madeleine Dinkel sighed, "I shall have to find someone to make a dress for one day."

8

People tend to describe Jacqueline in superlatives; Madeleine Dinkel says, "She had *more* than us. She had more of everything: more body, more heart, more talent, more energy, more soul, more emotion." During her Ladbroke Grove days, Jacqueline's energy seemed inexhaustible, her enthusiasm boundless. She also possessed a scatty side, illustrations of which recall those of her mother in Brompton Road. Kate Beare, a cellist who lived near by and knew Jackie only slightly at the time, got a phone call from her one day saying that she had to wash something, hadn't any washing powder and was terribly busy – would Kate mind bringing her some? "I thought, My gosh, if this girl is working so hard on her cello, she's not set up to be independent – not if she can't even go and get herself some washing soap, poor girl! She was obviously finding it difficult to cope. I thought she ought to be looked after."

Jacqueline liked to drop in on Jill Severs and her family in Hampstead, to chat with Jill and to play with the children. "She used to gambol up to see us. She adored Tania, my eldest daughter, who was very extroverted. She had the most wonderful whistle, she could do all sorts of trills. The children loved it. We once went for a lovely country walk together, sort of a romp across the country. Then I formed a chamber music group with two other friends of mine. Jackie sometimes came to hear us, with George Debenham. She was totally supportive and sweet, never sat in judgment or anything."

In the summer of 1964, Jacqueline went to a master class in chamber music taught by Nikita Nagarev in Sermonetta, where she and the other students lived in a castle. Back in England, she went to Dartington again and played there with harpsichordist George Malcolm, with whom she later played chamber music at his Wimbledon home and, the following year, at the Royal Festival Hall. Malcolm recalls playing the Bach Sonata in D with her at Dartington. "In rehearsing the twelve-eight Andante movement I said, 'Jackie, we're not actually going to play it as slow as this at the concert, are we?' She casually replied, 'Oh, I think so.' And we did, and it was *right*! John Amis summed up her subconscious message to audiences: 'Listen chaps, this is how it goes' – and it did! She had a wonderful sense of tempo, and I learnt not to argue with her." Malcolm, who had been organist at Westminster Cathedral, discovered that Jackie responded well to the same techniques he'd used successfully with the choirboys – "the same jokes, the same tone of voice, the same kind of badinage. She was very young for her age, and exactly on their wavelength. If I teased her too much and called her a 'wunderkind', she would throw cushions at me. Those were happy days."

In September Jacqueline played the Elgar at her third Prom, this time with Norman Del Mar conducting the BBC Symphony Orchestra. She had for some time had the idea that her technique was insufficient to convey the music she wanted to express, particularly the Dvořák and one of the Haydn cello concertos, and had struggled mightily to improve it. She had hoped that Tortelier would help her but he had contended that she had no problem, that she seemed able to do just about anything with the technique she possessed. In 1964 she studied technique briefly with the cellist Christopher Bunting, but soon discontinued the lessons. She played occasionally with Debenham, never in public; he says, "My playing was a bit of a joke. I could never keep up. We would play a Beethoven sonata, for instance, and go through it over and over because she wasn't happy with the tone or the way she phrased the opening bars." He can't recall ever going with her to other people's concerts; they went to the cinema, and to parties. "She'd never learned to dance but she could improvise, and that was the style at the time."

She occasionally cooked a meal for George, producing excellent food in huge amounts. Jacqueline always enjoyed food enormously; Debenham thought her "rather sensuous in that way". She once rang up a woman she'd met through mutual musician friends, asking how to make a fish pie for George. Like Kate Beare, the woman (who coincidentally married George years later and is now Jane Debenham) was surprised by the request from someone she hardly knew. "It made me think that maybe she didn't know very many people at all well."

With George, Jacqueline visited Alison's relatives in Wales, and Hilary in Ashmansworth. Debenham found Hilary to be a very good flautist, "quite different from Jackie. She had a much slighter build and was more even-tempered – more collected. I wouldn't describe Jackie as a collected person. She and Hilary seemed friendly enough. Christopher Finzi, known as Kiffer, used to tease Jackie unmercifully. He was building up a business in chicken farming and he had a strong musical pull as well; he used to conduct the Newbury String Players, a local amateur string orchestra."

Jenny Ward Clarke, who sometimes played in the cello section of the Newbury String Players, remembers an occasion when Jacqueline did, as well. "I think it was in 1964. We played Bartók. Jackie wore a kind of big flowery dress. From a distance she looked very striking and beautiful – but when you looked at her close, she was just sort of a puppy. She hadn't yet had time to grow into that wonderful kind of elegance that she had at the height of her career.

"Jackie and I were on the first desk. She wasn't very experienced at playing in orchestras, but she was *full* of enthusiasm. She sat there and played in her own soloistic way with tremendous zest, but she did get a bit carried away – she was about ten miles ahead of everyone, it was quite hard to keep up. She was such a powerful player. She was quite oblivious of the effect she was having on the regular members of the orchestra. A lot of them were quite elderly ladies. We used to call them the Newbury Fruits, after the little jelly sweets. There was one particularly marvellous character – a spinster, who had about fifteen cats. She had worked in the post office all her life and for as far back as I could remember, even when I was a child, she had played in the cello section. She wasn't very good, but it was just about the best thing in her life. I'm sure that quite the *best* day in her life, ever, was the day that Jackie played in the orchestra. Her face was like a child being taken to see the Queen."

In 1964 Emmie Tillett's list of clients included Stephen Bishop, an intense 25-year-old pianist from Los Angeles who had studied in London with Dame Myra Hess. Bishop had performed with the San Francisco Symphony when he was eleven, and made his Wigmore Hall début in 1961 – the same year as Jacqueline's. In appearance and temperament he was in many ways Jacqueline's opposite – of medium height (she was five feet nine inches), with dark eyes, hair and moods, and an analytical approach to music and life. Like Jackie, he looked about sixteen. Thinking that her two young clients would make an attractive duo, Mrs. Tillett persuaded the impresario Ivan Sutton to book them for one in a series of prestigious recitals at Goldsmiths' Hall in September.

Jacqueline needed and wanted a regular accompanist. "The cello is a lonely instrument," she once told a reporter. "One is incomplete because you have this lovely single line . . . but you need the harmony of the other instruments to tell you about direction and structure." She took her cello to the flat in which Bishop lived with his wife, to see whether their playing was compatible. Bishop had never played with a cellist before but he had been to Jacqueline's début and been "absolutely overwhelmed . . . A high proportion of musicians will say that she's the most musically gifted person they've ever encountered. Her talent was so beautiful, so strong. She had such an extraordinary physical identification with the cello. She seemed to be able to put all of her feelings into the instrument."

The combination of cello and piano has such potential for varied colours and textures that most great composers, from Beethoven onward, have written cello sonatas. At Goldsmiths' Hall Jacqueline and Bishop played sonatas by Bach, Beethoven, Brahms and Britten. They were warmly received – but the cello, perhaps the most difficult instrument to accompany, requires a pianist with a soft, sensitive pedal, and some observers felt that Bishop's forceful playing dominated the cello to the detriment of the music. The critics' cautious consensus was that the partnership was promising but had a long way to go.

Professionally and privately, the relationship went quite a long way. During the next two and a half years, Jacqueline and Bishop (who has since 1975 called himself Stephen Bishop-Kovacevich) played together all over Britain and in America, briefly, as well. Youth, proximity and their common purpose took their inevitable course, leading to what Alison Brown discreetly refers to as Jackie's complicated boyfriend situation. She says, "My poor old friend George loved Jackie deeply. He spent hours of time and trouble ferrying her everywhere, carrying her cello and really being her taxi. George was very solid, unemotional, dependable; he had qualities which were very precious to Jackie for a time. When she became involved with Stephen Bishop, George felt ousted and was deeply angry with her, so she had her first punishing setback from a man." When the end came it would be explosive, but for a time Debenham remained Jackie's "boyfriend" and the relationship with Bishop was purely musical.

Finally free of the very short lead on which she'd been kept at Portland Place, Jacqueline was, says Jill Severs, "like a wild horse that needed its head. Life was there for her for the first time, really. She sort of hurtled about, wanting to experience all of it. She was ready to live and play the field and find out what life was about." Even in the insular music world it was, after all, the Sixties, when rules were to be broken and limits exceeded. With characteristic zest, Jacqueline, who never did anything by half measures, plunged back into music, and into life.

She and Bishop played the provinces – a far cry from the glamorous ambience of the Wigmore and Festival Halls, but more relaxed. "We played twenty or thirty recitals together," Bishop recalls, "in places like Tunbridge Wells, Cambridge, Dublin. There are something like a hundred recital places in this country and each one puts on a series of three or four recitals a year. Jackie was what everybody wanted to hear; there had been so many waves from the recital at the Wigmore Hall, she was already a celebrity. The offers just poured in.

"I had a car, but we mostly travelled on British Rail. I remember once lifting her Strad from the overhead rack as the train pulled in to Victoria. I dropped the bloody thing and she took it out in the middle of Victoria Station and started playing. She wasn't fussed about it, and it was perfectly all right. Sometimes we travelled to where we were playing and came back to London after the recital. Sometimes we came back the next day. In those days the people who put on the concert would extend hospitality. After the concert there would be cold sandwiches and then they'd put you up for the night. I didn't have any money then, so I'd always accept hospitality if it was offered. I think Jackie did also; hotels are so cold. We used to split the fee – £150 or less. The halls were small, they might hold three hundred people. Of course I never knew what kind of piano I'd encounter.

"We played a few recitals in London: Goldsmiths' Hall, Chelsea Town Hall, Walthamstow Assembly Hall. At the Royal Festival Hall, I remember that we changed the programme at the last minute. We were supposed to play the Beethoven A major but it wasn't ready, and we changed to the D major on the afternoon of the concert, a Sunday afternoon."

The delicate balance of a musical duo requires that each partner maintain his or her individual personality within the limits of a shared concept of the work as a whole. Also essential is an almost clairvoyant sense of the other's timing, dynamics and rhythm. A sonata is an intricate dance, with the lead shifting continuously from one partner to the other. If one of them dominates for a single wrong second, it can only be at the expense of the music. Mutual dependence is total; together they succeed or fail. Bishop says, "We rehearsed a lot. We learned to make compromises. Everybody wants to play pieces in different tempi; it's very seldom that you agree. We learned that rather than compromise on a tempo in the middle it was better to say, 'Right, that movement is yours, we'll do it your way.' Then at least there is some conviction in the performance, and we might do the next movement my way. It's much better if you're going to give up an idea to just give it up completely. I don't work that way with everyone, but I did with Jackie. When you're young, as we were, you're perhaps more enthusiastic about your ideas."

9

"Inside a stringed instrument," Paul Tortelier wrote in his autobi-ography, "is a small piece of wood that nobody sees, but which is of vital importance to the quality of tone. It connects the top and back of the instrument and also compensates for the pressure of the bridge. It must be positioned with enormous care; a change of only a few millimetres can alter the quality of tone. The English and Americans call it the soundpost . . . the French and Italians call it *l'âme* and *l'anima*, which both mean 'the soul'. The cello is more than a piece of wood . . . it speaks with the voice of the soul."

Jacqueline once described the sound of the cello as "something basic and earthy, coming from one's guts and one's heart". It is a sound which, more than any other instrument, approximates to that of the human voice. In its upper register it can be poignant and touching; at the other extreme of its range, profound. Its middle and most frequently used register produces the more familiar smooth baritone sound. Whatever the register, the cello's sound, its shape, the warmth of its wood and the way the player virtually hugs it make it the most voluptuous of instruments. At the same time, cello and bow are merely wood, hair, gut and metal, and wringing beauty from them involves the entire body: feet planted firmly for balance, knees holding the instrument securely, arm muscles from shoulder to wrist for hours of bowing, and fingers like steel to span long stretches and depress strings which are thick and long and require pressure that can exceed twenty pounds. Casals, who spoke of bloody fingerboards at the end of some of his concerts, compared the physical exertion and dexterity demanded of a cellist to that of chopping down a tree and threading a package of needles at the same time.

The strong, lyrical tone of the cello and its often introspective quality have led many composers to write cello concertos; but although the cello is ideally suited to playing unaccompanied or with just one other instrument, in a concerto it is the least penetrating of all solo instruments. The essence of the form is the dramatic tension between the cello's resonance and the orchestra's power, and the cello's range merges too well with the overall sound of the orchestra.

Jacqueline had complained to Peter Thomas and others that much as she loved her Strad, she had to work terribly hard to get what she wanted out of it when she played a concerto. Her benevolent godmother, Mrs. Holland, had her solicitors instruct a London dealer in string instruments to look for an even finer Strad, to be purchased for Jacqueline as a gift. In 1964, word came that the "Davidov", considered to be one of the three or four finest cellos in the world, was for sale.

When Antonio Stradivari was born in Cremona in 1644, the cello was only a few decades old and had merely been used as an orchestral base. (Although Haydn and Mozart used and respected the cello, it would not be fully accepted as a solo instrument until Beethoven wrote his cello sonatas at the end of the next century.) Stradivari inherited from his teacher, Nicolò Amati, the secrets of more than a century of violin-making. In 1707, although he had previously made only one cello, Stradivari decided that the then-standard size was too big, and reduced the dimensions to a size that has served as a model for most makers since the beginning of the nineteenth century. The fifty Stradivarius cellos that survive today represent a standard of excellence that has never been surpassed. The exquisite workmanship, the combination of strength and elegance – especially of the F-holes and scrolls – will probably never be equalled.

String players claim they can recognise the sound of a Strad from behind a screen; even when played pianissimo, its unique quality carries it to the back of a hall. The sound owes a great deal to Stradivari's legendary varnish, the formula for which has been lost. Varnish that dries too quickly produces a hard, glassy tone colour, limited in range and sound. If the varnish is too thick and oily, it inhibits the wood's vibrations in a different, equally unsatisfactory way. Only after the varnish settles to its final consistency, which can take years, is it possible to assess the long-term quality of an instrument.

Stradivari's varnish dried to a light, delicate elastic skin. The Davidov, made in 1712, during what is considered his golden period, has a glorious rich, orange-red varnish, and a sound that pierces the heart. Its first owner was an Italian nobleman; after that there is a gap in its history until the mid-nineteenth century, when the Russian Count Wilhorsky bought it from another Russian count and then presented it, in 1863, to Carl Davidov,* a one-time child prodigy who became the greatest Russian player of his day. Davidov also

* Also known in the West as Charles Davidoff.

wrote some passionate and melancholy cello music, and was a major force in the Russian cello school.

After Davidov's death in 1889, the instrument acquired his name. It was taken out of Russia at the time of the Revolution, and later bought by an amateur French cellist, after whose death it was sold to a wealthy American businessman, Herbert N. Straus. In 1964, Mrs. Holland's representatives learnt that Straus's widow had put the Davidov on the market at a price estimated at $90,000. It was taken to London where Jacqueline tried it, fell in love with it and, for a price said to be the highest ever paid for a stringed instrument, became its owner. Guilhermina Suggia, who once wrote, "The finer the instrument, the more does it seem to require a great player," would have approved.

Stephen Bishop, asked whether any of Jacqueline's performances particularly stand out in his mind, instantly recalled the evening in February 1965, when she played the Dvořák Cello Concerto at the Royal Festival Hall. The Dvořák was one of her two favourite concertos, the other being the Schumann, and she was substituting at very short notice for Leonard Rose. Bishop can't remember who was conducting (it was Sir Adrian Boult), but does remember that the second movement had "that radiance, that rapturous quality that she could give". In a letter to the editors of the *Evening Standard* a few days later, Sir Malcolm Sargent objected to the *Standard* having headed its review TOO AGGRESSIVE, MISS DU PRÉ, and pointed out that the sub-editor who chose the headline "could with equal truth have quoted from the criticism – MASTERLY STYLE, MISS DU PRÉ."

At Antony Hopkins's invitation, Jacqueline went to Norfolk to play the Schumann Concerto with the Norwich Philharmonic Orchestra, an amateur group that Hopkins conducted. Dr. Ian G. Gray, a violinist in the orchestra at the time, was struck by her "youthful charm and intense musicianship. Jacqueline showed her insatiable appetite for music at the afternoon rehearsal. Not content with working on the concerto for an hour or more, she then expressed a wish to sit with the cellos for the remainder of the rehearsal. This she did, at the back desk, where she was happy to 'turn over' for the incumbent!" Hopkins recalls, "It was the first chance she'd had to play the *Polovtsian Dances* – and the first time the orchestra ever had a rear engine cello section. The piece is so physical and rhythmical, she loved playing it." After the rehearsal he and Jacqueline went to tea at the home of an orchestra member, but not without borrowing a supply of music from another cellist so that they could play Beethoven and Brahms together between cups of tea. Her performance that night, says Dr. Gray, was "absolutely glorious and unforgettable; I was at the third desk of fiddles and had a privileged 'view'. The audience of a thousand were ecstatic and recalled her many times; an encore was demanded and finally Jacqueline came on, stood at the front of the platform and modestly announced, 'a bit of Bach'. Whereupon she played an unaccompanied piece in an atmosphere which was at once electric. We were all unashamedly entranced."

Of the two conductors with whom Jacqueline was most closely associated during her career, the first, Sir John Barbirolli, had been her affectionate admirer since she had first auditioned for the Suggia, at the age of eleven. They never played together, however, until April 7th, 1965, when Barbirolli conducted his Hallé Orchestra at the Royal Festival Hall, and Jacqueline played the Elgar Cello Concerto.

Barbirolli had Sir Edward Elgar's music in his bones. Like the composer, Barbirolli was a romantic and, at times, a depressive. Elgar once described the Cello Concerto, his last major work, as "a man's attitude to life". Its four brief movements, from the haunting, lyrical opening theme to the poignant, elegiac ending, demand intense concentration from soloist, orchestra and audience. Barbirolli had been in the audience for the first ever performance of the concerto in 1927, and was himself the soloist at its second performance (with the Bournemouth Municipal Orchestra). Although the Edwardian Elgar was the first English composer of stature since Purcell, his work had initially been received with indifference and reservations in Britain; purists accused him of being overly emotional, even a bit vulgar – a musical counterpart of Kipling. After Elgar's death in 1934, Barbirolli had resolved to enlarge the public's appreciation of the composer's work at home and abroad. He subsequently conducted the world's leading cellists in the concerto, and was as sympathetic to it as anyone. Today it is rated as one of the greatest of all cello concertos.

Barbirolli, diminutive in stature, was artistically a giant. He had a volatile personality and an iron ego, but he was always willing to accept and support the interpretation of a soloist he respected, even if it differed from his own. He tried to tone down the natural exuberance in Jacqueline's playing, but only slightly, saying, "Jackie is sometimes accused of excessive emotions . . . but I love it. When you are young, you should have an excess of everything. If you haven't got an excess when you are young, what are you going to pare off as the years go by?"

At the Festival Hall concert, Jacqueline received the ultimate accolade: the orchestra's applause. Bernard Jacobsen wrote in *High Fidelity* of the extraordinary rapport between the twenty-year-old Jacqueline and the conductor who was in at the birth of the concerto and concluded, "The performance realised an ideal which the composer himself would have blessed." A few months later, Jacqueline recorded the work with Barbirolli and the London Symphony Orchestra at the Kingsway Hall.

It was her second recording of a concerto; the first, made a few months earlier, was by Delius, with Sir Malcolm Sargent conducting the Royal Philharmonic Orchestra. Jacqueline had recorded it on just a few days' notice, after spending a week at the beach with her family – without her cello. The concerto consists of just one long movement, and is as serene as Elgar's is passionate – a subtle, introverted reverie that Jacqueline privately called "diluted water". Publicly she played it, according to Bernard Jacobsen, "exquisitely . . . with a breadth and suppleness of phrasing that keeps the music moving". But the Elgar concerto had already become her trademark, the quintessentially English work with which the quintessentially English girl would remain linked for life. The record was released in the US as well as Great Britain, and was the beginning of her international reputation. In December the *Guardian*'s music critic, Edward Greenfield, called it the performance he had always dreamed of and the record of the year. "Not since Master Yehudi Menuhin recorded Elgar's Violin Concerto with the composer," he wrote, "has a young artist played with such profound dedication on record as Jacqueline du Pré." He credited her with "that rarest of all musical magics, the ability to command attention by sheer power of concentration".

During the next several years Jacqueline's recording of the concerto, combined with her performances of it all over the world, would bring the work such popularity that Elgar's music publishers would present her with an elegant gold-lettered, blue leather score. In twenty-three years, the record has never been out of print, and is now considered a classic. But although the Elgar meant a great deal to Jacqueline, it was never her favourite. The music critic Robert Anderson, who was with her when she first heard the recording, has written, "She burst into tears and said, 'That was not what I meant at all!'"

10

In the spring of 1965, Jacqueline and the 110-member BBC Symphony Orchestra visited the United States for the first time. The three-week tour consisted of fifteen concerts, all devoted to twentieth-century music. The more modern works were conducted by Pierre Boulez, who had an affinity for them; Jacqueline's concerts, at which she invariably played the Elgar, were conducted by Antal Dorati. Pianist John Ogdon and singer Heather Harper were the other soloists on the tour.

Off the stage, Jacqueline still looked like an overgrown, somewhat ungainly schoolgirl – but when she strode confidently onto the platform wearing one of Madeleine Dinkel's magnificent gowns, she was positively regal. In Boston, Philadelphia, Washington, DC and seven other eastern cities, audiences cheered and critics swooned. Michael Steinberg of the *Boston Globe* wrote, "Everything she does proclaims brio and authority . . . The lush post-Romantic world of Elgar's beautiful concerto suits her perfectly, and she plays this music ardently and with grandeur." She gave her final concert of the tour on the evening of Friday, May 14th, in the matchless ambience of Carnegie Hall. In the words of Leighton Kerner of the *Village Voice*, her performance "stood the audience on its ravished ear". John Gruen of the *Herald Tribune* wrote, "One must go back to the heyday of Casals, or to so singular an artist as Rostropovich for adequate comparison . . . To say that her technique is faultless would be an understatement – it is simply dazzling." Most smitten of all was Raymond Ericson of the *New York Times*:

A tall, slim blonde, Miss du Pré looked like a cross between Lewis Carroll's Alice and one of those angelic instrumentalists in Renaissance paintings. And, in truth, she played like an angel, one with extraordinary warmth and sensitivity . . .

Miss du Pré and the concerto seemed made for each other, because her playing was completely imbued with the romantic spirit. Her tone was sizeable and beautifully burnished. Her technique was virtually flawless, whether she was playing the sweeping chords that open the concerto, sustaining a ravishing pianissimo tone, or keeping the fast repeated-note figures in the scherzo going at an even pace.

Astonishing was the colour she brought to the concerto's dominant lyricism, the constant play of light and delicacy of emotion in a fresh, spontaneous, yet perfectly poised way.

At the end of the concert Miss du Pré was brought back to the stage again and again by the large audience, and she was applauded by her fellow musicians in the orchestra. One performance does not indicate the range of an artist, but at least in the Elgar concerto the cellist was superb.

Hugh Maguire, leader of the BBC Symphony Orchestra at the time, had first seen Jacqueline play in the BBC's Maida Vale studio in 1962. "Until that day, I'd been sceptical about dazzling young soloists. I believed in Yehudi Menuhin and I thought, Well, that's one that's come from up above, and there's not likely to be another like that. But of course when I saw Jackie play, and from only a few feet away, I was totally, *totally* knocked out. I was actually sort of choked; it was so beautiful and so inspired and so magical that I didn't speak to her. There was nothing one could say.

"The tour of America was relatively relaxed. I sort of looked after Jackie, made sure she had a good time. I introduced her to some of the young boys in the orchestra; they were all in awe of her. There was absolutely no pressure on her. She was a daisy, a free young girl. Without any bother she could play the Elgar Concerto. She could have played it lying on her back or standing on her head. Of course it was a marvellous thing for her to play in New York and Boston and other cities for the first time and have a new public and all that. I think she was hyped up all the time, but not overwhelmed by it. *She* was overwhelming."

After the tour, Maguire invited Jacqueline to his home in Willesden, where she met his wife, Suzie, and their five children. She became a frequent visitor, riding her bicycle up from Ladbroke Grove – perhaps four miles, all uphill – to see them. Maguire remembers her arriving at his house "with her hair flowing in the sunshine. Suzie took her to her heart, of course. Everybody did. The door was always open to Jackie. Sometimes she'd stay and have a meal, and slowly she began to be absorbed into my household. The children, all of them younger than Jackie, adored her and looked up to her. She was a very exciting girl to be with."

Musically, it was an exciting time in London. A new generation of young musicians had dramatically brightened the scene with their energy and enthusiasm, and three blazing British talents – Janet Baker, John Ogdon and Jacqueline du Pré – had particularly captured the public's imagination. Other exceptional talents were just becoming known: Ashkenazy, just arrived from the Soviet Union; Martha Argerich, from Argentina; Tamás Vásáry and Peter Frankl, from Hungary. They gave far fewer concerts than is customary today – twenty or thirty, as opposed to sixty or seventy, in a season – so there was time to attend each other's concerts, and to socialise. They were all extraordinarily good-natured – not competing but showing their wares, sharing one another's successes, attending parties that rarely ended without some chamber music having been performed.

Chamber music is a deceptively dry term for the intimate and infinitely challenging art known as "the music of friends". It generally means string quartets by Haydn, Mozart, Beethoven or Schubert; it can be performed anywhere, but a small room is ideal. It is the antithesis of orchestral music, in that instead of each section producing a mass of sound, each instrumentalist performs an individual line, complementing the others except when called upon to demonstrate his or her instrument's unique colour and facility. Chamber music can be lively or it can be profound, but never trite or obvious. Its success is as unlikely – and as rewarding – as a marriage of individuals who communicate and co-operate perfectly with one another – but with four or five partners in the marriage, each of them expecting equal rights!

Jacqueline played chamber music whenever and wherever she could – at Harry Blech's, at the pianist Fou Ts'ong's, at Hugh Maguire's – and no one who played with her will ever forget the experience. Whatever the hour, however worn out she might be, the fire was there. For violinist Trevor Connah, who was with the BBC Symphony during the American tour, "Playing chamber music with Jackie was the happiest time of my life. I remember Hugh saying, with his Irish twang, 'Sure, I've never played so loud in all my life!' Like all great artists, Jackie had a unique way of expressing things. You always could tell it was Jackie playing. She played so musically that you weren't even aware of her technical prowess. She seemed to have a heightened sense of awareness, maybe something like what you might get on LSD. She seemed to live on another plane."

Maguire says, "Everyone was taken under Jackie's spell. Her music was so overpowering, and there was such an abundance of it. One night at Fou Ts'ong's we played right through the night: Mozart, the Schubert E flat, the Mendelssohn D minor, various Beethoven,

95

all the big pieces. Jackie brought out the best in everybody when she played the cello. She had such wonderful intuition, such a wonderful way of playing. It was infectious. I've never played the violin as well as I did when I played with Jackie. We did a performance of the Brahms Double Concerto in the Festival Hall on one occasion and my friends said, 'This girl is a genius, she's in a different league from you!' And she was, of course! But somehow when I played with her I found myself sort of scrambling, climbing up into that league. She had this ability to bring out not only the best everyone could do, but even *more* than one could do!''

At Maguire's house, chamber music became a big activity. "Jackie would always want to play, sometimes at the most extraordinary times. It might be eleven o'clock at night; everyone else would be asleep, and she'd suddenly say, 'Oh, Hugh, let's play some quartets or piano trios!' We'd phone up somebody like Steve – I'd drive over with Jackie and fetch him. We'd come back to the house and play for an hour or two or three or four and then have some coffee and eventually go to bed. On those occasions it was absolutely obvious that Jackie had to spend the night. Eventually, she wound up living in my house. And that was how the music happened in my room.''

In June, Jacqueline played Haydn's Cello Concerto in C with the London Mozart Players at the Royal Festival Hall – a performance that inspired the young Prince Charles, who was in the audience, to take up the cello himself. Harry Blech, musical director of the London Mozart Players, accompanied Jacqueline on that and a number of other occasions, and remembers the extraordinary effect her playing had on people in the orchestra. "At the Festival Hall, one Swiss lady was in tears. Jackie's style of playing was so innocent then, extremely touching and moving. She was a completely intuitive, instinctive player. Some people have a touch so personal and so profound, nobody can explain what it is, why one artist has it. It may have something to do with the way the sound vibrates, like some wonderful voice that you immediately fall in love with. All music and all performing is about making love, anyway. Not sex, but in the deepest sort of way. When Jackie picked up the cello, it spoke to your heart.''

Before the Festival Hall concert, Madeleine Dinkel had received a letter, adorned with flourishes and addressed in Jacqueline's large, round, legible hand to Maestra Madalena Dinkalla. In it, Jackie thanked her for "the most beautiful dress in the world" and asked, in her most cajoling and self-deprecatory manner, if Madeleine had the time and inclination "to m-m-m-make me – hold it! – NOT another SUMptuous, man-smashing evening dress, but a posh short dress" to wear in Spoleto, Italy, where she was to give six concerts at what she understood was a "rather grand version of the Edinburgh Festival (if you can imagine that!)". The impassioned plea ended with a drawing of a heart with a fire blazing inside it and the playful signature:

JACKIE

A picturesque setting is almost as intrinsic to a music festival as the music, and Spoleto, on a mountain slope seventy miles from Rome, was as picturesque as a setting could be. Gian Carlo Menotti had founded the festival in 1958, to give young European and American artists an opportunity to appear in opera, plays and concerts. It was an informal affair; there were lunchtime and evening concerts, and parties in luxurious villas. In that visually and musically stimulating setting, wearing her man-smashing dress, Jacqueline met the pianist Richard Goode.

Jacqueline was a romantic, impetuous young woman who had by now discovered her very considerable sexual power and was experimenting with it. The 21-year-old Goode was physically very like Stephen Bishop: shorter than Jacqueline, with a compact build and dark colouring. Like Bishop, Goode was a powerful pianist, American, and represented in Europe by Emmie Tillett. The two men were temperamentally alike, as well – introspective, moody, analytical. When Goode got back to London from Italy, his friend Jeremy Siepmann – broadcaster, music teacher and amateur musician – met him at the airport. Siepmann says, "When Richard arrived, he at once began to talk about Jackie. We all met for an early supper, somewhere around Piccadilly, and I fell in love with her on sight. Her extraordinary openness, lack of stuffiness or any sort of 'side' or 'front' or manner. Her abundant youth. Her incredible long golden hair. She wasn't exactly beautiful, but at the same time she was. There was a kind of excitement, something about the combination of vitality, youth and fame. And this incredible possession when she played. Had I not heard her play, I doubt that I would have fallen in love with her. I fell in love with the music, as well. She was the greatest cellist I've ever heard. Musically I felt she was totally honest and didn't fake anything. Whereas I was aware that she did fake a lot socially.

"I wasn't blinded by being in love with her. I knew that underneath that sunny exterior there was a very complicated personality. You could detect it in her playing. A simple person could not have played the way she did. I could see that she was manipulative – she *told* me she was quite consciously manipulative – but that only added to the attraction.

"Apart from embracing her, I never had any physical relationship with Jackie. She was not overtly sexual. I was very timorous in the realm of sexual matters, and I have no idea how she would have reacted had I chosen to pursue it as something sexual. It always *seemed* to me that she left the door open, but that was only my impression. She had a way of gazing at you with a timeless, secret message – a long stare, as though she was in love with you, drawing you into her web. I saw her look at several people like that, people I know she wasn't in love with. I knew she faked that. I think I even knew she was faking it when she did it to me, but it worked. I knew I was in her power, as it were, but surrendered willingly.

"She had no shortage of admirers – myself, Richard, Stephen Bishop, Hugh Maguire, an American friend of mine who was a Rhodes Scholar at Oxford. I would say that Jackie did everything she could to encourage all of us – and certainly gave the impression that she was in love with Richard. There was no question that she loved knowing that we were all in love with her, and was playing us all off against each other. Sometimes we would all congregate in a restaurant, or in our flat. My wife, Joanna, who played the flute but was not a musician, found herself catering to this phalanx of lovelorn admirers, with Jackie as the queen in the middle. When Jackie wasn't entrancing all of us in one room, she would go through to the kitchen and talk to Joanna, whose quite considerable self-confidence she very systematically undermined. She told her what an inferior instrument the flute was and talked about her sister, Hilary – also a flautist – in a very denigrating way. I think her treatment of Joanna was bound up with her sister in some way. I would have thought that Joanna represented no threat to her whatever – unless she had a need to conquer everyone. I eventually told Jackie with some concern that what she'd been saying to my wife was making her really miserable – and then she said a very extraordinary thing. She said, 'I knew the moment I saw Joanna that I had to destroy her. I don't understand it and I don't like it, but I felt that I had to do it.' She was absolutely open about the fact that she felt that way.

"There was a lot of *Sturm und Drang*. One night about midnight the doorbell rang. I went downstairs and there was Stephen Bishop, whom I had never seen before – I recognised him from pictures – looking like Raskolnikov. Very grimly he said, 'Is Jackie du Pré here?' I said yes. He said, 'Would you tell her I'm here?' I asked him to come in; he said, 'I'll wait here.' So I went up and told her, and she went off with him. Leaving Richard upstairs. He hadn't realised he was in a hornet's nest. After that everything became extremely dramatic. I became a kind of go-between. Jackie would ring up and talk at great length about her feelings for Richard and about her feelings for Stephen Bishop, and I got very involved in this French farce. One door opening and another slamming shut."

In August, Jacqueline told an *Observer* reporter, "I enjoy it all – the music, of course, the travel, being solitary, all ties broken. But now I'd like to study again to catch up on the years spent playing." She had in fact accepted an invitation to study in Moscow with Mstislav Rostropovich. She had first met the Russian cellist at the home of her godfather, Lord Harewood, when she was fourteen years old. Accompanied by her mother, she had played a Beethoven sonata for him and he had made her perform a series of progressively more difficult exercises and figurations until she had reached the limit of her technique. Now, more or less as a formality, she was to audition for him. She asked Richard Goode to accompany her, and it was arranged that Rostropovich would come to the Siepmanns' flat to hear them play.

To Siepmann's surprise, Jacqueline seemed nervous about the audition; she told him and Goode that she wanted to play pieces with which Rostropovich was not too familiar, about which he would not have preconceived opinions. Goode pointed out that Rostropovich knew the cello repertoire better than anyone, probably even better than Casals did at that time, and that it would be futile to try to second-guess him.

Rostropovich arrived in the company of a translator. Siepmann remembers that he was "infectiously good-humoured, even though he couldn't speak a word of English at that time, and none of us could speak a word of Russian. He wore bright pink, practically fluorescent socks, and a bright tie and a funny-coloured shirt, and exuded energy like nobody I've ever seen. He seemed an absolutely unbuttoned character.

"Jackie and Richard played Beethoven. I can't remember the piece, only the effect of how they played, which was staggering. They were an electric combination; I've never heard anything like it. That wildness! And the chemistry between them! Jackie described him as 'the life force'. She certainly had good taste in pianists!''

After the audition Jacqueline went to the Lucerne Music Festival, where she performed with harpsichordist George Malcolm. During the first week in September she played two Prom concerts at the Albert Hall: the Elgar and *Schelomo*, with Sir Malcolm Sargent and Norman Del Mar, respectively, conducting. By that time, Richard Goode had returned to the States, and Stephen Bishop's marriage had ended.

11

Bishop moved into the London Musical Club, where Jacqueline became a frequent visitor. The club wasn't really a club at all, but rather a dilapidated house in Holland Park that had seen better days. About twenty-five young musicians – some students, some established performers – lived in rooms that were small and shabby, but equipped with pianos. The residents practised, shared dreadful meals, attended occasional concerts in the communal music room and socialised in the bar. Zamira Menuhin, who lived there for a time, recalls that it had "a very Bohemian atmosphere. The manager was a great English eccentric named Mrs. Armstrong, who would sit at her desk reading and holding an umbrella over her head as the rain poured through the ceiling. She certainly never batted an eyelid about anyone's morals when I was there. It was very open, with lovers and ex-lovers spending the night."

Alison Brown, with whom Jacqueline was still nominally living in Ladbroke Grove, says, "While Jackie was living with me, she did a lot of learning about boyfriends. It was a most intense period for both of us; I had just met my first husband, and Jackie and I were both very busy with our emotional involvements. I was good at listening, and she sometimes came to me for advice. I told her about a lady doctor who had helped me with contraception advice.

"Jackie's relationship [with Bishop] was never terribly deep on her part, I thought, but it was highly turbulent, a tense partnership. Jackie felt a great moral responsibility for breaking up his marriage, even though he told her it would have ended anyway. The whole thing got too serious for Jackie in the end, and it was she who broke it off. There were fireworks – with Jackie, nothing ever petered out. She *stormed* through her life, operating at a very high voltage. Everything that happened with Jackie was fast, fiery, larger than life."

Before the final fireworks, Jacqueline continued to perform with Bishop. At the Festival Hall on November 22nd, 1965, they played three transcriptions – Bach's D major Gamba Sonata, Franck's A major Violin Sonata and Schumann's Fantasy Pieces for Clarinet and

Piano – and closed with Beethoven's last Cello Sonata, No. 5 in D major from Opus 102. The reviews were excellent, and a few weeks later they recorded two Beethoven Cello Sonatas, No. 5 and also No. 3, for EMI. In close-up on the album cover, they gaze in opposite directions, Bishop glowering as he may have thought befitted Beethoven, Jacqueline with an enigmatic smile. It was the only record they made together; Bishop still considers it one of the best things he's done.

Although Jacqueline gave every indication of enjoying her post-Carnegie Hall status as an international celebrity, part of her yearned, and always would do, for the road not taken. In the summer of 1965, just after she had been at the Spoleto Festival, Jenny Ward Clarke spotted her walking in Ladbroke Grove and stopped her car. "I remember her coming up and saying how well I looked. I told her I'd been on holiday in Perugia. She wanted to know what we'd done there. I said we'd stayed on this farm and we hadn't really done anything – that we'd travelled around a bit and been with friends and met the local farmers. She listened to it all with great longing, and was obviously very sort of envious. She said, 'Oh, I've just been in Italy.' She'd been at a music festival. It had never occurred to me before to imagine that somebody with her success and the glamour of her life could possibly envy anything that other people did in an unglamorous way. It was obvious that to her that represented a side of life that she felt she would never have – that was simply not open to her. She seemed aware that she was confined to living, or expected to, or *had* to live this way of life, and that it wasn't possible for her to just sort of escape and be ordinary, and do exactly what she wanted."

Jacqueline continued to turn up erratically and unexpectedly at the home of Jill Severs. "She'd come to see me when she was fed up with being a jet-setter, or bored, or wanted to see the children, whom she loved. She sometimes came with the dressmaker, clouds of glory, making a great fuss over her – and we'd sit and simply eat bread and cheese. I think she felt that I'd known her all this time and I didn't set her up on a pedestal. Of course I admired her tremendously, but I wasn't bowled over by the glamour around her. I was far too busy in my own life, bringing up my children. Maybe that's why she sought us out – because we *weren't* rich and famous. We were an ordinary family, with children.

"Jackie was never spoiled by her success, I think because she had a sort of humility and wit and was so intelligent. But it may have been a terrible stress and strain – because she was such an ordinary sort of person, in a way, to have to contend with all that – playing the game, being a star. A soloist lives in a sort of cocooned state – you travel alone, a stranger meets you when you get off the plane and gushes all over you saying how wonderful you are dahling, doing the usual sycophantic stuff, taking you to some impersonal hotel. It must be a *terrible* burden. Rehearsal with people you may or may not have met before. Then a party, again sycophantic. Then back to the hotel room. Very lonely. I remember having a vivid picture of this young girl, in her twenties, doing this alone, carrying that cello . . .''

Just before her twenty-first birthday, in the depth of the Russian winter, Jacqueline carried the Davidov to Moscow. She was thrilled at the prospect of visiting the Soviet Union, which was then virtually inaccessible to Westerners, and hoped that the man *Newsweek* called the high priest of the cello would give her the technical help she had not found elsewhere.

The English cellist Liza Wilson was one of a handful of other Western students at the Conservatory. When Jacqueline arrived, Liza, who spoke fluent Russian, helped her get settled in the student hostel and introduced her around. Liza then proposed that they go to see Rostropovich, but Jacqueline said no, she needed to be alone with her cello for a while. She reappeared in half an hour, ready to meet the great man.

Russians consider the cello the king of instruments; in 1966 they considered Rostropovich, who has since been exiled, the king of cellists. At thirty-eight he had been playing professionally for twenty-five years, and held a professorial post at both the Moscow and Leningrad Conservatories. Tall, thin and prematurely bald, Rostropovich looked like a bank clerk but crackled with energy; his presence charged the atmosphere of any room he entered. Jacqueline admired the big, earthy lyrical sound of his playing. At one time she described him as a volcano; at another, as Cinerama. He gave the impression of being in perpetual motion, and had the dynamism and warmth to which Jacqueline had instinctively responded in Pleeth and in Tortelier.

Rostropovich taught his students as rigorously as an Olympics coach trains his athletes. He was an accomplished pianist and at the lessons he played the piano, never the cello. He used a great deal of imagery and, contrary to Jacqueline's expectations, paid little attention to technique. Liza Wilson, who spent four years at the Conservatory, says, "He had strong views about how a piece should go, how it should be shaped. He could be quite sensitive when he was in the mood, but he was very intolerant in lots of ways. He played all his scores from memory and he expected that students would play everything from memory. You had to give a performance. If you didn't, he would make fun of you or he would dismiss you. The room was always packed when Jackie played – not just by cellists but by all sorts of people, sitting two deep. No one had heard of her before she got there, but the word got around quickly. They all thought her playing was quite extraordinary. She was giving performances! Her playing was always very spontaneous and often very moving."

Rostropovich had promised Jacqueline two lessons a week – twice as many as the other students – but they had to be squeezed into his busy schedule of concerts and teaching. Sometimes she went to his flat, where they worked in a room with black leather walls – a privilege, by Soviet standards, of his position. Lessons might start at 10.30 p.m. and continue on into the small hours of the morning. Rostropovich reviewed her repertoire and set her new work, which she learned with astonishing speed. One of her first assignments was Prokofiev's difficult *Symphonie Concertante*; she played the first movement for him one morning and learned the second and third movements that afternoon. She learned the first Shostakovich Cello Concerto and played it in the class, but only a few times in public thereafter. Rostropovich told her that to be a great artist, one must suffer. "But that's Russian," she objected. "One must know happiness, too!"

She was expected to practise six hours a day, in addition to written work and Russian lessons. With Liza Wilson, she occasionally went to concerts and to play chamber music – on one memorable occasion with Pierre Fournier and his son, Jean Fonda, at pianist Sviatoslav Richter's flat. Liza thought her "gangly and clumsy in certain ways, and very graceful in others. She was very popular; there was a kind of aura around her. Lots of people were frightfully impressed by her and in love with her. All the students were always running around saying Jacqueline this and Jacqueline that. She was very sweet, and sort of untouched by it. She enjoyed it, but never expected it or asked for it. She could be lots of fun. We could have a good giggle, laugh about other people. And she could always sit down at the piano and just sort of play through something. She could also be quiet and subdued. I think she needed a lot of space for herself, and she probably found the hostel quite difficult because there was continuous noise, people coming in and out, and it was quite difficult to have any privacy. I think she missed her friends. Stephen wrote to her. She still talked about him as though he was her boyfriend. I think it was receding – but if she was heartbroken about it, she didn't show it."

Jacqueline wrote to Alison Brown and George Debenham, complaining that she was lonely and chilly. To Madeleine Dinkel, she wrote that when she went along the street with her long fair hair hanging down and her eyes streaming with tears from the cold, old ladies hissed at her because, it was later explained to her, only whores wore their hair down in public. She told Madeleine that the food was meagre, and that there were only twenty practice rooms for the four hundred students who lived communally in the hostel, in which trumpets "snarled" and pianos "scaled" all day long, from 5 a.m. Although her roommate, a Russian pianist named Tania, spoke no English, she learned virtually no Russian. She did learn to drink vodka, which she found "super", in the Russian style, extravagantly flinging her head back to swallow and then exhaling "with exotic fumes swishing up and down in and out of one! Mmmm!" She loved the parties with their countless toasts, and was overwhelmed by the two formal but warmly welcoming banquets Rostropovich gave in her honour. Her gold dress had been intensely admired, she proudly informed its creator, by at least thirteen different nationalities.

The atmosphere at the famous Conservatory was, she wrote, as serious as she had expected it to be, and she was impressed by the talent and professionalism of the students. She wrote effusively of her admiration and love for Rostropovich, who was "chipping away at the hysteria and extravagance" in her playing. She relished the opportunity to work with him, but by March, she was already counting the days until her return to "all my dear crumbs in England".

Her letters were warm and breezy, bursting with life. In the dark, icy Russian winter, she welcomed the brown streams and puddles of melted snow that signified the coming of spring; when that annual miracle arrived at last, turning the "barren snow land" into "the most graceful of blossoming plants and trees", her delight was palpable. She loved Moscow, where she said the sky seemed extraordinarily high – but Leningrad, she said, was the land of her dreams. A highlight of her "perfect" three days there was a concert, arranged by Rostropovich, at which one hundred student cellists played a hymn by Davidov. It was a tribute to Jacqueline and to her instrument – which she had left in Moscow. She spent the rest of her time in Leningrad discovering the choice art and architecture which surrounded her, visiting a great garden in sunshine after snow, and attending a thrilling concert. She concluded: "Can you imagine the drunken state I have been in? Oh, My God, the beauty."

The last weeks of the Conservatory year coincided with the Third International Tchaikovsky Competition, which took place in Moscow. Cellists had come from all over the world, and the distinguished jury included Piatigorsky and Fournier, who had brought their protégés and wanted them to win – as the Soviet Minister of Culture wanted any Russian student to win. Rostropovich, who wanted one of *his* students to win, suggested that Jacqueline enter, but she declined; the concept of competition was as foreign to her as anything she encountered in the Soviet Union. She didn't need the strain or, for that matter, the two thousand five hundred roubles. With Liza Wilson, she went to the great concourse where the contestants performed. She was impressed by the talent but dismayed by the tension and what she later referred to as the nastiness that breeds dislike for colleagues and "the terrible bitching that went on backstage".

On the final day of the Conservatory year, the graduating students gave a four-and-a-half-hour public concert in the Big Hall of the Conservatory. For the finale, Jacqueline played Haydn's C major Concerto, with Rostropovich conducting the student orchestra. The audience, which included many of the Tchaikovsky Competition entrants and jurors, was enraptured by Jacqueline's performance. Rostropovich whispered to Fournier, "Don't you agree that if she would compete, she just would swallow all of them like that?" Music critic Boris Dobrohotov wrote, "the virtuosity of the young artist is really astonishing. She does not overcome difficulties, they simply do not exist for her. And the sound, the fascinating sound of Jacqueline! . . . her playing is a vortex of exultant and all-conquering joy . . . the artist's *élan* – great, inspired, without any physical strain – won over the house. In her performance, Haydn appeared to us as our contemporary – young, exuberant, and very dear to us!"

After the concert, Rostropovich told Jacqueline, "Of all the cellists I've met of this generation, you are the most interesting. You can go the farthest – farther than me."

12

Jacqueline made no secret of her infatuation with Rostropovich, but it was never clear just how or to what degree her affection was reciprocated. She did make clear, more tactfully in public than in private, that his influence on her playing had been negligible. "All my interpretations stem from Pleeth's grounding," she told the press; "The other two [Tortelier and Rostropovich] just added their wonderful personalities."

Critics who had found her playing hysterical and extravagant before she went to Russia, would continue to do so afterwards – but passion can be mistaken for hysteria and extravagance, especially by those who find it unnerving. Jacqueline's passion was indisputably genuine; it was as apparent in Hugh Maguire's music room, when she played a simple Bach solo sonata for his children, as it was when she played in Carnegie Hall. The movement that some people found excessive was as natural and necessary to her as breathing, but it made her vulnerable to charges of overemotionalism and overindulgent mannerisms. One London critic said "She throws herself about a good deal, and sometimes throws the music about at the same time. When it works it's marvellous, but sometimes she pulls it about so that it's like chewing gum."

A concert is as ritualistic as any high church service; in the rigidly controlled, artificial and often sterile atmosphere of most concert halls, Jacqueline's impassioned playing was a dramatic contrast. Although she had played with uninhibited abandon in her teens, she had at the same time conveyed the pure, serene innocence of a child. Once she became a woman, the sexual element in her playing was unmistakable; it was said that Jacqueline du Pré made love to the cello in public, and certainly there was a voyeuristic element in watching her perform. But concert audiences, particularly genteel *English* concert audiences, are unaccustomed to the undiluted expression of emotions, from heartbursting ecstasy to ineffable sadness. When Jacqueline's face reflected the intense joy or anguish in the music, when her body rose, fell, swayed and lunged with the rhythm and her long hair flew wildly about, she could not have been more exposed if she had appeared stark naked. The vast majority of her audience stood and cheered, having gratefully allowed themselves to be swept aloft by the power and conviction of her fantasy; others, however, found her ardour distracting and dangerous – even worse, embarrassing – and could be seen primly tapping three fingers of one hand on the back of the other.

If Jacqueline's technique rarely reached the impossible standards she set for herself, she had little time to brood about it. Her career had moved into high gear, and Emmie Tillett was lining up engagements for her far into the future. She was committed to concerts in Warsaw, Prague and the Soviet Union with the BBC Symphony Orchestra in January 1967, to be followed by an extensive tour of North America as soloist with top American and Canadian orchestras. In the meantime, there were bookings in Edinburgh, Glasgow, Birmingham, London and, once again, the summer music festival in Spoleto.

Compared with the volcanic Rostropovich, other men now seemed mundane and dreary. A second flurry of a relationship with Richard Goode was short-lived, and Jacqueline's relationship with Stephen Bishop was, in his words, in diminuendo. Hugh Maguire's house in Willesden became her base, if not technically her home. Maguire loved having her there. "She was fabulous! She was like champagne, freshly uncorked, all the time. Terribly vivacious, lively – great, great fun. Everyone was in love with her. *I* was in love with her! She was absolutely scatty, totally unreliable – she thought nothing of taking a taxi from Sheffield to Leeds. Or she'd turn up an hour late because some crazy idea would get into her head and she *had* to go to a garden somewhere and lie down on the grass and look at the sky or something like that. She was still quite young; she didn't really understand the responsibility that was on her shoulders. I don't think she was aware that people were queuing up and paying good money to hear her play at seven thirty, and she had to be there. Her whole life was tied up with music but it wasn't tied up with working in music, it was tied up with loving music, enjoying it, discovering it, realising it. She had quite a cavalier approach, but you could never be angry with her. It never got her into trouble that I know of – she may have been late on a few occasions, but she almost always managed to get there. And when I came home in the evenings, I just had to get my fiddle out and away we would go, with some pianist or other."

Despite her husband's obvious adoration of Jacqueline, Suzie Maguire, a warm and generous soul, welcomed her into the family.

She remembers her being perpetually late, "always frantically calling a taxi and whisking off in it, flying around. She would burst out of her bedroom in the morning – '*Can* I use the bathroom?' – slam the bathroom door and then come out swinging her hair, bounding around. For breakfast she would boil herself an egg and make herself toast, and then stand there by the stove and eat it. Talking, talking all the time. Asking you questions, recounting little anecdotes that had happened to her . . . in that strange sort of slight accent. She always made a joke of everything. She was lovely to be with. She loved the children, and they adored her. My daughter Rachel is a cellist today because of Jackie. She turned to Hugh one day when Rachel was about seven and was trying to play the violin and she said, 'Look, Rachel's a cellist, so you might as well buy her a cello.' So of course he did – and she was right!

"She wore cotton summer dresses, even in the winter. She used to change her clothes after every time she practised. She rarely practised, but when she did, it had a very high quality and she used up so much energy that perspiration flowed. She'd go in and practise for twenty minutes or so and would come out and have a wash and change, then go back and do a bit more.

"She was generous to a fault – she'd go out and have a spending spree, buy people presents, come back with loads of bags of stuff. A dress for me, and for the children toys, puppets, dolls – she enjoyed them as much as they did! She loved the good things of life. She was always buying herself clothes: jumpers, cardigans and coats, the lot. I went shopping with her once to buy a coat, in Harrods. She wouldn't go anywhere but Harrods. Money was no object. She had the assistants in the store running after her, offering her this coat and that coat to try on – not because she was a celebrity, it was simply her personality. She just stood there – this tall, imposing figure with her long, long, thick fair hair and her wide smile – it was a rather toothy smile, but nevertheless brilliant and very striking. She bought a great big emerald-green cape; her hair flowed and the coat flowed, it was really dramatic."

To the Maguires, Jacqueline seemed unequivocally happy – "on the crest of a wave", Suzie says, "confident, carrying all before her." Then in September, quite suddenly, she became ill with what at first seemed to be flu, but was quickly diagnosed as glandular fever.

Glandular fever is a viral infection, not uncommon amongst young adults; it causes swelling of the lymph glands and spleen, general discomfort and severe fatigue. The only known treatment is rest.

Jacqueline cancelled her engagements in Glasgow, Edinburgh and London and retired reluctantly to a large, quiet bedroom that over-look the Maguires' garden. Suzie Maguire, although frantically busy with her own large family, was a willing and devoted nurse. She recalls that Jacqueline, whose only previous illness had been the usual childhood diseases, was a good patient, "cheerful and undemanding even though she was feeling rotten, but she was not too inclined to follow the doctor's instructions to rest. She was fighting it all the time, really. Every once in a while she would think she was better – glandular fever is like that – and sort of force herself to come downstairs. She'd talk to the children and do a bit of practice and walk round the garden, and then she'd suddenly feel rotten and go back to bed again. I remember her lying in bed with the cello on top of her and playing it."

The Maguire children brought Jacqueline flowers, picked in the garden; Suzie sat on the bed and kept her company. She told Suzie of her difficulties in making friends, dating back to her school years in Purley. Suzie believes that despite Jacqueline's sheltered life and limited experience, she had a core of common sense that carried her through – that she was far from naïve, and knew how to take care of herself. Her mother, however, still took care of her laundry; before she fell ill, Iris had driven up from Gerrards Cross occasionally with clean clothes for Jackie, taking a load of dirty laundry home with her. When Jacqueline's condition showed little improvement after more than a fortnight, Iris and Derek consulted with the doctor and it was decided that she would be admitted to hospital in Fulham, for closer monitoring.

She was released from hospital ten days later, still under orders to take things very easy. Iris phoned her old friend Mary May, who was living in France, near Toulon; she said Jackie had a low-grade fever, and needed a quiet place in which to spend a fortnight. Mary was willing, and Jackie arrived a few days later, bringing with her the Davidov and about thirty blouses – the latter, she told Mary, because she got hot practising and had to change frequently. Mary tried in vain to enforce the doctor's orders to rest; in her bedroom, Jacqueline sat crosslegged on the bed, like a Buddha, and practised. "It's all right," she told Mary. "I must keep moving."

Few people could resist Jacqueline in her pleading mode. When she said, "I must go to the sea! I can't go to the Mediterranean without going to the sea!" Mary agreed to take her to the port in Toulon. At the port, Mary was horrified when Jacqueline announced, "I must *bathe* in the sea!" It was October, and the sea was not warm.

" 'It's no use,' Jackie said, 'I *must* bathe in the Mediterranean.' She'd got her bathing suit on underneath her clothes. I said, 'If you must you must, but please go straight in and come straight out.' And she did. When she took off her clothes there was a long collection of wolf whistles from young men sitting along the sea wall. She wasn't beautiful but she had that wonderful colouring and she looked so alive, a bit like a Della-Robbia infant. When she came out of the water she produced a bright blue comb, with which she proceeded to comb her gorgeous thick long golden hair – to the absolute thrill of the gentlemen on the sea wall."

After the fortnight in France Jacqueline stayed briefly with her parents, but was soon back in London with the Maguires. In spite of the lack of energy that typically follows glandular fever, she resumed her activities at an only slightly modified pace. Through Hugh Maguire and Fou Ts'ong, who was then married to Zamira Menuhin, she had at long last begun to feel part of a musical community. She went frequently to Ts'ong's flat in West Hampstead. Between them, Zamira and Ts'ong knew virtually every young musician in the musical world at the time, and most of the older ones, as well. They kept an almost perpetual open house, where impromptu groups gathered for music, food, conversation and more music. Zamira would cook or they would go to a restaurant, usually Chinese. Zamira recalls, "There might be a dozen of us, whoever happened to be around. Someone would ring up and say, 'Shall we meet tonight? André's coming [André Tchaikovsky] or Jackie, or whoever – let's all go out together.' Then afterwards we'd come back to our flat in Canfield Gardens. On those evenings, there were lots of laughs. If they were playing music they might argue about interpretation, or about other musicians' ways of interpreting. We used to go to a lot of concerts together. There were great discussions about concerts that we'd heard. The arguments were never serious. Sometimes the subject wasn't even music, it would be films, or things we'd seen or read or done. Stephen Bishop used to play chess with someone; some of us used to play Monopoly."
  Zamira had first met Jacqueline at the Bath Festival, when she was "about seventeen, and extremely shy. She was very much under the domination of both her father and her mother, and hardly had a word to say for herself at all except when she was up there on the stage, playing. That's when she came completely alive. Later on, around 1963, I began to see her often. I think she was very lonely, and didn't feel very close to anybody. I think she wanted to feel close and

was experimenting with trying to get close to people, but she wasn't comfortable in that role. She was a person that one felt inclined to look after and protect. But she was totally, totally different the second she played the cello. Not when she talked about music, but when she was doing it. Even later, when she'd met Daniel and was in love, she was wonderfully warm and vibrant and smiling . . . but even then, she wasn't the sort of extraordinary creature that she was when she played the cello. When she picked up that cello she was in command. She could express exactly what she wanted to say, be exactly the person she wanted to be. But away from the cello, she hadn't *found* what she wanted to be. She definitely *felt* isolated. Whether it was because she'd been isolated from the others in her family because of her talent, because she was so different from the rest of them – or whether she wasn't really isolated and it was all in her mind, I don't know. But however lonely she was, she could be brought out of it. She would giggle at just about anything; one could always laugh with Jackie. She wasn't called 'Smiley' for nothing.''

On Christmas Eve 1966, Jacqueline went straight from a rehearsal to Fou Ts'ong's. Suzie and Hugh Maguire were there, and the pianist Peter Serkin, and another young pianist, small, dark and intense; Zamira introduced him as Daniel Barenboim.

Barenboim's base was London and he had known Zamira and Ts'ong for years, but he lived for the most part in his suitcase, on the international music circuit. Jacqueline had only had occasion to meet him once, very briefly, in the interval of a concert, when she had been too shy to say more than hello. More recently, he had obtained her telephone number from Ibbs & Tillett on the pretext of discussing a concert they were booked to play together the following spring; his real motive was to compare notes with her about glandular fever, which had confined him to the boredom of his room in the Westbury Hotel. Mutual friends of theirs had told him, with a lack of sympathy he found quite irritating, "If you think *you* have it bad, you should see Jacqueline du Pré! She has it *really* bad!" They had discussed their respective symptoms, and not spoken again until Jacqueline walked into Ts'ong's flat carrying her cello.

In a 1978 interview with Jacqueline for the *Sunday Telegraph*, Catherine Stott wrote, "She still described her first meeting with Barenboim eleven years ago with a sort of bewildered gratitude for his having noticed her." She told Stott, "I was very huge; I weighed 180 pounds, having been in Russia for five months eating nothing but bread and brown potatoes, and I felt like a great lump; I was horribly aware of my great bulk. This small, dark, lithe thing burst

into the room, stared at me and said: 'You don't look like a musician!'
I thought, being a very shy and somewhat insecure person at that
time, 'Oh, God, there's only one thing to do.' Mercifully I had my
cello, so I took it out and started to play. He joined me and, without
any doubt, that was it. It was . . . as if we had been playing together
all our lives. And the shock to me was enormous, that *I* could have
this degree of communication with another person."

What Jacqueline was unable to say in words, she said eloquently
through music. She and Barenboim played the Brahms F major
Sonata and the Beethoven A major Sonata, and went on playing for
a good part of the night, while the others listened or went into
another room. Suzie Maguire recalls, "Jackie was still very under the
weather and didn't have much energy – but Danny, who was supposed to be recuperating too, didn't seem to be suffering any lack of
energy at all . . . and of course once Jackie got going, she just got
totally involved. Danny was sort of starstruck by Jackie. It was quite
a memorable occasion, hearing them play together for the first time.
Just sort of uniting in the music. We must have eaten, but I don't
remember that at all. I just remember being in this room and seeing
the two of them, oblivious of the rest of us. I remember that before
he left, Danny made very sure he would see her again."

13

I t's likely that Daniel Barenboim was born a musical genius, and certain that he was raised as one. His parents, Enrique and Aida Barenboim, both taught piano in their tiny flat in Buenos Aires; when their only child was born on November 15th, 1942, he had been surrounded by music from the time of his conception.

During the first years of his life, Daniel quite naturally assumed that everyone in the world played the piano. His own piano lessons began with his mother when he was five, and he soon graduated to more advanced studies with his father. He gave his first public recital at seven, and during the next two years gave recitals in Buenos Aires and in other South American cities. When he was nine, the conductor-composer Igor Markevitch, who was on the faculty at The Mozarteum in Salzburg, Austria, suggested that his parents take him to study there. Accordingly, the Barenboims left their reasonably secure middle-class life in Argentina and took their son to Salzburg, where he was received as a *Wunderkind*.

The following year the family moved to Israel and settled in Tel Aviv, which was then little more than a shanty town, and a drastic change from the comparative sophistication of Buenos Aires. Barenboim claims that his childhood was normal – but normal children don't travel alone from the age of nine to give recitals in foreign cities, nor do they have the phenomenal talent, memory, concentration and energy that made him, like every prodigy, a freak. But although he told a reporter in 1976, "Music is an art that leads to precocity, and the divorce from other children can be lethal later," he probably had prodigies other than himself – Jacqueline, perhaps – in mind. If his talent isolated him psychologically or emotionally, if not physically, from his peers, he appears not to have suffered from it, or perhaps not to have noticed. Outwardly, he gave the impression of having the vulnerability of an armoured tank. A girl who went to school with him has said "God, he was cocky! Showed off all the time!" He had a lot to show off: he boxed, he played soccer, he studied Talmud and spoke, at the age of fifteen, five languages; in his spare time he liked to read songs and symphonic music in his father's music library, singing every role as he played through the repertoire of opera scores. He also practised intensively, and during his vacations studied conducting, chamber music and piano in Europe, where he met and greatly impressed his musical idol, Wilhelm Furt-wängler.

As an Israeli citizen, Barenboim was eligible for a scholarship awarded by the American-Israeli Cultural Foundation for musical studies in Europe. It enabled him to study theory and composition with Nadia Boulanger in Paris for a year and to attend the Accademia di Santa Cecilia in Rome, where he studied violin, theory and composition and graduated with honours at thirteen. That summer he also studied conducting with Carlo Zecchi in Siena, where Zubin Mehta and Claudio Abbado were fellow students. Daniel looked no more than eleven, like a midget conductor; Mehta, who was twenty, carried him around on his shoulders like a child.

The years of intensive study were punctuated by public perfor-mances throughout Europe, and it was said that because his father never allowed him to play the same piece in public more than twice, Daniel carried three hundred solo piano pieces (including all the Beethoven sonatas) and fourteen piano concertos in his head. He made his London début in 1956 – a chubby thirteen-year-old in short trousers playing Mozart's A major Piano Concerto with the Philharmonia Orchestra under Josef Krips. The press reported "the magnetism of his personal presence – skipping on to the stage with all the assurance of a young Beethoven . . . the vitality singing out from everything he did, tempered irresistibly in one so young by gravity."

He left school at sixteen. A year later, despite successes in Europe, America and Australia, he was not getting as many engagements as he wanted, and thought his career was over. But in the spring of his eighteenth year, the city of Tel Aviv invited him to perform the complete cycle of thirty-two Beethoven sonatas – a *tour de force* he repeated in London, Buenos Aires, Vienna, New York and, ultimately, on record. Like most critics, Edward Greenfield of the *Guardian* overcame his initial objections to what he perceived as ambition at the expense of humility. He wrote, "I was dead set against him. It seemed so cavalier to rush through the Beethoven cycle like that, so brash; another one of these get-along-quick young men. But by the end of the cycle I was kneeling at his feet."

In his early twenties Barenboim made London his base while he toured America, Australia, Western and Eastern Europe, tackling the most challenging works in the piano literature and establishing himself as one of the world's leading pianists. It wasn't enough; from the age of ten, he had wanted to be a conductor. His only professional experience at conducting had been from the keyboard with the Haifa Symphony Orchestra while playing a few Mozart concertos, and once taking over – uninvited – from a conductor during a concert in Valencia. In 1964, however, Ursula Strebi, owner manager of the English Chamber Orchestra, a player-governed group of top British instrumentalists, engaged him to play a Mozart concerto with the ECO. Afterwards, Barenboim nagged Strebi to let him conduct. In the spring of 1965, when another conductor had cancelled on very short notice, Strebi asked him to conduct two concerts in Reading and Cambridge. She did so with some apprehension: "Orchestras didn't like young conductors and I had no idea how the hard-boiled and pretty blasé members of the ECO would take to the idea of this boy, who was barely twenty-two. I was terrified that they might eat him alive. But the moment he stood in front of them there was no doubt who was in charge. Perhaps it wasn't perfect technically, but there was a sense of telepathy and it worked."

A year later, the ECO's management decided to promote their own concert for the first time. Barenboim and Vladimir Ashkenazy, who was a bit better known because of his widely-publicised emigration from the Soviet Union, would play Mozart's Double Piano Concerto, with Barenboim conducting from the keyboard. The venue would be the Fairfield Hall, in Croydon. To help pay for the concert they asked Christopher Nupen, a young trainee with BBC Television who had made several radio programmes with both Barenboim and Ashkenazy, if he could persuade the BBC to film the concert and thus obtain some money.

Nupen believed that a revolution was taking place in the world of performed music. "At what time in history, apart from Wolfgang Mozart, were there young musicians who would take on the most difficult works in the repertoire and confidently present them on the world's leading platforms and bring the house down? They *dared* more. They were more enthusiastic, more exuberant, more confident of their talents. Rubinstein, Segovia – at the age of forty, they had hardly been known; they'd had great careers, but they weren't international stars. Television was changing the world." Nupen sold the idea to the BBC saying, "Even if they don't play well – and they'll probably play better than anybody else – the quality of this youthful, exuberant commitment is going to carry through, and it's going to be a highly successful concert!" His film captured that exuberance and conveyed it to a television audience. Instead of the conventionally static, stuffy and reverential approach to serious music, Nupen used a hand-held camera to show the musicians rehearsing and socialising in informal settings, interacting with tremendous affection. He took viewers backstage and exposed them to the force-field created by Barenboim's demoniac energy. By the time the concert began, the audience shared the performers' excitement and anxiety, as well as their triumph. The film made international stars of Barenboim and Ashkenazy, practically over-night.

By the end of 1966, Barenboim had established himself as a conductor both from the podium and from the keyboard, and was being compared with Furtwängler as a leading interpreter of the classical and romantic repertoire. He savoured his new status, and all the accoutrements of success. He acquired a taste for Havana cigars, handmade Italian shoes and Krug champagne. Only five feet three inches tall, he had the disproportionate energy of a dwarf star. He claimed to need only two or three hours' sleep; arriving at the Westbury Hotel at 2 a.m. he would leave a wake-up call for four, in order to practise for a few hours before going to rehearse or record. He socialised as tirelessly as he worked, eating and playing chamber music with a group sometimes known as the "Barenboim gang" or the "Israeli Mafia"; it included Zubin Mehta, Itzhak Perlman, Alfred Brendel, Pinchas Zukerman and Vladimir Ashkenazy, as well as such older musical luminaries as Isaac Stern, Artur Rubinstein and Dietrich Fischer-Dieskau. On the periphery of this magic circle, women – wives and lovers – proliferated.

Zamira Menuhin and Fou Ts'ong had been friendly with Barenboim since 1963, and it was only by chance that his visits to Canfield Gardens had never coincided with Jacqueline's. Two days after their initial meeting, Barenboim was to be filmed playing Mozart's triple concerto; he invited Jacqueline to the studio to watch. During the next week they saw a good deal of each other. On New Year's Eve they went together to a party at Fou Ts'ong's, where Zamira observed an extraordinary "current" between them. After dinner, Jacqueline asked Barenboim to play the Beethoven Sonata in A major, Op. 69, with her – the work she had often played (and had just recorded) with Stephen Bishop. EMI producer Suvi Raj Grubb, who was there, still considers the impromptu performance one of the most notable he has ever heard of the work. When Grubb left the party at 3 a.m., Jacqueline and Barenboim were still playing as though the evening had just begun.

On January 3rd, Jacqueline left London with the BBC Symphony for a two-week tour of Eastern Europe. Barenboim took her to the airport and carried her cello to the plane. Caught up in the whirling hurricane that was Barenboim, Jacqueline was too dizzy to guess that at the centre of the hurricane was total, absolute control and determination – and that deep inside that centre, Barenboim had already made up his mind to marry her.

14

Jacqueline had begun 1966 in the Soviet Union as a student; she returned a year later as a star. With the BBC Symphony Orchestra, conducted by Sir John Barbirolli, she introduced the Elgar Concerto to packed-out audiences in Moscow as well as in Prague, Warsaw and Leningrad. Although the official Soviet position was that all twentieth-century music was corrupt, Jacqueline was received like a long-lost, much-loved member of the family.

January is the worst month of the year in Russia, and a foot of snow exacerbated the logistical snarls that complicate every orchestral tour. Schedules were altered without notice, rehearsal halls unavailable when promised, meals missed or inedible; at one point eight members of the orchestra took to their beds with stomach trouble. Jacqueline sailed happily through it all, buoyed by nightly phone calls from Barenboim; she said they cost him £200 a week. Her hotel room was a popular gathering place for some of the musicians after the concerts, but they were all instructed to leave before "Danny's" 2 a.m. calls.

If the statuesque English rose and the diminutive Israeli cactus seemed, on the face of it, the unlikeliest of couples, their differences only reinforced their attraction for one another. His talent amazed and fascinated her, and so did everything else about him, from his Olympian confidence, decisiveness and vitality to his heterogeneous accent and his two-tone pointed Italian shoes, "Daniel," she said, "includes absolutely *everything*!"

Naturally extravagant with her emotions, Jacqueline held nothing back when she fell in love. After she returned to London on January 16th, the Maguires seldom saw her; when she wasn't working she was with Daniel at concerts, parties, restaurants or the Westbury Hotel. On February 4th, after three hectic weeks that left her spinning even more rapidly than before, she bade Barenboim a tearful farewell and embarked on the most extensive tour she would ever make of North America. In eight weeks she would perform with orchestras in fourteen cities, and give recitals with Stephen Bishop in four.

The first concerts on her tour, with the Columbus (Ohio) and

Oklahoma City and Dallas Symphony Orchestras were wildly successful. On Valentine's Day Jacqueline arrived in Los Angeles, where she would give four concerts with the Los Angeles Philharmonic. Martin Bernheimer, music critic for the *Los Angeles Times*, interviewed her in her hotel room and was completely captivated when she asked plaintively, "Do we have to do this? Couldn't we just go to the flicks?" Bernheimer noted that although the first concert was less than twenty-four hours away, Jacqueline had had no rest the previous night, had consumed only soft drinks and canapés, and had neither met the conductor nor rehearsed. He found her a bit bewildered by all the fuss being made about her, and breathless about the rigours of a first jet tour of America. She referred to one of her much-admired show pieces as "a beastly old thing" and told him she had no use for the avant-garde, but would some day like to play the Hindemith Concerto and Britten's Cello Symphony, which Bernheimer described as "the exclusive property, at least for the time, of Rostropovich, an old man of forty or so. It will be amusing to see how many comparable works become the exclusive property of Jacqueline du Pré – by the composer's dedication or by her own interpretive supremacy – during the eighteen years that separate her from a similar statistical milestone."

The following week she introduced the Elgar to Cleveland, playing it three times with the Cleveland Orchestra, conducted by Louis Lane. One of the several rave reviews was headed TALL, BLOND AND BLAZING, SHE PLAYS WARM CELLO. From Cleveland she flew to New York and her début with the New York Philharmonic, conducted by Leonard Bernstein. She played the Schumann Cello Concerto in A minor, and the reviews were worshipful. Under the heading UPSTAGING LENNY, Harold C. Schonberg wrote in the *New York Times*:

For the last few years, everybody in music has been talking about the young British cellist Jacqueline du Pré, now twenty-one years old. She came out, tall, blonde, assured, in a red gown, listened attentively to the short introduction and launched into Schumann. Her performance was very fine: big tone, lyric approach, security of finger and bow arm. Also a set of gestures and physical movements that all but merged her body with the cello.

Miss du Pré is a cellist in the modern vein. There is plenty of strength to her playing, and a good measure of romanticism without the romantic string mannerisms of portamento (sliding from note to note) and a fast, wide vibrato . . . She can produce a mellow sound of unusual size, and clearly was born to play the cello.

. . . Miss du Pré, like all young instrumentalists today, has tone and technique; but in addition she has something rarer, the ability to transmit. There might be reservations about this or that aspect of a given performance of hers, but there can be no reservations at all about her personality and innate sensitivity.

Newsweek reported that she left behind her "a wake of frothy reviews and broken hearts. Technically, she is a marvel. For a woman, the power and quality of her tone are stunning . . . Her musical instincts are uncanny in their maturity and independence, as if she were born with them in her fingertips. Even when she fearlessly and confidently takes liberties with the tempo or dynamics, she is uncommonly persuasive about accent, phrasing and color." The article quotes Zubin Mehta as saying, "Women usually have a small tone – they are all Mozart specialists. This girl plays like five men. No bar of the orchestra covers her tone. It's flabbergasting."

Jacqueline told *Newsweek*'s reporter, "I love to play the cello . . . when I'm playing, I'm happy. It's that feeling of happiness when one makes music and the joy of feeling the music as well as playing it." *Newsweek* said, "She spoke of a clan – 'people like Vladimir Ashkenazy, John Williams, Itzhak Perlman, Fou Ts'ong, Stephen Bishop and Daniel Barenboim'. Her eyes lit up at the in-ness of it all. 'We keep together, go to each others' concerts and never miss a chance to play for ourselves. Aside from music, seeing friends like these is the most important thing in my life.'" She added, "I value my private life too much to continue such long and demanding tours. I hope eventually to limit my travel. I'd like to marry and have children. But I'll never give up my career as a cellist. Why can't the two go together? I know it will take careful planning. But I think there is – there has to be – time for everything." Barely concealed between the lines was a secret: Barenboim had met her in Cleveland, and they had become engaged.

They planned to marry in September; not until then would they both have a few free days in their schedules. The engagement would not be made public until Jacqueline returned to England, but she was palpably in love, and it added a new dimension of drama to her playing. *Time* reported that when she played Schumann's Cello Concerto, "One instant she looked like a puckish milkmaid, the next like Ophelia going mad . . . It was a performance to be seen as much as heard, for du Pré couldn't sit still a minute. Swathed in acres of floor-length red chiffon, she attacked her cello in ungainly frenzy, reaching forward to take a massive chop with her bow, arching her back, tossing her head, closing in on the cello again and again." *Life's* reporter wrote, "Jackie performs with rapturous fury . . . In concerts her wheaten mane of hair flails about, sometimes tangling in the pegs, and she seems to be sawing the cello in two with her bow. But she has a grace and glow. In the midst of a skittering crescendo she suddenly draws out a sound of burnished gold and, looking up, throws a smile at her conductor."

Jacqueline's happiness lit up her surroundings, from hotel rooms to concert halls. She was twenty-two, but the child in her still came out to play at every opportunity. On the afternoon of March 14th, before a concert with the Toronto Symphony, a seventeen-year-old cello student named Christine Newland skipped school in order to meet her idol, Jacqueline du Pré, at the Park Plaza Hotel in Toronto.

Newland, now principal cellist of Orchestra London Canada, writes, "When I arrived for the meeting, which had been arranged by my cello teacher, Jackie popped out from behind the door with a playful 'Boo' in her typical girlish way. Jackie was bouncy and happy and smiling from ear to ear. The mirrors in her hotel room were literally plastered with pictures of her new boyfriend, Daniel Barenboim. She was madly in love with him. I was too young and naïve to understand her enthusiasm about wanting to marry this fellow, but she assured me I would understand when I was her age.

"She asked me to play on her famous Davidov Stradivarius, which for me was a thrill. Then we sat and chatted about music and pets and such, and she ordered up some hot chocolate and biscuits. She got me tickets to her concert. What a concert! She played the Saint-Saëns concerto at Massey Hall to an audience who received her with open hearts. You could literally feel the warmth and love radiated by Jackie when she played! She had a special ability to fill her audience with the same joy which she herself was experiencing."

It was not unusual for young men to present themselves in Jacqueline's dressing-room after a concert, proposing dinner and, sometimes, marriage. On this occasion, Christine Newland recalls that smitten male admirers awaited Jacqueline backstage and "poured out their feelings for her. She would smile that radiant smile of hers and thank them for their compliments. They would ask her out but she, being faithful to Daniel, would decline. Then Jackie, my mother and I went back to her hotel room. She talked on the phone with Daniel, who was on the other side of the globe, while cuddling her stuffed koala toy."

Jacqueline's final orchestral engagement of the tour was with the Canadian Broadcasting Symphony in Montreal, where one critic said she played the Elgar "as tho it had been written for her alone", and another compared her with Glenn Gould: "There is the same irrational intensity to every note, the same conviction, the same feeling of communication with the gods. The force of her personality sweeps all reservations aside. You live each note with her as she breathes fire into the music, and she makes the [Elgar concerto] vibrate with an intensity I did not know this music to have."

The recitals with Bishop, which had been scheduled many months in advance, took place in Ann Arbor, Michigan; Pittsburgh, Pennsylvania; Fort Wayne, Indiana and the New York Town Hall in Manhattan. Bishop was admittedly and understandably envious of the star treatment Jacqueline received. His perception was that she was neither impressed nor overwhelmed by her celebrity, but thoroughly enjoyed it. "She of course suffered from the fatigue and dislocation that comes from travelling, but most soloists find it more nerve-racking than she did. Jackie didn't get nervous. Rubinstein didn't get nervous. I don't think Daniel does. But all the rest of us, to a greater or lesser degree, have to fight the negative aspects of walking on a stage to play well. Whereas Jackie actually thrived on it. She *loved* performing." Although Bishop is American, he has lived in England long enough to master British understatement. "We played together a few more times after we came back to England," he says, "but it was different . . . she and I had changed. And then we went our separate ways."

Twenty years later, Bishop has not played professionally with any other cellist. "Playing with her makes it difficult to play with another cellist, because you remember what it was like. Her instincts were so strong, they incorporated her intelligence. It was infallible. She didn't need the props that most people need, didn't need to articulate or analyse." Sometimes at parties, his friends play a game called "Who's-the-most-wonderful-person-you've-ever met?" The name most often mentioned, by himself and others, is Jacqueline du Pré. He says, "People fell for her – not necessarily romantically, but she had that overused word, charisma. I've never met anyone who didn't like her. She was . . . sunshine. A really radiant person. Not all the time, of course, but that's the primary image. She was so gifted and attractive; she enjoyed everything, and people loved her. If there were any pressures on her, I honestly wasn't aware of them. I used to think, This is really one of the most fortunate creatures I've ever met."

15

In March 1967, Iris du Pré mentioned to a colleague at the Apsley Grammar School in Hemel Hempstead, where she was teaching, that Jacqueline would need a flat in London when she returned from America. The colleague owned a small flat at 27a Montagu Street, near Baker Street, and it was available. At the end of the month, Jacqueline and Daniel moved in.

The flat was the basement of an eighteenth-century terraced house. It measured only thirty feet from back to front; Barenboim's Steinway baby grand (which he was buying in instalments) filled the sitting room, and the bedroom was barely big enough for a double bed. They were so cramped that when Daniel practised at the piano, Jacqueline had to practise sitting on the bed or on the toilet. But it was Jacqueline's first real home of her own, and she was thrilled to have it.

The engagement was not yet official, but it was apparent to everyone who saw the radiant Jacqueline that Barenboim was her accompanist of choice, in music and in life. She had lost the weight gained in the Soviet Union, and was down to 140 pounds. She looked shorter as well as sleeker, for she tried to de-emphasise the six-inch difference in their heights by wearing only flat shoes, and slouching a bit. In Russia she had acquired a rather exotic, Garboesque accent; in the United States, an American drawl. Now she sounded as though she might have emigrated, as a young child, from Israel.

Jacqueline and Barenboim gave their first public performance together in Northampton, playing Beethoven and Brahms sonatas on very short notice. At their first orchestral concert together, in April, at the Festival Hall, Jacqueline played the Haydn Cello Concerto in C major, with Barenboim conducting the English Chamber Orchestra. The sparks that flew between them electrified the audience. Barenboim seemed to use his entire body as a baton, at times vibrating like an engine or rapidly leaping up and down like someone feverishly skipping with a rope. Joan Chissell wrote in *The Times*, "It was as if each work was being created on the spot, instead of merely reproduced for the ten-thousandth time . . . Miss Du Pré's playing exuded happiness in every bar, through tingling rhythm, radiantly lyrical tone and the keenest imaginable characterisation of every small detail." The *Daily Mail*'s reviewer observed that Barenboim "sometimes folded his arms and stared at her as she played; at others, told her to stop stamping her foot," and added, "They are a strangely assorted pair. She, for all her maturity and experience, still looks like a big schoolgirl, sweeping her bow across the strings as though drawing a sword. He, tiny, almost Chaplinesque from the back." Two years later, long before there was any tangible basis for his feeling, Christopher Booker would write in the *Spectator* of his "acute sense of foreboding" at the concert. "It was all going too well," he wrote, "like a hectic spring so green that it is painful."

Interviewers observed that when Jacqueline mentioned Daniel, as she did at every opportunity, she glowed with a touching, girlish delight. David Pryce-Jones wrote in the *Daily Telegraph*, "There is a slight foreign intonation in her voice and I ask if this is linked to her name. The accent, she says, has been picked up from some Argentines she is seeing a lot of and with whom she will be flying after the [Festival Hall] concert to Berlin for five days of rest." The unidentified "Argentines" were Daniel, Aida and Enrique Barenboim.

No one has recorded how Enrique Barenboim received the news of his son's engagement; he was known to be difficult with everyone, and there is no reason to believe that his son's fiancée was an exception. Aida Barenboim, however, welcomed her daughter-in-law with open arms and heart. The family's overblown rhetoric and blatant expression of emotion was a revelation to the young woman reared in a house where raising one's voice had been unacceptable, and emotional censorship a way of life.

Perhaps in reaction to her conventional English upbringing, Jacqueline loved to shock people – and there was plenty of shock value in Barenboim, especially where her parents were concerned. When she introduced him to them, she informed them that before the marriage she would become a Jew.

If she had announced her intention to become a man, her parents could not have been more horrified. In their provincial, Protestant, middle-class world, Jews existed outside the periphery of a clearly defined circle. Iris had told her young daughter not to talk to William Pleeth except about musical matters "because he's a Jew". And there is no evidence that Derek's experience of Jews had expanded since he wrote in *When Poland Smiled* of his discomfort on encountering a group of Orthodox Jews on a Polish train. In the tone of an anthropologist discovering a primitive tribe, he recorded how they reeked of garlic, fingered his clothes, peered at him with their noses practically touching his, and questioned him "in a weird mixture of languages". Confronted with the prospect of a Jewish son-in-law, a Jewish daughter and Jewish grandchildren, he objected strenuously – to no avail.

When the engagement was made public in April, Jacqueline told the press that her conversion would be for Daniel and their children, but also because she had since her childhood admired and felt an affinity for many Jewish musicians, beginning with William Pleeth. Iris rose to the occasion; when reporters visited her in Buckinghamshire, she said she liked Barenboim enormously and was delighted with the match, and proudly showed them the latest cuttings in her famous daughter's scrapbooks. Jacqueline said she and her husband-to-be hoped to live in Israel, although their way of life would prevent their spending much time in any one place. The following day, between concerts with Barbirolli and the Hallé Orchestra in Manchester and Sheffield, Jacqueline visited Margo Pacey and her family, who lived near Sheffield. Her parents were there as well. "Jackie was over the moon," Margo Pacey recalls. "We all drank champagne, and walked on the moors."

Jacqueline spent the next weekend in Brighton, where Barenboim performed at a new music festival. On Monday morning they were at EMI's studios in London together, to record two cello concertos with the English Chamber Orchestra; the classical Haydn in C major, and the romantic Boccherini. As at the Festival Hall concert, the extraordinary rapport between soloist, conductor and orchestra produced an inspired performance. After the session a group of fifteen exuberant people, including Itzhak Perlman and others who had come simply to watch, went out for a meal. Barenboim, famous for his generosity, probably picked up the bill. After all the years of feeling as isolated with people as when she was alone, Jacqueline basked in a sense of belonging to an extended family far more congenial than her own. "With Daniel," she said, "I got used to being with people."

Due to engagements booked months ahead, she was with Barenboim far less than she would have wished – but their time apart was filled with work, and warmed by anticipation. However many miles were between them, they spoke daily and at great length on the phone. In London they played together at every opportunity – everything from Beethoven sonatas to small nineteenth-century pieces written for other instruments, which they instantaneously adapted for cello and piano. Jacqueline's life had shifted into an even higher gear, and Hugh Maguire realised that the idyllic evenings of chamber music at his house were over. "I was a bit resentful. Danny was a very powerful influence, and he wanted Jackie for himself. He was in a different league from us altogether. He was already a big international star, very established. Jackie was, too, but Danny had the *mentality* of a big star." Maguire went to the Montagu Street flat a few times to have supper and to play, "but then she faded away from my circle. Jackie became a big superstar and all her activities were channelled into Danny's. Not at first – for a year she was on one side of the earth and he was on the other – but eventually they channelled it all together."

On Saturday, May 27th, 1967, Jacqueline and Daniel both happened to be in London when Barenboim's parents phoned from Tel Aviv with the news that the city was blacked out, and a full-scale war was imminent. Daniel's immediate response was that he had to go. He lived in London but he was a committed Zionist, and Israel was his spiritual home. He felt that his adopted country's existence as a nation was in peril, and that his place was there. Jacqueline's reaction, just as immediate, was that she would go with him. Within half an hour Daniel had cancelled a performance of *Così Fan Tutte*, they had packed a suitcase and were en route to the airport.

Arriving in Tel Aviv at 3 a.m. on what they thought was the eve of the war, they were surprised to find the city lit up and apparently normal; but by the time they reached the Barenboims' flat, where they were to stay, they could feel the tension. They told reporters that they would perform anywhere, either with the Israel Philharmonic Orchestra or in recital, for the troops and for civilians. It would be their gesture of solidarity with and support for the cause; all proceeds would go to the Soldiers Welfare Fund.

The Israel Philharmonic quickly rearranged its programme for the week's subscription concerts so that Jacqueline and Daniel would appear along with the previously scheduled Moshe Murvitz and Sergiu Commissiona, the Romanian-born conductor and former director of the Haifa Symphony Orchestra. The first concert would take place on Monday evening, May 29th, at the Mann Auditorium in Tel Aviv. Jacqueline would play Schumann's Cello Concerto, conducted by Barenboim in his first appearance as a conductor in Israel. He would also play Beethoven's Piano Concerto No. 3. Just before the performance began, a representative of the orchestra arrived from London carrying Jacqueline's Davidov, "so that the

Jackie with other pupils of the London Cello School in 1951 (middle row, second from left).

Jackie accompanied by her mother, Iris.

The photograph that Jackie gave to William Pleeth.

With Stephen Bishop.

With William Pleeth.

Above: The Barenboim
quintet. *Left to right:* Itzhak
Perlman, Daniel Barenboim,
Jacqueline du Pré, Zubin
Mehta and Pinchas
Zukerman.

Left: Jackie and Daniel at
the time of their marriage.

Right: Charcoal drawing of
Jackie by Zsuzsi Roboz,
1969.

Rehearsing for a Prom in 1967.

With Sir John Barbirolli and Suvi Raj Grubb during a recording playback at EMI Studios.

With Barenboim after
the concert at St. Paul's,
1976.

The public face,
February 1976.

The ecstasy of music.

sounds will be as pure and as clean as the heart of the people of Israel in these difficult days".

The next morning Jacqueline cabled her mother, SITUATION COM-PLETELY UNDER CONTROL FEELING VERY RELAXED DON'T WORRY MUCH LOVE JACKIE. She worried that Iris might read it as "Don't worry much" and asked if "Much love" could go on a separate line. In London, the *Evening Standard* reported that although she was scheduled to play at the Norwich Festival two weeks later, neither her agents nor the Festival's producers had heard from her, and were anxious about her safety. Emmie Tillett, who felt strongly about the sanctity of engagements, told a colleague, "Jackie really is *very* naughty." Antony Hopkins, director of the festival, recalls a tele-phone call from an exhilarated Jacqueline, telling of playing to troops from the back of a lorry: "She made it sound almost as though playing in that environment was some sort of drug."

Israel is a small country; they performed in the north, south, east and west, often giving two concerts a day at kibbutzim, army camps and concert halls, sometimes on improvised outdoor stages. They played sonatas by Beethoven and Brahms in Tel Aviv on May 30th and 31st, in Haifa on June 1st, in Jerusalem on the afternoon and evening of June 2nd, and again in Tel Aviv on June 3rd. On Sunday, June 4th, they performed with the Israel Philharmonic at a camp in Beersheba, not far from the Dead Sea. Jacqueline again played the Schumann Cello Concerto and Barenboim the Beethoven Piano Concerto No. 3, with Sergiu Commissiona conducting. On Monday, the war began.

Once hostilities were official, large gatherings of people became risky and their concerts were limited to one a day. Jacqueline called it a terrific experience. "We were playing for people either about to go to war, or just come back from it. Or they had sons and husbands and brothers about to go. They came to hear us, because they needed something very badly. There was a need which nothing else except music could perhaps have answered at that time. We felt that we were playing with tremendous purpose . . . Being in a period of crisis brought out the best in everybody. There was such a strength in the people, such a lack of panic, that my respect for them was unbounded. I don't think I met anyone who, on the surface at least, showed any kind of fright. There was an optimism – a feeling that the war would be won."

On the morning of the first day of the Six Day War, Jacqueline's rehearsal with Barenboim and the Israel Philharmonic in the Mann Auditorium was interrupted by air raid sirens. The musicians adjourned to the spacious shelter in the basement, where Jacqueline and violinist Moshe Murvitz played gypsy music while the sirens wailed. That night the city was blacked out and the performance cancelled.

Zubin Mehta arrived in Tel Aviv that night and made his way through the blackout to Orchestra House, a guest house for visiting artists. He found Jacqueline, Daniel, Enrique and Aida Barenboim, and Sergiu Commissiona and his wife in an improvised air raid shelter in the basement. Even though a raid was unlikely, as the first Israeli attack had destroyed the entire Egyptian air force, they all spent the night there, talking and joking to break the tension, and planning the programme of a concert to celebrate the victory of which they had no doubt.

After ten days in Israel, Jacqueline told a *Jerusalem Post* reporter she felt she had lived there for ever: "It has become a home." Barenboim added, "Jackie is going to convert to Judaism. She is very British, and the British have always associated with Lawrence of Arabia. So now we have Jacqueline of the Jews! Isn't that wonderful?" They were both intoxicated with the tension and excitement of the war. Then on June 10th, victory came with stunning swiftness. Euphoria swept the country; everywhere there was celebration and rejoicing, and the awareness that this was an historic time. In the wildly emotional atmosphere, getting married seemed the most natural – and romantic – thing in the world to do.

On Tuesday, June 13th, Jacqueline telephoned her mother and told her the wedding was to take place on Thursday, in Jerusalem; could she come? With mixed feelings and considerable difficulty, for the airlines were not operating to any normal schedules, Iris, Derek and Piers arrived in Tel Aviv the next day.

In the meantime, the concerts continued. On June 11th Jacqueline played the Saint-Saëns Cello Concerto, with Mehta conducting the orchestra, at the Mann Auditorium. The "victory concert" took place on the 12th, in the Armon Theatre in Haifa: Jacqueline again played the Saint-Saëns, Barenboim played the "Emperor" Concerto, the orchestra played Beethoven's triumphant Fifth Symphony and Mehta conducted. On the afternoon of the 13th, Jacqueline played the Schumann in Tel Aviv; Barenboim played the Mozart Piano Concerto in D minor and conducted Beethoven's Symphony No. 7. On the 14th they gave what was advertised as a farewell concert, again in Tel Aviv; Jacqueline played the Saint-Saëns, Barenboim the "Emperor", Mehta conducted. The following morning, Mehta borrowed a car and drove Jacqueline and Daniel and a rabbi through Jerusalem streets teeming with soldiers and tanks to the ritual *mikvah*, or purifying bath, for the bride.

Israel does not acknowledge civil marriages: only a religious ceremony is considered kosher, and this was to be an Orthodox one, so that any offspring of the marriage would be indisputably Jewish. Jacqueline's knowledge of Judaism consisted of a few Yiddish expressions and one visit to the West London Synagogue, where Rabbi Hugo Gryn had explained to her that converts must complete a course of instruction which normally includes learning Hebrew and takes at least a year – but that he would work with her to accommodate her complicated schedule. The Jews, however, are above all a practical people, and the Israelis, at least at that time, were quite flexible about such matters. Accordingly, friends and admirers in places as high as the prime minister's office waved a magic wand that granted Jacqueline a highly unusual, if not unheard-of, one-day conversion. Between concerts and rehearsals, she received some basic tuition on which she was examined by rabbis who quizzed her through an interpreter. Although it was technically called a conversion, in actuality she was made an honorary Jew.

Jacqueline found the ritual of the *mikvah* a bit archaic but she loved the drama of it, the symbolic cleansing of the outer and inner woman. "I had to have an ordinary bath and wash my hair and nails," she later told a reporter, "and then, with no clothes on, I had to be totally submerged in this sort of mini swimming pool. You are taught how to bend in a certain way, so that the water goes right through you. Then a rabbi said a Hebrew prayer and I was given a Hebrew name, Shulamit. And so I came out with dripping hair and rushed off to the wedding."

The rabbi's little house was near the Wailing Wall, practically on the dividing line between the newly reunified Old and New Jerusalem. Jacqueline said, "It was as white a wedding as we could make it. There'd been a war after all, and it wasn't a good time to do shopping – you just try finding a wedding dress on an occasion like that! Luckily I'd brought a fairly simple white dress with me, and from somewhere – heaven knows where – my mother-in-law managed to get a veil. So it felt white." Barenboim's wedding gift to Jacqueline was a fur coat, and Mehta gave her a matching fur hat.

Ancient Jewish tradition holds that there is a preordained partner for every person in the world, and that when they find each other they are a *zivig* – a heaven-blessed couple. On the afternoon of June 15th, 1967, Jacqueline and Daniel stood underneath the *chuppah* – the bridal canopy – in a white walled courtyard, in the full heat of the

Israeli summer afternoon. As is customary, the women sat back around the perimeter of the courtyard, and the men in the centre, around a large table. Children and chickens wandered in and out; Iris found it "rather like a painting out of the Old Testament". The cantor sang, "He who is Mighty . . . may He bless the bridegroom and the bride." The rabbi said a benediction and praised God for the laws of chastity and for the institution of marriage. Barenboim placed a ring on Jacqueline's right forefinger and said in Hebrew, "Behold, thou art consecrated unto me by this ring, according to the Law of Moses and of Israel." The rabbi pronounced six more benedictions, blessing God and the couple and their children to be. Then Jacqueline drank wine from a glass that Barenboim crushed with his foot, as a reminder, even at that most joyous moment, of the destruction of the Holy Temple in Jerusalem. After that, they were man and wife. The rabbi's wife led them to a little bedroom, locked the door – a purely symbolic gesture – and then released them.

The ceremony was private, but the celebratory luncheon afterward, at the King David Hotel, was attended by a large crowd that included Prime Minister David Ben-Gurion, Jerusalem Mayor Teddy Kolleck and Defence Minister Moshe Dayan, who used the opportunity to discuss the future of the country. Despite the exigencies of the recent war, there was plenty of food and drink and a proper wedding cake. Sir John Barbirolli, coincidentally in the country for an engagement, proposed the wedding toast "to these young geniuses".

The bride and groom rushed from their wedding luncheon to Tel Aviv, for the rehearsal of what was billed as yet another farewell concert, which took place that evening. Barenboim conducted and played Mozart's Piano Concerto in D minor, and Jacqueline played the Schumann Cello Concerto. The audience, more than half of whom were in khaki, overflowed the Mann Auditorium and gave the newlyweds an overwhelmingly emotional reception.

The next morning, Evelyn Barbirolli, who was staying with her husband at the small hotel provided for guest artists, saw Jacqueline carrying her cello to a waiting taxi and asked, "How's married life?" Jacqueline said "It's wonderful!" and waved her cello in the air. She and Barenboim were on their way to the airport and a flight to Spain; they had been invited to honeymoon in Marbella, at the villa of Artur and Aniela Rubinstein. In all the excitement, Jacqueline left behind the first and grandest dress Madeleine Dinkel had made for her – the gold silk she had worn at her Festival Hall début – and never saw it again.

On June 26th the *Daily Mail*, in the only notice of the wedding in a national British newspaper, ran this story in its entirety: "One-time infant prodigies cellist Jacqueline du Pré and conductor and pianist Daniel Barenboim, who announced that they would marry in September, found themselves in Israel with unexpected time on their hands. So they have married out there."

16

Christopher Nupen filmed Jacqueline for BBC Television a number of times – playing Brahms's sonatas and trios, Bruch's *Kol Nidrei* and Bloch's *Schelomo* – but none of those programmes still exist, for the BBC inexplicably destroyed them. Only Nupen's unforgettable sixty-five-minute television film *Jacqueline*, made in the autumn of 1967, survives.

Nupen says that in order to make a great documentary, the film-maker must have affection for and an intimate knowledge of the subject. For *Jacqueline*, he had both. He had been a devotee of her playing since first hearing a radio broadcast of her 1962 recital at Fenton House, and had met her soon afterwards when his flatmate, guitarist John Williams, accompanied her on one of her early recordings for EMI. At their first meeting, "This great striding thing came bounding into our flat. She was simultaneously a shy English girl and, in her movements and her being, radiantly confident. An interesting dichotomy." Nupen came to know her better when she joined the Barenboim clan, of which he was also a member. He considered her the finest cello talent on earth. He and his cameramen were Jacqueline's friends; she played to their cameras as to a lover.

Nupen employed the same intimate approach that had been so successful in the Barenboim–Ashkenazy film, adding background material to make it a full-blown documentary. He filmed Jacqueline on planes and trains, and clowning around with Barenboim; still photos showed her in infancy, childhood and adolescence, and there were brief comments by her parents and Barbirolli. Her husband praised her for "not only living for her career, like so many lady musicians who have this almost complex about it, that they have to go at it almost harder than a man. She's interested in being a happy person first of all." He added, "The fact that we feel music so much alike has nothing to do with the fact that we got married. It sounds so romantic – they're in love, so therefore they play well together. I know lots of people who play very well, they are not in love; and I know a lot of people who are in love and don't play very well together." His logic overlooked the fact that in this particular marriage music was, in Jacqueline's words, "the spine through it all", the cement that bonded their life together. All this is prologue to the heart of the film, in which Jacqueline performs the Elgar Cello Concerto before a live audience, with Barenboim conducting the New Philharmonia Orchestra.

Jacqueline loved to play the Elgar; she loved the depth and breadth of the sound it allowed her to produce. She said she had first played the work "because it happened to fit in with a concert programme. I don't know why it's become so popular abroad. Perhaps because it's an English girl playing an English concerto." The film gives a more convincing explanation; it glows with the fire of a love affair between Jacqueline, her cello, Barenboim, the music and the camera. Visually as well as aurally it is pure, glorious gold.

Jacqueline, never beautiful in repose, was bewitching when animated and transfigured when she played. Although the film is black-and-white, her face reflects every shade of emotional colour in the music; her heart seems to beat in unison with Elgar's as she dances on the high wire of intuition without a net. Eyes open wide, she listens raptly and obediently to private voices and visions that require physical release – nodding, weaving, shaking her head fiercely, tossing her hair, and flourishing her bow; she and her cello and the music are one. In the brooding slow movement she takes her sweet, sweet time, as the music yearns like Keats's "god in pain". In the second movement, there is wit – Jacqueline liked to quote Donald Tovey's description, "dignity at the expense of a banana skin" – and in the finale, with what she called her sumptuous glissandi (gliding downward slides), she drenches the audience in great waves of ecstasy and love.

Music is a language, encoded; its essence is not in the score. Even when composers play their own music, there are discrepancies with the markings on the page. Without betraying the essential quality of the piece, the interpreter must make innumerable choices: How loud is forte? How fast is allegro? How long is a pause? What are the nuances *between* the notes? In previous centuries, composers were relatively casual about indicating tempo, dynamics and the like. Elgar's notations were more explicit, but still left innumerable questions of shading and timing. As she leaped through the blazing hoops of her fantasy, Jacqueline's uncanny phrasing surprised and delighted with its originality while seeming the only, inevitable choice.

The cellist Gregor Piatigorsky called vibrato the window of the soul; its speed and quality are what give colour to the tone. Throughout this near-orgiastic performance, Jacqueline's vibrato was perfectly

135

controlled, her technical mastery absolute, her legato as smooth as though her cello had but a single string. Her idiosyncratic, seemingly impossible fingerings were executed with such apparent ease that she might have been born holding a fingerboard. Arm, strings and bow seemed indivisible, belying the fact that the latter weighed over one hundred grams. Indeed, the entire instrument seemed an organic part of her body; when the music called for it she could attack it with fury, but more often she stroked, caressed or coaxed it, or cradled it like a child. Her tone was rich and vibrant, from her biggest, most opulent sound to the unearthly pianissimo played by her exquisitely slow, clinging bow. It could be intentionally jarring but never ugly, and was, to a musical ear, immediately recognisable.

The smiles she flashed at her husband would have melted stone. Barenboim, whose artistic roots were in the Germanic tradition, had never even heard of Elgar until he had heard Jacqueline play the concerto. She had quickly and completely converted him, he said, to Elgar's music. In the film, asked what it was like to accompany her, he said, "Difficult . . . in the sense that it's so natural to her that it doesn't dawn on her sometimes that we mortals have difficulties in following her. She doesn't even realise the difficulties involved. But it's the sort of difficulties that make music-making interesting and adventurous. She has sometimes a very free idea of tempi and of tempi fluctuations. But it all comes so much from inside with her – it's not something that she searches for – and I'm sure most of the time she doesn't even realise she is fluctuating. But we who have to beat, of course, find it sometimes rather hard."

The film, put together in three hectic weeks, retains all the heat with which it was made. Jacqueline's performance projects something universal, beyond words, evoking wonder and tears. The *Daily Telegraph*'s reviewer called *Jacqueline* a stirring programme and wrote, "The voltage of [Jacqueline and Barenboim's] present relationship and their musical talents looked in the film so extravagant as to suggest that they must surely burn themselves out before their time, that this is the sort of thing which cannot last. Insofar as it can be preserved, perhaps Mr. Nupen has done so."

Nupen's film catches Jacqueline in full bloom, when the bright side of her life was very bright indeed. By focusing exclusively on that limited dimension, the film set in concrete the myth that had surrounded her since her début. Seeing it, one would imagine that she lived an enchanted life on Mount. Olympus, dining on ambrosia in the fascinating company of other musical jet-setters. It looked and sounded like the fairy story that some reporters literally labelled it to be, and made a satisfying meal for the media, from the tabloids to *The Times*. Her romance and marriage provided the dessert. There were endless comparisons with Robert and Clara Schumann, and speculation about how talented their children would be. Newspaper and magazine stories written in the late Sixties were headed MARRIED TO MUSIC; THE MUSIC OF THEIR MARRIAGE; THE CHARISMATIC CELLIST; THE GIRL WITH THE MOST FAMOUS CELLO IN THE WORLD; and, in the *New York Times*, TRIANGLE: DANIEL AND JACQUELINE BARENBOIM AND THE CELLO. They spoke of "the golden girl of the music world with her eloquent cello and her wild, wheaten hair, and the stormy-eyed, dark-haired pianist turned conductor", and portrayed a glamorous whirl of engagements followed by wild applause, curtain calls, bouquets, autograph hunters, late suppers with the fascinating members of what *Time* called "a musical Camelot, with Daniel as its King Arthur". Photos show Jacqueline jauntily carrying the Davidov (booked as Miss C. Stradivarius) and a teddy bear onto jets. Mentioned in passing is the fact that she had during the past year travelled over 40,000 miles for concert engagements with a dozen different orchestras and conductors; not mentioned at all was her increasing dread of flying. There was never a hint that there might be more to her, or to her life, than what one would expect of or for a golden girl, the phrase the media bestowed upon her with a Midas kiss.

Golden girls, golden boys – for whatever reason, we everlastingly invent them. We expect golden girls to brighten our lives with their light, to fulfil our fantasies by remaining smiling, innocent girls for ever (one never hears of golden women). We admire and envy lives that seem somehow exempt from the rules that limit our own. And when a golden girl's mortality becomes apparent – when her marriage fails, or her mind or her body breaks down – we find a perverse satisfaction in the revelation that she is, after all, what we refused to allow her to be: as human and vulnerable as ourselves.

Seen in a certain light, Jacqueline was as golden as anyone can be – which is to say that she was utterly, sometimes painfully, human. Her *joie de vivre* was genuine, and the early years of her marriage were in many ways idyllically sunny, but there were, as in every life, shadows. Shadows are taken for granted in an ordinary life, but golden girls are expected to live in perpetual sunshine. Everyone who knew Jacqueline, even casually, noted her ubiquitous smile and accepted it at face value. Her husband called her "Smiley" because, he said, he had never met anyone who smiled so much; but only an idiot smiles all the time, and there was nothing idiotic about Jacqueline. She had discovered early on, in Purley, that a smile conceals the pain of rejection and disguises the anger that her mother had taught her, if only by example, was unacceptable. She had a naturally sparkling smile and it was, to be sure, often spontaneous. But throughout her life, it was, when necessary, a convenient and impenetrable mask.

Even before their marriage, Barenboim had begun to arrange their future bookings so that they would do all their long tours together, and be as near to one another as possible the rest of the time. Previous commitments in different parts of the world had to be fulfilled, but they played together whenever they could, beginning with their honeymoon. Mme. Rubinstein recalls that during their ten days in Marbella, "They made music every evening. Jacqueline gave herself to it completely, until she was exhausted. Then she would swim in the pool – we had a big swimming-pool and she loved to swim, and the evenings were warm – and I would give her a hot bath and she would sort of recover. After she went to bed, Daniel would stay up with my husband and make more music. Jacqueline spent herself entirely when she was playing. She really was all music."

From Marbella they flew to London and then almost immediately to North America for hastily-arranged concerts in New York, Cleveland and Toronto with Zubin Mehta and the Israel Philharmonic. The programme replicated that of the "victory concert" and all the artists donated their time and talents to the war-depleted Israeli treasury. On September 23rd Jacqueline was in Vienna to perform the Schumann Cello Concerto with the Scottish National Orchestra in the hallowed halls of the Musikvereinsgebäude; the Vienna *Kurier* called it "a ravishing performance". Two days later she played the Brahms Double Concerto in the Royal Festival Hall; Alan Blyth wrote in the *Daily Express*, "Jacqueline du Pré and her cello wanted to make it rather more emotional than did her violinist partner Hugh Maguire."

Meanwhile, Barenboim completed a successful provincial tour. As a foreigner, he had been permitted by the Home Office to perform no more than twenty concerts a year in Britain. Now he was officially designated a "foreign husband", and could work in the country as much as he liked. He also embarked on a heavy recording schedule; that year he would record piano sonatas by Beethoven and Mozart, piano concertos by Mozart, Beethoven, Brahms and Bartók, wind and string concertos by Haydn, Mozart and Boccherini, symphonies by Mozart, orchestral works by Wagner and Schoenberg and the Brahms clarinet and cello sonatas, the latter with Jacqueline.

On October 4th, Jacqueline played the Elgar Concerto at the Royal Festival Hall, with Norman Del Mar conducting; on the 21st she played the Schumann, with Barenboim conducting the English Chamber Orchestra, at the Queen Elizabeth Hall. In November she was in Munich to play the Elgar; on December 13th she was back in London to perform the Haydn D major Concerto with Sir John Barbirolli and the London Symphony Orchestra, again at the Festival Hall. A week later she and Barenboim left for Israel to celebrate the holidays with his parents, and also to work: between December 23rd and January 4th, in Tel Aviv, Jerusalem and Haifa, Jacqueline gave a total of eleven performances of Haydn's C major Cello Concerto, with Barenboim conducting the Israel Philharmonic Orchestra.

Jacqueline ended this most momentous year of her life playing sonatas by Beethoven and Brahms with the love of her life, in the Mann Auditorium, in Tel Aviv.

17

In 1968 Jacqueline spoke with writer Maureen Cleave, for an article in *Nova*, about her "soppy and stupid" love of nature. "Like a bumptious English girl," she said, "I love to walk. I love the rain and all the things Danny can't stand. It's boring to be too much in the sun. I love the physical thing of being on the earth that bore you, the longing to get in touch with something that's more infinite. I have the same feeling when I walk in a very beautiful place that I have when I play and it goes right." But however much she loved and longed for the outdoors, she lived indoors, in impersonal settings – planes, taxis, restaurants, hotel rooms, rehearsal and concert halls.

The sustained pitch of excitement at which she had lived during her first year with Barenboim would not diminish during the year to come. In 1968 she spent three nights in hotel beds for every one in her own, on the international music circuit in the United States, Canada, Italy, Germany, Austria, Spain and Portugal. "Sometimes Daniel may be in one part of America and I in another," she said, "but at least we're in the same country and can communicate. This is very important. Otherwise, we'd go in different directions the whole time. We wouldn't have any chance to get to know one another, or build up a life together."

She was often alone or with strangers, with whom she was still so shy and uncomfortable that she ate meals in her hotel room rather than downstairs in the dining room. When she wasn't performing or practising or rehearsing she was shaking countless hands, meeting masses of people; agents' representatives, concert organisers, orchestra managers, society presidents, friends of friends, unknown admirers. She enjoyed the company of many of the musicians with whom she worked, but dreaded the artificial social activities that were peripheral to a concert; she had no conventional small talk, nor any interest in it.

A tour was a musical treadmill on which the days, hotels, cities, and even countries were in many ways interchangeable. Performances consumed vast amounts of energy, and few allowances were made for jet lag or other exigencies of travel. The Davidov was a burden as well as a joy; Jacqueline had to cope with its extreme sensitivity to the temperature, the air conditioning, the lack of humidity and the poor acoustics of a hall. The instrument was more fragile than a violin and as highly strung as any thoroughbred; it had to be protected from radiators, heaters, hot-water pipes, extreme cold and other shocks. It required frequent, expert, minute adjustments: its bridge and its soundpost had to be precisely positioned, and the distance between strings and fingerboard exact. Tight pegs required lubrication; loose pegs needed chalk. Open seams, cracks, a slackness of the inside lining or a loosely wrapped string could cause rattles, buzzing or other unwelcome sounds.

In London, her life was no less hectic; there were rehearsals, concerts in and out of town, television appearances, broadcasts, recording sessions, interviews and practice, meals eaten at ridiculous hours. Although she practised far less than other musicians liked to believe – she claimed that too much study destroyed spontaneity, and she also hated to practise – some time for it was essential. "Those lonely hours are so important," she said. "It is lovely when you go into a room or onto a platform to play, but this is such a tiny part of one's musical life . . . No one ever pays to hear scales!" To learn a new work, she would embrace the whole of it, intuitively, and only later looked at it bar by bar. "Then I come down to the ground and look at it more carefully – or perhaps you could say that out of the chaos I put the bits together again."

Barenboim found it necessary to practise even less than she did, but away from the keyboard he was constantly studying, memorising and absorbing new works to conduct. His approach was logical and analytical, his views articulate and persuasive. By 1968 he was a prominent presence in British musical life – "Mr. Music" some called him, with as much envy as sarcasm. He divided his time about equally between playing and conducting; when he played the roles simultaneously it was generally with the English Chamber Orchestra, with which his rapport had become remarkable. He was also blossoming as an accompanist, notably with Janet Baker and Dietrich Fischer-Dieskau, and his recording schedule for the year included the Beethoven sonatas and Mozart piano concertos, the late Mozart symphonies with the ECO, and the Beethoven and Brahms cello sonatas with Jacqueline.

He kept the details of their bookings three years in advance in his legendary memory. He dealt with their fan mail, requests from composers who wanted them to play their works, travel arrangements, record companies, agents, lawyers and accountants, and spent hours on the phone, discussing professional and social plans. "Daniel manages his life very well," Jacqueline said, "and now he can manage mine, too. He likes to be the one making decisions, and I like having them made for me. I can't think a week ahead, but he has a very clear mind." Music, she said, was "not the most important part of their life; it *is* life."

In an interview at home with writer Patsy Kumm, Jacqueline said that because of their early success, both she and Barenboim had already fulfilled their main ambitions. "Now we're free to organise our life so that we *enjoy* it," she said. "Of course we'll always be working towards perfection. But at least we can do things in our own time, and when we feel ready to put down roots and raise a family, we can do it with the minimum of problems." Living out of suitcases was a bit of a bore, she said, because clothes constantly needed cleaning or pressing, "which is annoying when you like them as much as I do". Barenboim, who encouraged her interest in clothes and enjoyed buying them for her, chimed in like a sitcom husband: "I'll say she does. She thinks of them twenty-four hours a day. When she wakes up she thinks of a dress she wants; she knows just how it should look, and the shop where she can get it. So off she goes. While she's shopping she thinks of something else she'd like to wear and she buys that too. By the time she's finished she's starving, so she hurries home and has an enormous lunch, changes into one of the dresses and starts to practise. Only to realise with horror that, because she's been on tour, her concert dresses are all at the cleaners and she needs one that evening. So off she goes again – and that's the end of her practice."

The Montagu Street flat resembled a rather shabby, untidy hotel room – without room service. Shelves, tables and all other available horizontal surfaces were covered with piles of scores, papers, laundry and assorted objects. Jacqueline made sporadic efforts to keep the place clean; although they could well afford help in that department, she claimed to enjoy it. She and Barenboim had inherited their parents' conventional middle-class role definitions; it would have been unthinkable for Barenboim to have washed a dish. She slipped willingly into the traditional role, telling friends that she intended to be a good wife, mistress and mother – an impossible expectation. A musician on the international circuit needs a wife, or servants; Jacqueline had neither, nor had she the time, energy or organisational ability to keep house in any consistent way. She also told friends she looked forward to having babies, lots of them, and bringing them up on a kibbutz. Alison Brown was astonished when her formerly undomestic friend sent her advice about stews, and recipes for quick, easy, delicious meals. She occasionally experimented in the kitchen, with mixed results, but they usually ate out. Barenboim, famous for his generosity, often hosted large post-concert dinners at a nearby Italian restaurant for the "Barenboim gang". Its core now consisted of Itzhak and "Toby" Perlman, Zubin and Nancy Mehta, Vladimir ("Vau-va") Ashkenazy, Pinchas ("Pinky") and Eugenia "Genie" Zukerman, Christopher ("Kitty") and Diana Nupen. Barenboim was "Pear Tree" and Jacqueline was, of course, "Smiley".

The parties and chamber music at Fou Ts'ong's continued; Zamira Menuhin has amongst her souvenirs a 1967 photo of Jacqueline draped over her husband, dancing. An autograph book contains the inscription, in Jacqueline's large, generous hand, I SIMPLY MUST STEAL AWAY. She signed it "Shulamit Barenboim, née du Pré – and her ex-fiancé", and illustrated it with a whimsical cartoon. On the same page, Barenboim wrote I AM ONLY WRITING IN THIS BOOK AFTER BEING THREATENED WITH NOT BEING INVITED AGAIN.

The evenings never ended before two or three in the morning. Zamira recalls that Barenboim, with his remarkable metabolism, had the energy of ten men and was never tired. "He had so much energy, he wore her out. We'd say, 'Please tell us when you're tired,' but she never would. I remember Jackie often having to be poured into a taxi, or Danny taking her home in a great heap at three in the morning. But she so adored him that it didn't matter."

Madeleine Dinkel was concerned. "In Jackie's early years," she says, "it seemed that she had the constitution of a horse. She was built on pretty sturdy lines – I should know, having pinned her into her dresses. But as she got busier and busier, to get her for a fitting became a nightmare! She was rushing round the world faster and faster. She was always leaving things all over the place. I used to make her these grand petticoats of moire, ten yards wide down to the ground to support these wonderful skirts, and she'd leave them in some hotel somewhere, harum-scarum. I couldn't be cross with her, she was under such a strain, so much pressure.

"She didn't complain at all, but she did evince signs of exhaustion. I was distressed that she should have so many engagements and be so overworked. I said, 'Jackie, do you have to do all this? Can't you limit the number of concerts you do? Can't you take a few weeks or a few months off? Couldn't you talk to your agent about it?' And she'd say, 'But Madeleine, you don't understand at all! Once you're on this level' – she didn't say international stardom, but that's what it was – 'that's what you have to do! That's the way it works! Your agent fixes it up . . .' and she explained it to me. But I wasn't convinced. She seemed to feel there was no way out. It seemed to me dreadful she'd got onto the rails of this faster and faster, never-ending, demanding routine, from which she couldn't escape. She used to get very exhausted. I remember her just lying down on my couch and passing out. Or sometimes I'd say, 'Get into my hot bath.' Other times she was very exuberant. She loved to play, she adored her audiences. In a way I suppose it acted like a drug, where you've got to have it – you don't come alive fully unless you're on the stage."

It was obvious to everyone who observed Jacqueline during the first years of her marriage that she was incandescently happy with her husband. "Apart from all the normal joys of marriage," she told a reporter, "it's marvellous, when one has a musical problem, to be able to nudge someone in bed and say: 'Hey, what about this or that?'" At last she had the affection she'd always longed for – and not always in private. When they performed together, she whispered "naughty things" to him in plain view of the oblivious audience. On an aeroplane during a tour with the ECO, they became so amorous that the air hostess had to reprimand them. Their delight in each other, combined with their talent and youth, enthralled packed houses in Europe, North America and Israel, and reduced hard-boiled journalists to shameless sentimentality. Roger Kahn wrote in the *Saturday Evening Post*, "observing their triumphs, watching the counterpoint between them, one thinks of lines by Joseph Conrad: 'I remember my youth and the feeling that I could last forever, outlast the sea, the earth and all men.'"

There was a great deal of laughter, some of it undoubtedly to relieve the tension of their pressurised life. Jacqueline's imitations of a Russian accent always got a laugh; otherwise, her humour remained on the level of surprising people by popping out from behind doors, or warming up at a rehearsal by fiddling the theme from *Dr. Zhivago*. Barenboim's imitations of Klemperer, Barbirolli and others were polished and very funny; otherwise, his humour ran to practical jokes such as swapping the breakfast orders in an hotel corridor, and was not always in the best of taste – but Jacqueline, too shy to be shocking herself, appreciated a rude joke as much as her husband did. She loved his gregariousness and his apparent lack of neuroses ("no corns to be trodden on"); he never experienced the pre-concert nerves that were familiar to most artists (and had even begun to plague

Jacqueline), and his dressing-room was always full of friends before he went on stage.

Barenboim was a small man with a towering talent and *chutzpah* to match; he seemed to assume, if he thought about it at all, that everyone's ego was as indestructible as his own, and was capable of blurting out, at a dinner party arranged especially for him, "I'm dying for a proper meal!" Jacqueline, always considerate and impeccably courteous, was horrified by his rudeness to waiters and other unlucky underlings who incurred his wrath. In a musical situation he never threw the tantrums for which some conductors were notorious – he was far too controlled for such behaviour – but he could be so rude and impatient that only his colleagues' overwhelming respect for his musicianship kept the situation in hand.

In the rarefied, élitist world of classical music, Jacqueline was never an élitist. Success never made her world-weary or smug or superior, or lessened her childlike curiosity and delight in what she could see, touch, feel, hear and taste. Abstractions intimidated her; she remained self-consciously aware of her lack of formal education and during "intellectual" discussions, depending on the company, either became shy and tongue-tied or clowned around like a charming but silly child. Barenboim loved to discuss almost any topic; he spoke six languages, and was articulate and opinionated in all of them. He shared Jacqueline's strong convictions about music but had reached them with analytical efficiency, whereas she had followed an intuitive path. He had his pompous moments – perhaps an attempt to compensate for his youthful appearance, which he believed prevented some people from taking him and, more important, his work, seriously. He was capable of making such statements as "The power of music is precisely that of expressing the eternity of feeling, not transient or subjective emotion." She was capable of starting a mock fight by throwing paper pellets across the table in a posh restaurant.

In 1968, Ian Hunter, Barenboim's agent and also director of the Brighton Music Festival, suggested that composer Alexander Goehr write a piece for Jacqueline which she could première at the festival, with Barenboim conducting the New Philharmonia Orchestra. Until then it had never crossed anyone's mind that she would play a new piece by a modern composer, or that Barenboim would conduct one, except by someone as well-established as William Walton or Benjamin Britten. Jacqueline disliked most modern music because it contained "anti-string" sounds and was not melodic – "Bartók," she said, "is about as far as I go." But the staples of the orchestral cello repertoire were the handful of concertos that were always in demand:

145

Elgar, Schumann, Haydn, Dvořák, Saint-Saëns, Lalo and Boccherini. Only in chamber music, for which there was a limited demand, could Jacqueline find a great variety of works to play. Barenboim had had no experience at all with modern music, but he was intrigued by Hunter's idea. He agreed to help Jacqueline learn the new piece, and to conduct it.

Goehr wrote *Romanza*, a substantial twenty-three-minute "novelty", as a showpiece for Jacqueline. It consisted of a single lyrical movement with a long opening theme for the soloist. Realising that Jacqueline's relatively small classical repertoire had not required that she learn the complicated counting required for modern music, Goehr cast the work like an aria for an opera singer: once she started she would play straight through to the end, and so couldn't get lost. Goehr thinks it a pretty glum piece, but Jacqueline said it suited her "down to the ground". She played it in April at the festival, in the Brighton Dome, and again in October, at the Festival Hall, to reviews that were warm for her, mixed for the work.

Goehr subsequently wrote a difficult piece for Barenboim to play and conduct – he learnt it, Goehr says, "in a minute" – and a warm friendship developed between the two men. In 1968, 1969 and 1970, Goehr and Anthea, then his wife, saw a good deal of the Barenboims in London and intermittently, when their travels coincided, in Boston, New York, Philadelphia and Los Angeles. The relationship was more than casual but less than close; there was, Goehr says, "a situation difference. One was a bit shy, because they were very well off; one was very conscious of not wanting to be a hanger-on. It was complicated. Daniel is the life of the party – you can hardly take him out, he's always paying the bill. I was happier when we were at home, theirs or mine, where they were very unbuttoned, or when we'd go to some local place or get a take-away, more like one's normal life." Goehr, who is ten years older than Barenboim, says that he sometimes felt twenty years younger. "When Daniel was nine, he was playing with Furtwängler; so he was an old man as well as being a young man."

Goehr says, "You couldn't describe Daniel as well-read – I was always struck by the absence of books in their houses – but he was moderately in touch with what was going on, he was not uneducated or uninformed. I flatter myself that he liked to be with me because he could talk about things with me that he wouldn't have talked about with Pinky, with whom conversations would either be about which towns he was playing, musicians' talk, or big-time stuff. He was wonderful company, exciting to be with, whether serious or messing about. He was terribly witty, full of Jewish jokes. Never boring or repetitive. But difficult to talk to because the telephone rang all the time, you were always competing with the transatlantic phone for his attention. No conversation ever went on for very long unless you went to a restaurant.

"I thought that for a big-time showbiz marriage, it was bloody good. In those days Jackie was all vanilla, Daniel all vinegar. She had a quality of complete innocence, never any nastiness or sharpness. Daniel was very taken by that quality in her, he was entirely enchanted. He could be vinegary and sharp and harsh, but he is also one of the most generous men in the world, and not only putting his hand in his pocket and paying the bill. He genuinely cared about all those people, the Zubins and the Pinkys. He was always recommending people for jobs, going to their concerts – there was never any jealousy. Well, I suppose there was nothing for him to be jealous *of*. And Jackie was generous in a very English way, a very *kind* person who deeply cared about not hurting people's feelings. Once she married Daniel she was completely overwhelmed by his very powerful personality. He was clearly the dominant partner, and he provided the ambience of their lives. Her role was to be Smiley with the pale English looks in a world of dark men, in which Daniel was the centre of attention. But she contributed to him as well, and seemed to be doing more so until she got ill. He grew as a person under her influence; everyone remarked on how much softer and amenable he became. He even took time to think about what he said, which could be devastating. When he was being awful to some menial person, he could be a bit rough, and she wouldn't take it. She would say, Danny, you just can't behave like that! He was progressively nicer, more caring of people – that he surely got from her. He became a deeper and more happy man with her – until her illness.

"About two days before her illness was diagnosed, I was driving along Finchley Road and saw her standing on a traffic island, looking totally disoriented. I pulled up and she got into the car. She was ice cold. I took her to my mother's in Hampstead, and gave her some tea. Then I took her home. For me, for ever after that, she was a poor thing. But I wonder whether I didn't think she was a poor thing when she was famous, and being courted by the world. I suppose I thought of her as a poor thing because she couldn't really get that much pleasure from her life. Jackie was happy at certain times, on certain days, but generally I don't believe she was happy in that world. Even in the Beverly Hills Hotel, getting the Hollywood treatment, she wasn't at home. The only place she ever seemed at home to me was in the basement flat in Montagu Street. It was rather dirty – it had no polish. Danny was just making his reputation with gramophone records and he had a terrible little square gramophone that was cracked. They were young, they'd just got married, there was lots of sex in the air. There was a relaxed atmosphere which I never remember around them after that. She possessed this great talent, but had to take it for a walk, like a dog. She lived, to her disadvantage, in a fake world, a trap, in which any kind of reality was swept under the carpet.

"I remember her sitting in a New York hotel room, overtired. She just seemed to have had enough – of traipsing around to parties and concerts and dos and restaurants and all this stuff that goes on in that life. Daniel was mostly on the telephone, or sitting and waiting for transatlantic phone calls. She was going to play a concert, and she had strapped round her middle this ridiculous sort of disgusting woolly vest with holes in it to absorb the sweat when she played, so it wouldn't show through onto her elegant gown. She was giggling because underneath this tralala with the New York Philharmonic was this simply disgusting object. It struck me as quite a good symbol. You dress up and do these great things, and you take one familiar object with you that you wear underneath, to prove that you're a real person, and not just the object that they're watching."

On another occasion, in another hotel room, Anthea Goehr found Jacqueline improvising a replacement for the dilapidated vest. "Jackie showed me her newest concert dress – gold silk with a tight bodice, full skirt, low neckline. Then she showed me a tiny, very pretty and expensively made sewing kit she'd bought at Harrods. She was cutting up Marks & Spencer's "fully interlocking cotton knit" knickers – the plainest, most utilitarian women's underwear. The kit was to sew the pieces into the bodice of her dress, so the perspiration wouldn't show through. We giggled a lot; we were both young and slightly immature, and terribly relieved to be alone in this hotel room." For Jacqueline, it was a rare moment of decompression in an increasingly stressful life. Her persistent fatigue was beginning to make playing, which had always been a welcome release, a source of anxiety. She worried about her health, but looked so well that friends accused her of hypochondria; they told her, and she told herself, that her weariness originated in her mind. She kept smiling, and tried to ignore it, but it was as real – and as invisible, except to her – as the perspiration she went to such lengths to conceal.

18

On July 3rd, 1968, thirty-six hours after having returned to London from engagements in Europe, Jacqueline and Daniel were at Heathrow airport with the members and management of the English Chamber Orchestra, boarding a plane for New York. During the next two weeks the orchestra gave nine concerts in eight cities; Jacqueline was the featured soloist (playing the Haydn cello concertos) in only six of them, but attended every rehearsal and performance in the strenuous schedule. They used New York as a base, commuting by coach to Katonah and Brookville, New York, and Columbia, Maryland, rarely returning to their Manhattan hotel room before 4 a.m. "This is our life," Barenboim told writer Roger Kahn. "Rehearse, perform. I give now thirty-five per cent of my time to piano, thirty-five per cent to the [English Chamber] orchestra and the rest to other conducting." He said he hadn't had a vacation in four years; his 1968 holiday had been scratched when he'd taken the London Symphony Orchestra to America in April, at a week's notice, for his New York conducting début. "It's hard work," he said, "but I love it."

On July 11th Jacqueline, elegant in an emerald-green dress, played the Haydn Concerto in D major at Lincoln Center. "During her cadenzas," Roger Kahn wrote, "Barenboim leaned back on the podium rail, legs crossed at the ankles, in a posture that bespoke approval mixed with pride. Sometimes, after difficult runs, Jacqueline looked towards him and smiled. He nodded and in the end, with the orchestra playing forte, she spun through the difficult arpeggios and there was all that long blond hair flying. The sold-out house erupted in a cry of triumph." Another critic wrote, "I lust for her."

Jacqueline played with the ECO at festivals in Ravinia, Illinois (her midwestern début) and Stratford, Ontario. When the orchestra returned to London on July 15th, she and Barenboim flew to Los Angeles, where she played the Saint-Saëns Cello Concerto with the Los Angeles Philharmonic at the Hollywood Bowl. After the concert, *Los Angeles Times* music critic Martin Bernheimer wrote, "She ripped into the bravura vehicle like a fury, but – a big but – like an ultra-musicianly, intelligent, warm-hearted fury. Hers was a radiant performance, built on gorgeous, mellow tone and total immersion in the pleasure of recreation. Barenboim and the orchestra followed with seeming awe and discretion." The occasion was marred by the theft of Jacqueline's wedding ring, which she had left in her dressing room when she went on stage.

In August, Barenboim presided over a mini-festival advertised as "the outstanding new musical event of 1968". The eleven-day "South Bank Summer Music" had been his idea for an alternative to the weightier Proms, performed in the vast Albert Hall and emphasising orchestral programmes. South Bank Summer Music took place in the relatively intimate Queen Elizabeth Hall and consisted primarily of chamber music and works within the means of the English Chamber Orchestra. As musical director, Barenboim organised the programme around his friends: Ashkenazy, Perlman, Janet Baker, John Williams and clarinettist Gervase de Peyer. The result was an exciting and incredibly high level of music making, so successful that it was repeated in 1969 and 1970. At one concert Jacqueline played Brahms's Trio for Clarinet, Cello and Piano with Barenboim and de Peyer, and the Brahms Second Cello Sonata with Barenboim; *The Times* reviewer carped, "Miss du Pré attacked with too unrelenting an intensity; when everything is so much emphasised, and the tempi so unsettled, there is no room for the degrees of contrast that are essential in what is perhaps the tersest of Brahms's chamber pieces."

Within the week Jacqueline was at the Edinburgh Festival, where she played the Dvořák Cello Concerto so energetically that she broke a string in the first movement. She and Barenboim stayed in a big rented house with some core members of the clan. She had arranged for the group to fly in a private plane from Edinburgh to the Isle of Mull and then on a three-day holiday to Fingal's Cave, but the holiday aborted when Barenboim agreed to perform with his wife at a benefit to be held in London on the afternoon of September 2nd. The concert, "Czechoslovakia 1968", was sponsored by the United Nations to aid Czechoslovakian students stranded in Britain after the Russian invasion of their country. Jacqueline was to play the cello concerto by the Czech composer, Dvořák.

At seven o'clock on the morning of the concert, the telephone rang in the Montagu Street flat. Barenboim answered the phone and was told by an anonymous caller that the concert was an act of provocation, that he would be shot if he appeared, and that it would be impossible to find the assassins in the crowded Albert Hall. Daniel

Barenboim did not tell his wife, nor report it to the police; he did mention it to some friends, and they alerted the authorities. That afternoon, Jacqueline, oblivious of the plainclothes detectives who mingled with the seven thousand members of the audience, gave what *The Times* reviewer said must have been one of the greatest performances of her life – "passionately felt, yet controlled in every minute detail, a flood of glorious evocative song". After the concert, which took place without incident, Barenboim told the press he'd been tempted to look over his shoulder during the concert, but had managed to concentrate. He said, "I was a little anxious, but when I started to conduct and I was not shot, it went out of my head. It was not until afterwards that I told my wife of the threat."

If the situation had been reversed – if it had been Jacqueline who took the phone call – it is inconceivable that she would not have told her husband and allowed him to make an informed decision as to the degree of risk, and whether or not he would subject himself to it. Jacqueline was denied that right, for reasons which stemmed as much from her background and personality as from her husband's attitudes and values. Although Barenboim had a forceful father and she did not, they were both products of a culture and class in which the husband's authority is absolute. And if Barenboim felt it his duty to protect his wife from the harsher realities of life, such as decisions, her behaviour was in part both cause and effect. At the age of twenty-three, Jacqueline retained a naturally child*like* quality which was often mistaken for child*ishness*; as a result, she was perceived as a carefree and endearing, if sometimes exasperating, little girl, to be patronised and indulged. It was the role in which she had been cast since childhood; she played it well, and may not have been aware of an alternative.

By 1969 the Barenboims were a touring couple, seldom apart for more than two days in a row. Jacqueline lacked the ambition and energy for as heavy a concert schedule as her husband's, but he liked to have her at his rehearsals and concerts, and she loved to watch him work. During the 1968–69 concert season they travelled throughout Europe and to Canada and the US, where she performed as soloist with various orchestras and also in recital, playing mainly Beethoven – duos with Barenboim, or trios with Perlman or Zukerman on the violin. On April 2nd she played the Haydn Concerto in D major at the Festival Hall with Barenboim and the ECO and then, despite her dislike of flying, accompanied them on a world tour that included New York, Australia, New Zealand, Israel and Italy. She took her cello along, but did not play until the penultimate concert, in Florence on May 12th. Throughout the trip, Ursula Strebi says, Jacqueline was tremendously tired. "Everyone said Daniel was wearing her out. I think she had a concert scheduled in Australia and had to cancel. But she came to all our concerts and was very supportive. And when I was ill during the trip she sent me lovely, thoughtful, sympathetic little poems."

It was not her husband but her incipient illness that was wearing Jacqueline out. She often complained of needing more than eight hours' sleep, when Daniel needed so little. Jet lag left her exhausted but not always able to sleep, while Daniel, to her great annoyance, nodded off immediately, snored deeply but briefly and awoke ready for another twenty action-packed hours. While not entirely unsympathetic, he believed, as he had told Suzie Maguire when he was recovering from glandular fever, that a professional should have the discipline to work through anything.

In its earliest stages, multiple sclerosis is diabolically difficult to diagnose. Symptoms come and go unpredictably and can be mild, fleeting and easily forgotten – or, as in Jacqueline's case, misinterpreted as signs of nervous strain. When she consulted a doctor in Australia about her tenacious fatigue and occasional double vision in her right eye, he dismissed the symptoms as "adolescent trauma" and suggested she take up a relaxing hobby.

Immediately after the tour with the ECO, Jacqueline performed the Brahms Double Concerto with Pinchas Zukerman at the Brighton Music Festival, with Barenboim conducting the New Philharmonia Orchestra. Two days later, the Barenboims gave the first of two programmes of Beethoven's sonatas and variations for cello and piano at the Festival Hall. "The whole of musical London turned out," Joan Chissell wrote in *The Times*, "to hear what was probably the most accomplished duo of the century playing the works of one of the world's greatest composers . . . In the Sonata in F major, [Jacqueline] supported him like a tigress in several of the finale's climaxes."

A week later Jacqueline was in New York again, to play the Elgar – a performance that moved Pablo Casals, who listened from the wings, to tears. The following week she played in Rome with the St. Cecilia Orchestra, conducted by Barenboim. Parthenope Bion Talamo, Jacqueline's one-time schoolmate in Croydon, was in Rome and arranged a meeting with Jacqueline at the Grand Hotel. Parthenope, now a psychoanalyst, says, "The thing that most struck me about her was her sadness and her loneliness; I got the impression that her marriage was not going so well. During the interval of the concert, the Barenboim clan clustered round Daniel, very much leaving her out. I couldn't help wondering what happened to her when they gave concerts in cities where there didn't happen to be old acquaintances around. Did she get completely left alone? What made this so painful to me was what she had said previously at the hotel, when she had clearly and urgently expressed the need to belong to the group she had adopted, and was very enthusiastic about the kibbutz upbringing which she envisaged for her future children."

Jacqueline's marriage was a very public affair. In a reflective moment in 1969, she told writer William Wordsworth, "There seems always so much activity and so many people with whom we have to be involved that days upon days go by without us being able to sit down for a quiet talk to one another. It's all most enjoyable, although there does come a longing just to be left on our own sometimes." If Barenboim had any such longing, it was subordinate to his insatiable appetite for socialising with high-powered, highly talented people. His motor was always racing; he had no interest in the kind of ordinary domestic scene in which Jacqueline had felt so comfortable at Jill Severs', at the Maguires' and later, after her marriage, at the home of Kate and Charles Beare. At a Thanksgiving Day party given by Kate, who is American, Jacqueline had a wonderful time playing with children, mashing potatoes and otherwise amusing herself with mundane matters. Kate was aware of "a side of her that was so normal, even supernormal – you could imagine her on a farm. But that life wasn't accessible to her. She was wonderful with our children, and with the children of other people who were here. She had fun just having a normal day, because you don't get that many chances when you're busy with an international career. But that wasn't really Daniel's scene. It was boring for him, and he didn't like turkey. And Jackie went along with his lifestyle. She always said that he got everything he wanted. But she came down here a lot when he was away."

Jacqueline seemed to long for the kind of ordinary friendship that was precluded by her lopsided, peripatetic life. She talked more easily away from the social occasions that were invariably dominated by Barenboim and his male friends, where wives literally took a back seat. When the Barenboims, Nupens and Goehrs drove to Coventry for a concert Daniel was to give, the men sat in front having their own conversation while Jacqueline sat in the back with Anthea Goehr (now Anthea Hogan) and Diana Nupen. Anthea recalls, "We just giggled and said silly things, letting off steam. One had to be persistently female in the way the men wanted you to be female in order to survive. It was impossible to be assertive. You just accepted what people wanted you to do and be. If Daniel wanted Jackie to do her imitation of someone to amuse his friends, an imitation that she might have done for him in private, she would be embarrassed, because she was very shy, but she would never put her foot down. She just giggled and shrugged her shoulders and did it, to please him.

"There was a very strong feeling of goodness about Jackie. Her whole inner nature shone through whatever she did. That never changed. It wasn't because of the chemistry in the room or the people she was with. She didn't make jokes herself, but she laughed a lot. So people might have thought she was just a smiley, laughing girl who played the cello. Later, the things she said about her illness showed there was far more to her than that."

Playing was both means and end for Jacqueline; she had no taste for glory. Jan Theo says, "From the time Jackie married, she wanted kids. Daniel wouldn't have wanted it, not at that time. I felt she'd have been quite happy to be wife and mum, not a superstar – that persona never came naturally to her. She didn't have that sort of personality, and to be married to one must have been a hell of a strain. She wasn't reared as one; Daniel was. He wore the role very naturally; Jackie always seemed uneasy with it."

In the third year of her marriage, Jacqueline's public enthusiasm for having children had waned. When asked – and every interviewer seemed bound to ask the question – she spoke of the incompatibility of children with her lifestyle. She told Alan Blyth of *The Gramophone* that she wanted several children, but that she could never stop playing for any length of time, that she couldn't live without it. She made the same statement to a *Sunday Times* reporter, adding that if a child happened, she would adapt. That reporter then asked an extraordinary question: how would it affect her or her husband if the other one were to die? "It would affect one normally," she said – "humanly, as it would anyone. We both have this talent which is also our life – in a sense, our blood . . . it could possibly help."

19

In August, Jacqueline gave six concerts at the second South Bank Music Festival, and Christopher Nupen filmed her in live performance with Barenboim, Perlman, Zukerman and Mehta at the Queen Elizabeth Hall. The music was Schubert's "Trout"* Piano Quintet in A major; Zukerman played viola, and Mehta played double bass.

Nupen, who had left the BBC to form his own company, used the technique which had worked so well in the 1966 Barenboim–Ashkenazy film. He filmed the musicians off guard in informal situations, separately and together, preparing for the concert. Viewers saw Zukerman cracking jokes while buying a new viola, Perlman relaxing with his family in their temporary Hampstead home, Mehta anxiously watching his bass as it rolled (in its case) down the trestle at Heathrow. For laughs, before a filming session at a rehearsal, the performers all switched instruments, to see what the film crew would do. Mehta played the piano and showed Barenboim how to manage a few notes on his string bass; Perlman took the cello; Zukerman, who was playing viola, took the violin, and Jacqueline played the viola. Nupen and the crew pretended not to notice, got it on film, and left it in.

Like Nupen's other films, *The Trout* is glossy and glamorous; even the dreary concrete exterior of the Queen Elizabeth Hall is somehow made to look exciting. The film sparkles with the high spirits, the joy in making music and the affectionate affinity of the young musicians (all of whom, except Mehta, were still in their twenties), and its television showing was a great popular success.

Jacqueline's two recordings of the Beethoven cello sonatas, with Stephen Bishop in 1965 and with Barenboim in 1970, illustrate certain changes in her style. With Bishop she had lost some of the classical finesse she had had under Pleeth's steadying influence, and her energy verged on excess. With Barenboim, who was the epitome of control

* So nicknamed because its fourth movement is a set of variations on the melody of Schubert's song "Die Forelle" – the trout.

at the piano, she began to get it back. She believed that her playing improved after her marriage and attributed it to her husband's influence, saying that although they sometimes disagreed strenuously about performance, they shared the same absolute respect for the music. Barenboim also introduced her to a world of music beyond the cello; incredibly – for a musician – she had never heard opera until he played her a recording of Wagner on his cracked gramophone. She reciprocated by opening his eyes, as he said years later, "to a whole dimension of sound which, as a string player, she was in total command of, and a whole variety of colours in the music and in sound, not just in Elgar but in other music, too. I don't think I have ever met a more natural musician than she was. She had a totally perfect musical instinct. She saw two notes, and they were inevitably right the way she felt them and the way she did them, and that was quite flabbergasting." From Jacqueline he learned to notice fingering more carefully than other conductors do – enough to say to a cello section, "Start vibrating before you play the note, so as soon as you start making the sound, it's lovely."

The year 1970 was the two hundredth anniversary of Beethoven's birth, and the composer was a presence in Jacqueline's life throughout the year. Observances of the bicentennial began two months before the year did, when the Barenboims performed Beethoven's "Ghost" and "Archduke" Trios with Pinchas Zukerman at Carnegie Hall. *Vogue* called them "Super Trio – Super Brio" and said, "Not since Rubinstein, Piatigorsky and Heifetz has there been such a trio as this. They bolt onstage with the verve of a coltish troika, attacking their instruments like priceless, loved toys." In December, in Manhattan's Philharmonic Hall, Jacqueline and Barenboim repeated the two Beethoven programmes they had given in London the preceding May. They were compared for the umpteenth time to the Schumanns and also, by *Time*, to the Lunts. On New Year's Day and the four days around it, they took part in an astonishing marathon at EMI studios. With Pinchas Zukerman and Gervase de Peyer, they recorded all of the Beethoven piano trios, variations for piano trio and the clarinet trio, filling both sides of five long-playing records. *Look*'s Joseph Roddy, who attended the sessions, wrote that while Barenboim and Zukerman discussed the playbacks in rapid-fire Hebrew, Jacqueline sat "as uncomprehending as her chair".

By August, Jacqueline had played Beethoven sonatas with Barenboim to packed-out houses in Toronto, Los Angeles, Oxford, Brighton, Tel Aviv, London and Edinburgh. She had also played the Haydn C major Concerto three times in San Francisco, with the

San Francisco Symphony Orchestra conducted by Seiji Ozawa, and the Saint-Saëns Concerto four times in New York, with the New York Philharmonic conducted by Claudio Abbado; of the latter concerts, Harriett Johnson wrote in the New York *Post*, "She used her bow and fingers as if she were ecstatic at the privilege. With Miss du Pré one cannot speak of technique or gorgeous tone or any single facet of her incredible art. She makes everything culminate in the drama of the music." Other reviews ranged from fawning adulation to the familiar complaints (Robert Commanday wrote in the San Francisco *Chronicle*, "There can be such a thing as too much soul, if by soul one takes the contemporary definition of a complete unburdening of one's emotional insides"), but were predominantly positive.

At the third annual South Bank Summer Music Festival she performed Beethoven's piano trios, Bach's chamber music, Beethoven's Triple Concerto (with Barenboim and Zukerman), *ad libitum* music for Dietrich Fischer-Dieskau singing Beethoven's arrangements of folk songs, and, with Ashkenazy, a cello transcription of Franck's Violin Sonata. Christopher Nupen filmed her playing the "Ghost" Trio with Barenboim and Zukerman, and EMI recorded her live performances of the cello sonatas, with Barenboim, at the Edinburgh Festival.

In September she and Barenboim again flew half-way around the world, to participate in Australia's celebration of the Beethoven bicentennial.

They were received like royalty, and billed by the organisers of the concert series as "the golden couple – the musical love match of two child prodigies". They stayed for a month, during which Barenboim gave twelve concerts and Jacqueline only three. She played the Elgar in Sydney and the Dvořák in Melbourne with the local symphony orchestras, and gave a duo recital with Barenboim in Melbourne, where they drew the largest audience ever to attend a cello-piano recital in that city's history; every seat in the hall was filled, and another hundred people sat on the platform. Eva Wagner wrote in *The Australian*, "The Barenboim concerts were an exhilarating experience, one that made me feel that the world despite everything is not such a bad place to live in."

Jacqueline zigzagged from Australia to London to Toronto to New York to Michigan, and back to New York. When she played the Schumann Cello Concerto with the Toronto Symphony, conducted by Karel Ancerl, the *Toronto Star*'s William Littler wrote:

Miss du Pré can easily crush a concerto in the bear-hug of her embrace. She is one of two cellists, Rostropovich being the other, who put almost too much love into the act of playing. Each of them has been guilty on occasion of leaving passion in tatters.

This time she did not. The romantic spirit which forms the concerto's opening theme and guides the soloist's entire course, was kept in proportion. She made the music sing without sobbing or shouting . . . She found in Schumann's concerto not the evidence of an erratic muse but all manner of lyrical intimacies, tied into beautifully arched melodies. She is, in short, the singer to make a song.

Between her own engagements, Jacqueline joined Barenboim, who was booked solidly for a three-month tour of the USA. The media reported his energy and staggering accomplishments with awe: his thirty-six records, his two hundred concerts a year on five continents, his master classes on British television. *Time* called him "not the best pianist in the under-30 group", churlishly described the way "his pudgy little hands fly over the keyboard", catalogued his successes and failures (superficiality, glibness, and an emphasis on technique that made him "sometimes bland and bloodless"), and concluded that he was "one of the most intriguing figures in music today".

At the year's end Jacqueline was recorded twice in live performance, both conducted by Barenboim: the Dvořák Cello Concerto with the Chicago Symphony Orchestra in Chicago, and the Elgar, with the Philadelphia Orchestra, at Carnegie Hall. Jacqueline identified strongly with Dvořák's deep love of nature, which comes through in his music, and this recording was one of her favourites. The Elgar recording is less controlled than her earlier one with Barbirolli, but she preferred her later interpretation, and the immediacy of the live performance – for which she had used a brand new cello, made especially for her.

Jacqueline loved her Strads – the earthy, peasant sound of the first and the fine clarity and silky tone of the Davidov. She also loved a Francesco Goffriller that she had acquired in 1968 and had used on many of her recordings. When both she and her instruments were on their best form, in a room of reasonable size, the result was sublime. But the combination of her forceful playing and the hypersensitivity of her cellos necessitated frequent adjustments and caused her considerable anxiety, particularly in a large hall. She worried that her sound might not carry above the orchestra, or that the cello would get – her expressions – a terrible "wolf note" or "buzz", or start "kicking" or "bubbling". She needed a louder, sturdier, more stable instrument – and Barenboim found one for her. He had heard Pinchas Zukerman play a violin made by Sergio Peresson, a Philadelphia instrument maker, and was so impressed that he commissioned Peresson to make a cello for his wife. Surprised and flattered, Peresson, who had previously made only two cellos, went immediately to work, and delivered the instrument just in time for the Elgar recording. Jacqueline wrote to him a few months later saying, "Everyone has fallen in love with your cello and I continue to love playing it." It was very healthy, she said, and "strong like a tank".

Imperceptibly to everyone but Jacqueline, her own health was breaking. She looked well, and most of the time she felt well; then all at once, without warning, her energy would drain away, as in a dream when one tries to run with leaden legs. She consulted doctors about it, and about other mysterious and wildly erratic symptoms – a tingling and numbness in her fingers, a sensation that her foot was frozen when she awoke, ambiguous aches and pains. There were times when she hadn't the strength to open a window or fasten her suitcase. The symptoms were fleeting – but when she was on stage, the object of intent scrutiny by thousands of people, a minute could be an eternity.

In the clarity of hindsight, there had been portents – wispy shadows, washed out by the dazzling sunshine of her success. She had always had a slightly ungainly, almost clumsy, gait; as a child, in Purley, she'd been teased for falling down. In her teens she had complained to Peter Thomas of numbness in her thumb – but musicians, especially string players, are notorious for complaining about the discomforts of playing, and Peter, whose neck often hurt after hours of violin practice, was not terribly sympathetic. Alison Brown remembers Jacqueline's vision problems, and that she wore cotton gloves when she practised because her hands got so cold. Liza Wilson saw her take a peculiar and rather spectacular fall when she was a student in Moscow: descending a staircase, she had suddenly and inexplicably dropped her cello and fallen down the last bit to the bottom. She had gone to a hospital, worried that she'd broken or sprained her wrist, and had been told that no damage had been done.

During a performance, when concentration is intense and every emotion is engaged, adrenalin races. Afterwards, whatever the hour, artists need time to unwind, preferably in a convivial atmosphere with musical colleagues, before they can sleep. But by 1970, Jacqueline was often too enervated after a concert for more than a bowl of corn flakes in her hotel room and an early night. Although none of the doctors she consulted found evidence of any physical problem, her strength and endurance were dwindling – but her commitments were not.

The stakes were high. Of all the high-flying members of the Barenboim clan, Jacqueline's name was the biggest draw, and her fees, which ranged anywhere from £1,000 to £2,000 per concert, the highest. After her marriage she had left Emmie Tillett for Barenboim's agents, Harold Holt Limited. The change facilitated their joint bookings and also assured her of better fees and more personal attention.

There are probably no outright villains in the music business; individual agents and managers may be dictatorial and sycophantic, but they are not inherently evil. They operate, however, in an extremely messy arena. The big orchestral circuits are controlled by record companies whose business is governed, like every other business, by laws of supply and demand. The product is people. A musician must be marketed when she is hot, even at the risk of turning her into a touring freak. As a soloist, Jacqueline was a gold mine; when she and Barenboim appeared together, they were platinum. Any agency would have been horror-struck at the thought of cancellation of a tour, unless there was a demonstrable medical reason. If they believed the artist to be neurotic, or temperamental, or even overtired, they would agree to a rest only after the completion of a tour that was in progress.

The constraints were psychological as well as financial. With certain exceptions that prove the rule, artists know that if they step off the international music treadmill, they will need to run at least twice as fast to regain their position. Jacqueline was running faster and faster just to stay in place. She knew that *something* was affecting her speed and co-ordination, and that her playing was not up to her normal standards. When she could no longer ignore her symptoms, she tried to counter them by extending her warm-up time before concerts. She had no way of knowing that physical exertion, by raising the body's internal temperature ever so slightly, can produce rapid and disproportionate fatigue in one who has multiple sclerosis. For the same reason, the hot baths she thought therapeutic were also counter-productive. The greater her efforts, the less she achieved, and the greater her emotional stress – which in turn probably contributed to the symptoms that produced it. Her confidence was badly shaken; when the symptoms suddenly and unaccountably disappeared, she wondered whether, and when, they might return.

Her predicament would have been hard on anyone; it was particularly so for someone whose husband was totally absorbed in himself and his music, whose stamina was considered superhuman, and who accepted more work than anyone in the business, while complaining that there were only 365 days in the year when he would have liked to work five hundred. Jacqueline looked tired but otherwise well; her anguish was difficult to comprehend. With no medical diagnosis, Barenboim was sceptical, rather than supportive. It was easier to believe that her problem was emotional than that it could be a chronic physical disease.

When her husband was away, Jacqueline saw a good deal of Kate and Charles Beare. She would arrive by taxi at their Richmond home, play with the children, help Kate in the kitchen, have a meal, and play duets with Kate, who is also a cellist. The two women were the same age and startlingly alike physically, with the same long, straight blond hair, light blue eyes and fair complexions. Kate says, "Jackie told me she was exhausted. She said, 'Nobody understands me when I say it's so difficult to play.' There were two times when she wanted to quit a tour, but they were going to sue her if she didn't continue her commitment. She needed so badly to rest, and she wasn't allowed to rest. Would the illness have been so bad if she'd been given that liberty? One of the awful things about MS is, you look at the person and you don't see anything. It's all hiding on the inside! You don't *see* all that damage! She complained that people would say she was crazy and neurotic, and she *knew* there was something else wrong."

Kate Beare speaks with special authority on the subject. Ten years later, she began to experience similar symptoms, which have since been diagnosed as multiple sclerosis.

20

Jacqueline and Daniel both felt a strong sentimental attachment to their cramped basement flat; leaving it would symbolically end their honeymoon, and they remained there long after they had outgrown it. Finally, late in 1970, they bought a spacious two-storey red brick house at 5a Pilgrim's Lane, in Hampstead.

Jacqueline had always liked north London; the air seemed fresher, and sprawling, woodsy Hampstead Heath was the next best thing to the countryside that she loved. The house was just steps away from Hampstead Village. On the ground floor were sitting-room, dining-room, kitchen, a small conservatory and an attached garage, which they converted into a studio for Daniel; upstairs there were three bedrooms. Best of all there was a wonderful back garden, behind which lay the quiet grounds of the Rosslyn Hill Chapel. It seemed an auspicious new beginning.

Jacqueline decorated the house with her husband (who is colour blind) in conventional, suburban style. They had little time for or interest in personal touches, for they spent less than a quarter of their time in London – a week here, a few days there – and that time was crammed with demands on their attention. Early in 1971, Barenboim again toured the US; when he played the Brahms Piano Concerto No. 1 with the Los Angeles Philharmonic, conducted by Zubin Mehta, Jacqueline played in the back of the cello section, hidden from the audience by the violas – their private joke. But behind the smile, she was bewildered and frightened. At the end of May, after a concert in California, she cancelled concerts in the USA and Israel and flew home, doubting her talent and her sanity.

There is no specific diagnostic test for multiple sclerosis. Its early symptoms – fatigue, loss of sensation, weakness and visual changes – are frequently misdiagnosed as psychoneurosis or an even more severe psychiatric disorder, such as hysteria, particularly in women. When doctors could find no organic cause for her complaints, they prescribed a year's rest, and referred her to a psychiatrist.

Gossip is the compost of social intercourse in the music world, and speculation about Jacqueline's sabbatical was rife. As she had feared, it was rumoured that she was neurotic, that she was having a nervous breakdown, that her marriage was falling apart; some people even attributed her impaired co-ordination to a drinking problem. Because she looked well, it was easy to interpret her weakness and fatigue as laziness or depression.

Jacqueline was in fact deeply depressed, but it was the result, not the cause, of her illness; she thought she was losing her mind. Always before, she had had the cello to help her cope with emotional difficulties. She had once written to Christine Newland, the young Canadian cellist she had met in Toronto and with whom she occasionally corresponded, saying that one of her favourite things was to go into a room all alone and play some Bach, "keeping on until I am utterly wrapped up in the music, the thrill of drawing the bow over the strings, and the feeling that I am fit to burst with the beauty of it all." It had always given her a feeling of strength, she said, in difficult times. In 1970 she wrote to Christine saying that she had had an unhappy time, but assured her that it was over, and she was well. She would not be playing for a few weeks, she said, but would rest, and "quietly learn some more repertoire – perhaps try and get all the Bach suites in better shape. I do find them hard."

It was not weeks but months before Jacqueline played again, even for her own comfort. From June to December, she did not touch her cello. With no evidence to the contrary, she assumed that whatever was wrong must be her fault – that her mind was subverting her body and disrupting her life. Friends were solicitous, but most of them made the same assumption. Few of them knew that five times a week she saw Dr. Walter Joffe, a Freudian psychoanalyst. In 1970, psychiatric treatment was considered a shameful secret in unenlightened Britain. Jacqueline had always liked to walk, and she walked the mile and a half to Joffe's office every day – but when she got there, she resisted. Music was her element, her first and truest language. How could she begin to convey her frustration and guilt and anxiety in mere words?

Barenboim took some time off for her sake, but was nevertheless away a good deal. She spent some time at her sister's ménage in Berkshire – but although she enjoyed Hilary's children, and even admitted publicly that she coveted them, her relationship with "Kiffer" Finzi was strained, and it was not the refuge she sought. Nevertheless, when the Finzis went on holiday to their house in the south of France, Jacqueline, and her parents, went along. Writer Robin Golding, who was there as well, recalls that the household was dominated by Finzi's forceful personality. Iris seemed sweet,

Derek old-fashioned, the atmosphere pleasant, but all in a superficial, *arti*ficial way. "On the surface, Jackie was full of fun. She liked rude jokes, such as discussing the size of the turds in the very primitive loo. But underneath she seemed sad. Lost. Bewildered. She was taking sleeping tablets. She told me that she and Daniel didn't need to talk about music or about anything else – that they just understood each other instinctively. She missed him very much."

In December, in the middle of her sabbatical, Jacqueline awoke one morning in Hampstead feeling so well that she took her Peresson out of its case and began to play as though there had been no interruption. For four days, she and a delighted but cautious Barenboim worked on Chopin's Cello Sonata in G minor, Op. 65, and a transcription of Franck's Violin Sonata in A. Barenboim and EMI producer Suvi Raj Grubb quickly reserved a recording studio, and they recorded both sonatas in two remarkably smooth sessions. When they finished, early on the second day, Jacqueline exuberantly suggested that they begin to record the Beethoven cello sonatas, a project that had often been postponed in the past. She and Barenboim played through the first movement of Op. 5, No. 1 and then, suddenly looking very tired, she put her cello in its case and said she was afraid that would be all for that day. At twenty-six, an age when most musicians have barely begun making recordings, she had made her last appearance with a cello in a recording studio.

Jacqueline's symptoms abated during her year of rest, and by June 1972 she seemed so much improved that Harold Holt Limited held their collective breath and announced that she was completely re-covered and would return to the concert platform in the autumn. Her schedule would be "not too heavy", and she would not play with an orchestra until the new year. Friend and photographer Clive Barda, who went to Pilgrim's Lane to shoot the publicity photos that accompanied the announcement, thought she seemed cheerful and perfectly fit.

In July she went with Barenboim to Tel Aviv, where they played the Tchaikovsky Trio, Op. 50, with Pinchas Zukerman. Her London "come-back" took place at a Prom on September 24th; she was nervous, and told her old friend Sybil Eaton, "It's a big wall to climb after so long." She played the Tchaikovsky Trio again and Beethoven's "Ghost" Trio, and all went well. A week later, at another Prom, she and Barenboim played the Franck Sonata they had recorded together. Her friend Rosie Barda said, "We all came out in tears; it was *so passionate*. I don't know if she knew by then that it was all going wrong. It was an amazing performance. *All of her was in it – everything."*

She did know that it was going wrong. She was experiencing the same symptoms, but attributed them to the stress of resuming her career, and tried desperately to believe they would go away. Instead, they were probably aggravated by her anxiety. The one constant in her life had been her faith in her talent, on which she could no longer rely. Her control was precarious; the concert platform on which she had always felt so at home had become a threatening and perilous place.

During the first week of 1973, she managed two successful performances of the Lalo Cello Concerto, in Cleveland, Ohio; but when she played the same work in Toronto a few days later, one reviewer wrote that although Massey Hall was packed,

> It turned out to be merely another concert – not an inferior one, but rarely more than mildly exciting . . . There were only a few moments, as in the finale of the middle movement, when there was a suggestion of her accustomed fire and vitality. Elsewhere one could command only remote admiration for the quality of a sound that seemed surprisingly small for this artist . . . This was outstanding cello playing, musically and technically. It was just not great du Pré.

On January 25th, at Philharmonic Hall in New York, Jacqueline gave what was to be her last public performance with Barenboim. Puzzled and disappointed, the *New York Times* reviewer wrote,

> Taking sonatas by Brahms (No. 1), Debussy and Chopin as a starting point, Miss du Pré charted a course that included a good deal of raspy tone, wailing shifts, pouncing upon (and often missing) notes and a wide vibrato in pizzicato passages that had about as much charm as a twanging rubber band.
>
> Along the way there were isolated phrases of revelatory beauty, but they never seemed to fall into an overall pattern of logic and consistency. Each piece was propelled with plenty of impetuous energy that only generated a kind of thoughtless and finally meaningless excitement.
>
> Through the technical lapses and interpretational eccentricities, one can still discern a musician of great talent, and a personality of communicative vitality. Perhaps Miss du Pré should consider

tempering self-indulgent abandon with a little hard thinking about the notes and where they are headed.

Jacqueline had never needed critics to judge the quality of her playing. She knew better than anyone when she was on form, and she needed no one to tell her how far off she was now. Fighting the impulse to panic, she returned to London and Dr. Joffe, whom she had grown to love and to trust. With his help, she shored up her confidence for a February concert at the Festival Hall. It went well, and the audience of hardcore fans received her affectionately. The *Guardian*'s Neville Cardus, who had written so glowingly of her début twelve years before, now wrote a touching and unintentionally appropriate eulogy for her career:

> It was good to have Jacqueline du Pré back at the Royal Festival Hall last night, playing in the Elgar cello concerto. Though time and poor health have momentarily taken something from her art of technical certainty, much has been returned to her in maturity of understanding and inwardness of thought as she goes through this most private and troubled music Elgar ever composed . . .
>
> Jacqueline has always played this concerto beautifully, but often with a sort of virtuoso love of her instrument dispelling withdrawn reflection. On this occasion Jacqueline went to the heart of the matter with a devotion remarkable in so young an artist, so that we did not appear so much to be hearing, as overhearing, music which has the sunset touch on it telling of the end of an epoch in our island story and, also, telling of Elgar's acceptance of the end. The bright day is done, and he is for the dark. Towards the close of the concerto Elgar recalls a theme from the slow movement and the falling cadences are even self-pitying. Jacqueline du Pré got the wounding juice out of this self-revealing passage: her tone came from her sensitively quivering fingers [and] . . . brought home to us the poignancy and what Thomas Hardy would have called the loving-kindness of the concerto.

A few days later, Jacqueline flew to New York, where the nightmare she most feared came to pass.

She was to play the Brahms Double Concerto with Pinchas Zukerman and the New York Philharmonic, conducted by Leonard Bernstein, at Philharmonic Hall. When she arrived for rehearsal, she needed assistance to open her cello case; during rehearsal, she couldn't feel the strings of the cello or properly command the bow, and the opening cadenza, difficult at the best of times, was a disaster. Feeling frightened, guilty and ashamed, she told Bernstein that she wouldn't be able to manage the performance – but Bernstein, believing the problem to be nerves, persuaded her to go on.

Jacqueline walked onto the platform that night feeling, she said later, as though she was walking to the guillotine. Her arms had no strength, and her fingers were numb; she had no idea what sounds she was going to produce, or even how she would find a key. She realised that her only hope was to use her eyes to see where her fingers were, and to estimate visually how many inches she had to move them from note to note. At the end of the interminable performance, she was excruciatingly aware of the audience's disappointment.

After the concert, Bernstein took her to a doctor. Again, the diagnosis was stress. The next day, she cancelled other engagements in America and flew home. No one, including Jacqueline, knew more than what the *New York Times* reported – that she was suffering from paraesthesia, a nerve disorder, in her bowing arm. Seven terrible months would pass before she would learn that her body, not her mind, had betrayed her.

Part Three

21

The onset of multiple sclerosis is so baffling that its victims typically begin to question their sanity. Diagnostic procedures are unreliable and slow, as doctors consider the patient's history, conduct neurological exams, perform specialised procedures – spinal taps, X-rays of the brain, electrical tests – and observe the patient over a period of weeks or months, until they have ruled out every other possibility. During their interminable observation of Jacqueline, the depth of her anxiety, disappointment and despair could probably only have been expressed, ironically, in music.

"A really great genius finds its happiness in execution," said Goethe, an authority on the subject. Jacqueline herself had said that playing was more than a way of life; it was life itself. Now, when she tried to play, the sounds she produced only added to her frustration. She continued with Dr. Joffe on the premise that her unconscious bore some responsibility for whatever was wrong with her – but if the search through her psychic past shed any light on her present difficulties, her physical condition did not improve.

In April, she was scheduled to perform the Dvořák concerto, with Barenboim conducting, in Tokyo. They made the journey together, but her performance was cancelled at the last minute. The body that she had always taken for granted had become a source of anxiety and self-consciousness. Walking was an effort, for her legs did not always respond to her brain's commands. She had to concentrate on maintaining her balance, on putting one foot after the other, on consciously bending her knees and watching the pavement.

In September, Isaac Stern replaced her at the Edinburgh Festival. She went to Edinburgh anyway, to be with Barenboim, who was making his belated operatic début conducting *Don Giovanni*. She attended every rehearsal and most of the social activities, but her mysterious ailment made people uncertain how to behave; it was difficult to believe she was ill when she seemed cheerful and looked well. When she occasionally staggered, or dragged her feet, or dropped things, friends were uncomfortable, and joked that she'd had too much to drink, or that the Scottish mist must have got into her bones. She was in her twenty-eighth year – precisely the age at which Beethoven had written to his brothers, "You must forgive me if you should see me draw back when I would gladly mingle with you. My affliction is all the more painful to me because it leads to such misinterpretations of my conduct."

On the evening of October 5th, Liza Wilson was at Pilgrim's Lane with her then-husband, pianist Radu Lupu. It was the eve of the Yom Kippur War. Liza recalls, "Jackie was making this wonderful dinner, and Daniel was terribly upset about the war starting – he was phoning a hundred people and trying to get there. He kept saying 'I've got to leave! I've got to go!' Jackie obviously wasn't sharing his anxiety to the same degree. At a certain point, when he was in the middle of a phone conversation, he asked her to please go upstairs and get his address book. She said, 'No, I won't.' He got quite put out about it and said, 'Can't you even do that for me?' She said, 'No, I can't, sorry.' She didn't tell anyone until afterwards that she couldn't, because her legs were not going to take her up the stairs. She was too frightened to tell anyone about it.

"She would often go out on her own; she might go shopping or walking on the heath, and she would fall down and have to wait for someone to come along and pick her up. She'd come home late, and Daniel would say, 'I thought you'd be back ages ago.' She'd say, 'Oh, I saw something in the shops that I wanted to try on.' Finally she fell down somewhere, I think it was in the street, and couldn't get up, and ended up in hospital."

Although Jacqueline's doctors must surely have suspected multiple sclerosis for some time, they had never mentioned the possibility to her. To do so could have spared her years of doubting her sanity, but could also have unnecessarily curtailed her career. She was in the Lindo Wing of St. Mary's Hospital, Paddington, on October 16th when she was finally given the diagnosis. Barenboim was in Israel, playing for the troops with Zubin Mehta. When the news reached him, he had no idea what it meant until a doctor friend of Mehta's told him what little is known about the disease. Within days he was back in London, reeling.

Multiple sclerosis is a chronic, progressive disease of the central nervous system which destroys the insulation of nerve fibres in scattered areas of the brain and the spinal cord. At the sites where the damage occurs, the myelin sheath that encases the nerve fibres is replaced by dense, hard, "sclerotic" scar tissue, so that messages from the brain to the muscles and organs are short-circuited.

Depending on which part or parts of the nervous system are

affected, the result can be muscle weakness, poor co-ordination, giddiness, loss of balance, blurred or double vision, slurred speech, numbness, tingling sensations, difficulty in swallowing, problems with bladder, bowel and sexual function, and spasticity (involuntary muscle contractions that stiffen the knees and hips, push the feet down, and make walking and mounting stairs extremely difficult). People with MS may have one or any combination of these, at any time, without warning, in degrees ranging from mild to extremely severe, lasting for minutes or years. Unusual fatigue, by far the most common symptom, has specific physical causes, and can also be a result of the depression and frustration of having a chronic disease.

Attacks – a short period of acute symptoms – are typically followed by remissions – an easing or disappearance of symptoms for weeks, months or even years. The disease is not fatal, but it can shorten one's life by reducing the body's ability to fight off other diseases, most commonly lung or bladder infections. It is not contagious, but its cause is unknown; there may be genetic, environmental or viral factors. Its cure is also unknown. During its early stages, remissions that verge on the miraculous often occur, either spontaneously or coincidentally to some treatment. It is not uncommon for the disease to be inexplicably arrested, or burned out, during its first five years. Most people with MS have a mild form of the disease and are able, like Kate Beare, to lead active lives with only occasional disruptions. At the other end of the scale, fifteen per cent of the cases progress rapidly and lead to complete paralysis.

Jacqueline's first reaction to the diagnosis was one of enormous relief that her symptoms were real, after all. She immediately phoned William Pleeth, Suzie Maguire, Diana Nupen, Liza Wilson, Alison Brown and a great many other friends and calmly told them the good news: she wasn't going crazy. She said that MS was a serious illness and could some day lead to a wheelchair existence, but that she had a mild case and would have long remissions, and they were not to worry. She said she had wanted them to hear it from her, not to read it in the papers.

When the story did break, the shock rocked the music world. On November 6th, the front page of the *Daily Mail* carried the headline, JACQUELINE DU PRÉ WILL NEVER PLAY IN PUBLIC AGAIN. That morning an anxious, unshaven, furious Barenboim interrupted a rehearsal with the London Philharmonic Orchestra at the Festival Hall to tell reporters, "We were sitting at home having breakfast this morning, which my wife had prepared, when we heard the news on the radio that she was gravely ill. In fact, she is coming to my concert at the Festival Hall tonight." He called the news reports greatly exaggerated and said, "She has been in the London Clinic for tests for three weeks. She came home from the hospital last Friday. No doctor has ever said she will never play again. She has been leading a normal life at home and doing the cooking and tidying up the house." He pointed out that someone with MS could lead a normal life for a long number of years and said angrily, "It is absolutely no help at all to say she is gravely ill." The next day the Harold Holt organisation issued a statement saying, "Jacqueline is making a fantastic recovery and is in great form," but would not say when her next concert appearance would be.

Jacqueline told herself, and friends understandably reinforced her hope, that her career was not over and she would play again – but after the initial relief came desolation, and what she later called "very deep doldrums". She said, "My husband was away a lot and I had relied on him for everything. There came a period when I couldn't move at all, when I would stare at the ceiling and indulge in despair." The feelings of isolation from which she had suffered as a child returned a thousandfold, and were relieved only fleetingly during her sessions with Dr. Joffe. When she could no longer walk to his office, he went to Pilgrim's Lane.

In her first months with the analyst Jacqueline had been almost inarticulate, finding words a pathetically inadequate substitute for the cello. Now, in her third year of analysis, the diagnosis had clarified the problem – but in order to deal with it, she would have to find out more than just the facts of her neurological condition. She had to learn more about herself. She clung to the hope that Joffe could help her recover, and tried to take a more active part in the painful process. Talking about her deepest feelings was still difficult, but silence, she knew, was worse. At the same time, her continued analysis implied that her unconscious had somehow colluded with the disease.

Her condition, particularly her energy level, fluctuated from day to day. Attempting to deal with perfectly normal feelings of anger, depression, loneliness, self-pity and grief was in itself stressful, and may have exacerbated her symptoms. Barenboim cancelled engagements with the Chicago Symphony and New York Philharmonic in order to be with her, but although he did his best to look after her, he was not by nature a caretaker. He was also grieving, and struggling with his own emotions – but instead of sharing them with his wife, he was more paternalistic and protective than ever. At a time when open, straightforward communication between them was imperative, unexpressed anger and sorrow made it impossible. Each felt that to openly acknowledge the extent of the catastrophe would unfairly burden the other. As Jacqueline turned to Joffe, Daniel turned to his friends, precluding the intimacy and shared vulnerability that is difficult enough to achieve at the best of times. They both suffered from the strain of mixed and conflicting messages, sent and received.

Barenboim cancelled a number of concerts in order to be with his wife, but he could not do so indefinitely. He desperately needed help in the house – ideally, a housekeeper who could cook. In February 1974, he and violinist Rodney Friend walked into a London restaurant for a bite to eat. Olga Rejman, a Czechoslovakian kitchen worker and avid music lover, recognised him and introduced herself. She told him that she had attended the 1968 benefit concert for Czech students – the concert that had prompted the death threat – and had enjoyed his performances many times since then.

Barenboim said, "You know about my wife."

"Of course," Olga said. "It is a tragedy."

He asked if she knew anyone who could help in the house; she said she would ask around, and did so, but with no luck. Barenboim returned to the restaurant the next day, and the day after that; on his fourth visit, he asked Olga if she would come to his house to cook dinner for Isaac Stern that night. She agreed, and the dinner was so successful that Barenboim asked her to stay. Olga declined. "I was already sixty-two years old. I was tired. I told him, 'It is too much, I can't cope any more.' He said, 'You are not strange to me, you are really like my family.' His eyes were wet, he was so unhappy. So I said, 'All right, I will stay.' And I stayed six years."

Olga had led a sheltered, privileged life in Czechoslovakia until she was thirty-six. Then her husband died, her family's business was nationalised by the Communists, and she served a three-year prison sentence for hiding political offenders. After that, with no work experience or technical skills, she survived as a labourer in the sugar-beet fields. Eventually she taught herself to cook, and in 1964 made her way to London, and the restaurant job. Concerts were a link with her past, and her only luxury.

Olga filled the Pilgrim's Lane house with plants, and with her generous personality. Jacqueline was recovering from a severe attack. She could still stand and walk, but her legs had become so inflexible that she could only descend the stairs by scooting down in a sitting position, and there were times when she was unable to move at all. Olga thought at first that she had a bone disease, and offered to give her a piece of her own; "but nerves I could not give her, because I don't have them.

"We were always laughing together; I always managed to say something to take her away from the sorrow. I was terribly sorry for her. I loved music, and she was such a marvellous musician. She played with such gusto, such *panache*. Her playing went into your blood, into your heart."

Olga liked Jacqueline, but she loved Daniel. "He was in a terrible state. He needed support, as well. He got it from his friends, but not from Jacqueline. He was not able to make a cup of tea. He was able to make some eggs, that was all. He was sweet to her; he really loved her. He was heroic. He loved to surprise her by taking in her breakfast tray. They understood each other. When she got very ill, he cancelled his concerts. He was like an angel to her – he brought presents, books, flowers, and he phoned every day. He should have a halo around his head.

"When we were in Hampstead, he played a lot. After she went to bed, from about eleven o'clock at night until maybe half past one. The neighbours sometimes complained. She was jealous that she wasn't able to have this glory and he was. After we moved to Knightsbridge she would say 'Don't, don't play!' She couldn't listen any more; she was really jealous. So then we listened to *her* records.

"Aida Barenboim taught piano in Tel Aviv, but she came during the school holidays. She would come down the stairs and every step was shuddering. When she and Daniel were in the house, it was rocking. These tiny little people, when they were in a room they made it full. When she came, she did everything for Jacqueline. I used to tell her, 'I know that I am one horse, but you are three horses!' She laughed. Only once I saw her down, when Jacqueline was really not well. She came downstairs saying 'Olga, that this has to happen to my son! What a tragedy!' When Enrique came along, it was tense; he and Aida had rows, and Daniel always took her side."

Iris du Pré's role in her daughter's life, once so essential and well-defined, was now marginal. She had taken her daughter's conversion to Judaism as the rejection that it was meant, at least in part, to be. Now, she was unable or unwilling to witness the conflagration of all her dreams. Derek had retired, and the du Prés still lived in Gerrards Cross, not far from Hilary and their grandchildren. When they visited Jacqueline, Olga was appalled. "They lived not so far away, but she had to bribe them to come, and give them money for petrol. And so bad they were not off. They came in emergencies, but sometimes not for a month. They were strangers to each other, this family. They did what was expected of them, but there was no love or understanding. Iris was heartless, like an icicle.

"Jacqueline told me her parents' marriage had been unhappy but now it was better, and she was pleased. She said she was so sorry for her mother – but her mother was never sorry for her. She was helping her family a lot; many times I had to go to the bank to get money when they came – it probably added up to thousands. Her mother was never able to tell her something that would make her feel better. She told me, 'You are better than my mother,' and everybody knew it. She was so hungry for love. We were extremely near to each other, because I was so terribly sorry for her. 'You are my Edengarten,' I told her. I came with the breakfast to her, I was sitting on her bed, I was holding her hands or she was holding mine, and she was speaking, speaking, speaking. She never stopped. She told me about her unhappiness at school, her shyness – that she had not been a good pupil, and the other children laughed at her."

Jill Pullen, one of the first nurses to look after Jacqueline at home, says that Iris and Aida Barenboim were "poles apart. Aida arrived at the door and you could see in her stance, in her whole being, that this woman was going to be effective. Jacqueline's family may have been well-intentioned but when they stood at the door, there were just question marks everywhere. Aida could produce a meal from nothing – once from boiled eggs and green peas, with a white sauce on it. With Jacqueline's mother you had to have the food, the instructions, and also help her; she gave the impression that it was all much too complicated for her. Iris seemed *irritated* that Jacqueline was in this situation."

Training and temperament kept Jacqueline smiling when she wanted to scream; only in her sessions with Dr. Joffe could she remove the mask without feeling guilty. She had never felt accepted as a person in her own right, and she was grateful to Joffe for perceiving her as neither child nor cellist, but as an intelligent adult woman. She trusted him, and depended on his non-judgmental ear. As her life collapsed, her desperation and need made him indispensable. No one was more aware of that fact than Barenboim, who told Olga, "We would not be able to bear it if she didn't have him."

On May 8th, 1974, a stranger phoned with shattering news: the fifty-year-old Joffe was dead, without warning, of a heart attack.

22

J acqueline was inconsolable; she felt abandoned, in a dark, dangerous universe inhabited only by herself. Only with Joffe had she
felt free to divulge her rage, her guilt at being a burden, her terror
of the unpredictable future. He was, she believed, irreplaceable.
But within twenty-four hours, into the void stepped a colleague of
Joffe's, who would support her through the next thirteen years.

Psychoanalyst Adam Limentani was an Italian Jew with aristocratic
features and a powerful, steadying presence. He was in his late fifties,
tall in stature and in his field. Like Joffe, he was a Freudian. "When
Joffe died," he says, "Jacqueline felt totally betrayed. He'd been
someone who showed an interest in her for *her* sake. She appreciated
that neither Joffe nor I were really interested in her music, that we
did not want her to perform. I did not *want* her to be anything special.
That was the crucial bit of the relationship. She needed to feel accepted
as a woman, not as Jacqueline du Pré. For all her greatness as a
musical genius, she still had the feelings and the interests of a woman.
She was a very *human* human being. Sensitive, vulnerable, and needy
of love. Success had given her applause and love. Suddenly it was
gone.

"She had a tendency towards depression, which had been extremely
well taken care of in the music. A passage in the Elgar, for instance,
which she always felt was a little tear. [Dvořák's] 'Silent Woods'
appealed to her because of its sadness. And Schubert's *Death
and the Maiden*, which she loved. The cello had been her way of
getting in touch with what was inside her. It was a part of her, an
extension of herself. She loved the audience as much as she loved
her cello. The whole thing was a unit; cello and audience were nothing without the other. I was a kind of replacement for the audience
she had lost – and I was a faithful audience. She could count on my
presence."

Dr. Limentani does not believe that Jacqueline's life was particularly
stressful until the illness made it so. "First the symptoms, and we
can't know when they started, made engagements stressful – and
then the stress, when the engagements ceased, of the extremely drastic

change in her life." He had a preconceived idea that MS would respond to a psychological approach. "Some physical illnesses, psychosomatic conditions, respond well to psychoanalytic intervention. Cancer . . . even AIDS. So why not MS? Although there is no cure for her condition, I feel that somehow we [her doctors] failed, because we couldn't do more for her. I don't feel I did anything for her except help her fight to stay alive.

"I have always been the analyst who didn't ask questions. I *interpret.* In the beginning I had a difficult time, because I expected her to do more work. I was strict. I wasn't going to have silence. When her music was taken away, she had to find another outlet. Words. And eventually, as the music receded, language flowed back into her subconscious."

Five sessions a week were not enough. "She would fill in between them by writing notes that she would give me. Revelations, containing such depth of feelings. She knew nothing about me, but she insisted on calling me by my Italian name, Amadeo. No one else calls me that. It made her feel a little closer. She idealised me, as many patients do. She thought I was the greatest analyst in the world – that I was a sort of guru. She needed to feel she had someone who could make her go on fighting."

In May 1975, Jacqueline was admitted to the Rockefeller Institute in New York, where an experimental programme of treatment for MS was under way. She made the trip reluctantly, on the recommendation of her neurologist, Dr. Leo Lange; she had never liked travelling much, especially in a plane, and once she became ill she hated to leave home, even for holidays. "When she left for New York," Olga recalls, "there was a terrible moment. She came downstairs on her bum and they got her into the car. Someone was passing by carrying a cello. Rodney Friend was standing next to me; he knew what I was thinking: that it was finished. We were both thinking it was finished."

While she was in hospital in New York, Jacqueline explained her reason for being there in an affectionate, reassuring and seemingly serene letter to Christine Newland. She wrote that the researchers were testing the possibility of a connection between multiple sclerosis and the measles virus. Like many other people with MS, Jacqueline had had childhood measles, but appeared not to have developed natural antibodies to the disease. The theory was that the virus had remained in the system and continued to cause damage, sometimes in the form of MS. The experimental treatment was "to feed one's blood with the healthy serum in the hopes that it will remove the naughty serum". It had worked on a limited number of people, she said, but it had not worked on her. She wrote that although she was not very well and tired easily, her spirits were "excellent". There was no reason for her to tell Christine, an adoring but casual acquaintance, the truth: that she had never been more miserable, or terrified, in her life.

Dr. Limentani says, "New York was a landmark in her medical history. She didn't want to go. But if you are Jacqueline du Pré, people do the very best for you. They felt she should try everything. She was very isolated there – doctors and nurses rushing in and out doing tests and different things to her. No one seemed to realise her predicament. They made her do what chronic patients do in hospital. She hated the occupational therapy. For her, it was the cello or nothing. To be given a piece of leather and told, 'See what you can do with it' made her cross. She made a huge belt and inscribed a passage from Elgar on it and gave it to me as a present. That was her response to that sort of thing."

After three weeks of tests, the doctors in New York told Jacqueline that she would never walk again, and that the disease could eventually affect her mind. Dr. Limentani believes that only then was she directly confronted by the gravity of her illness. "It was a crisis. When she went to New York, she walked onto the plane, and she walked off the plane. Three weeks later, she could hardly walk at all. There was a sudden, dramatic deterioration. At that time she was not given long to live, but she wasn't told that. Her doctors told me. She lived another twelve years, because of her will to live."

When Jacqueline was given the devastating news, she wanted to go home immediately. Piers du Pré happened by chance to be in New York at the time, and it was he who brought his sister back to London. Olga believes that Jacqueline hadn't realised until then that the illness really was incurable. "Selby [Dr. Leonard Selby, her GP] and Lange and Limentani had always given her hope. She *hated* those doctors in New York! They were so insensitive! Could they have realised how talented she was? How much she had to lose?" Jacqueline told Olga, "They were so rude to me! They told me that to the end of my life I will be in a wheelchair! They never should have told me." Olga said, "Better to be in a wheelchair than not to move at all. And you will not be the only one."

After that, Olga never saw any improvement. "Jacqueline would say, 'Today I'm much better, I can move much better' – but I never saw it. Dr. Selby told me that she had galloping MS, like galloping

TB, and wouldn't live long. But then it stopped galloping and went slowly, slowly, slowly."

The Pilgrim's Lane house had become an obstacle course, in which the steep interior staircase made Jacqueline virtually a prisoner in her room. Olga had to take meals up for her and her guests. But in New York, Jacqueline had serendipitously met Dame Margot Fonteyn. The dancer was married to a quadriplegic, and they owned a three-storey house in Knightsbridge which had been adapted for his wheelchair. The house had a lift into which a person could be wheeled from an upstairs bedroom, to re-emerge in the downstairs hall. A ramp provided easy access to the street. Fonteyn and her husband now lived elsewhere, and they offered to rent the house to the Barenboims. Daniel quickly accepted; Pilgrim's Lane, so bright with promise four years earlier, was the graveyard of his hopes. Olga and Aida worked frantically to get the new house ready and in July, while Barenboim was touring in Greece, they moved into 2 Rutland Gardens Mews – and Jacqueline moved into a wheelchair.

Denial is a natural and sometimes necessary coping mechanism, and for a time it allowed Jacqueline to avoid acknowledging the magnitude of her disaster. The wheelchair represented the reality that she might not get better, and made it harder for her to believe that she wouldn't get worse. In it, she knew the panic and despair of a bird that has lost first its song, then its wings. In it, she dammed up an ocean of tears.

   Losing her cello was an amputation from which Jacqueline had not even begun to heal. Losing the use of her legs meant an end to the taken-for-granted activities of ordinary life: impulsively taking a walk, getting a snack, making love. What had been a pleasantly disordered existence became one in which medical considerations dictated a strict routine. The minutiae of her life assumed dramatic proportions, with every action demanding conscious attention. If she could write, read, dress and feed herself today, would she be able to do so tomorrow? Some simple tasks that were achievable when she was rested were impossible when she was even slightly fatigued. Could it be the onset of an attack, or was she just tired?

   MS requires the diligent conservation of one's energy and at the same time imposes enormous psychological stresses that drain that energy. Maintaining a degree of optimism – trying not to worry, or to anticipate the next loss or indignity – can be an effective coping strategy, but the effort exacts a price. No less stressful is the pressure, both external and self-generated, to alleviate the burden one feels oneself to be by *never complaining*. Like fat people who are expected to be jolly, people with disabilities are expected to bear their lot meekly and cheerfully. They may be drowning in a sea of anger, fear, sorrow and bitterness, with an undertow of self-pity – but in polite society, the honest expression of such emotions is as acceptable as throwing up on the carpet. Cursing God, like hammering one's pillow, is to be done in private – unless one can afford an analyst.

MS patients have been stereotyped as euphoric – the medical term for cheerful. Some MS patients *are* euphoric, perhaps as an emotional reaction to the physical effects of the disease, or a result of damage to the nervous system – but Freud showed how exuberance can be a cover-up for depression, and studies of people with MS indicate that depression, not euphoria, is typical. They quickly learn, however, on pain of real or imagined abandonment, to protect those around them from embarrassment, from their guilt at being well, and from the fearsome thought that such a random calamity could happen to them. The overriding obligation is to *comfort other people* by pretending that *everything is fine*. Healthy, able-bodied people need the illusion that a severe handicap need not prevent one from having a complete, happy life. Not until Helen Keller was seventy-seven did she admit publicly that she had always pretended that being blind, deaf and mute had not excluded her from living. Jacqueline's friends needed her smile, and she obliged.

Visitors arrived with kind intentions and hearts full of sympathy, but their fear of saying the wrong thing inhibited spontaneity, strained communication and magnified misunderstandings. As the threads that had connected Jacqueline with their world frayed and broke, she felt their growing estrangement. She felt estranged from her own body, as well, as it regressed towards infancy and forced her to rely on others. Her perception of herself shifted and blurred. Our culture encourages and rewards self-reliance and, particularly in women, physical perfection. When Jacqueline thought about how she must look to others – especially to men, whom she had been trained to please – her self-esteem shrivelled, and she wanted to hide. Everything she had been seemed to be slipping away.

The demons of shame, guilt and self-hate torment every victim of chronic illness. When one hates the illness, one can easily hate oneself for having it, and feel ashamed. Guilt is the cleverest demon. The innocent instinctively feel that where there is what appears to be punishment, there must have been a crime, and Jacqueline was obsessed by the question that haunts every victim of an incurable illness: *Why did this happen to me?* She confided to Liza Wilson that as a child, she had always been frightened of being ill. "She told me many times that she had some deep-seated fear that she couldn't have all this talent without having to pay for it – some idea of retribution. I remember her telling me once how she regarded the cello when she was little – that it had a kind of mighty power, like a god of some kind, and she would actually worship it, get down on her knees. That it was not only a means of expression but some sort of totem pole, a phallic symbol. It was very much a psychoanalyst's kind of jargon, which I was surprised to hear her use. Perhaps she got it from her analyst."

With Dr. Limentani, she surveyed the ruins of her life. As she struggled with the necessary and protracted process of mourning her losses and contemplated those that might lie ahead, her depression deepened; she asked Liza and other friends whether they thought she should kill herself. Limentani found her "much more genuine when she was depressed. I could get closer to her then. Depressed without tears. Struggling to get tears out. She was more depressed than people thought. But wasn't that a natural reaction to her situation? She did consider suicide. But a reasonably good analysis can mobilise the life drive, the life instinct, if it does anything."

Jacqueline was afraid of dying, but she wondered whether there might be worse things than dying. She decided that there were not.

23

There have been hundreds of experimental treatments for MS, and once Jacqueline's illness was made public, suggestions came from all over the world for remedies, therapies, cures. She tried many of them, from acupuncture to megavitamins, hoping for a miracle of any magnitude. A suit which had been developed for astronauts allowed her to stand when it was pumped up with air, but it made her look and feel like a robot, and was quickly discarded. Steroids – powerful anti-inflammatory drugs – may have slowed the progress of the disease, but they had distressing side-effects: her face puffed up like a pink balloon, and her hair began to fall out, growing back only after a specialist told her to rinse her hair in cognac every day. A bland, boring diet named for a Dr. Grier had allegedly enabled people to rise up from their wheelchairs and play tennis; Jacqueline followed it steadfastly for more than a year, to no avail.

The consensus in the medical community is that the best that can be done for MS is to manage the symptoms and minimise complications, such as urinary tract infections. Physiotherapy is a conventional method of management, and shortly after Jacqueline's disastrous trip to New York, she was introduced to physiotherapist Sonia Corderay, a providential source of support. "The first time I met Jackie," Sonia recalls, "she was sitting up in bed, knitting, fast and furious – to keep her fingers active. We each agreed to try the other out, and for the next seven or eight years, I went to Rutland Gardens three times a week. We would spend an hour together, doing exercises and discussing feelings, and I would regale her with stories about other patients.

"She would ask me about multiple sclerosis, what it meant. She'd say, 'My muscles are getting weaker, do these exercises help keep them strong?' I'd say, 'They keep you going, but I can't arrest the disease. I can only hope to slow its progress.' She didn't suffer fools gladly – there was no point in giving her vague answers. She liked an honest answer or 'I don't know, I'll find out for you.'

"I soon grew to love her. Apart from her obvious genius for cello playing, there was this very loving girl underneath. She was totally generous, with thoughtful little gifts on my birthday. When my sister committed suicide, Jackie gave me a little icon with an engraving of Christ – she'd been given it in Russia – with a note that said, 'Hold it close and rub it every now and then, and you will find that it will give you great comfort.'

"Jackie worked very hard with me. She knew that if she didn't, she would probably get worse. She was diligent – and the exercises were damn boring. When I met her, she hadn't walked for some time. We got her a walking frame, and she learned to walk in it. It was a great thrill for her to walk across the room on her frame for Daniel and others at Christmas. When her arms still worked fairly well she enjoyed swimming, it gave her a lovely feeling of freedom. But then it became too tiring, and she had to stop.

"She never complained. She never was cross, she never exploded. She was always the same, except when Limentani was away. Then she would seem a bit down. I'd say, 'Lemon drops isn't here.' She'd say, 'Yes, I miss him.'"

The only interruptions allowed during Jacqueline's physiotherapy sessions were Barenboim's telephone calls, at which times Sonia would discreetly leave the room. She says, "I asked Daniel if he could help me find a key to Jackie, so I could help her. He said, 'I can't help you, Sonia; I don't know.'

"I think that basically what I gave her was love. I gave her as much as I could. She lacked love; she was a person who soaked it up like a sponge. She couldn't get enough of it. She grew up like a strong plant with just one stem, which was cut off. Other people have lateral shoots that then begin to grow. Jackie's didn't. It was as though she was bleeding from that main stem all the time. I tried to encourage her to get out, to spread her wings. I wanted to give her a sense that life would go on, that she had something to give."

Popular myth has it that the crisis of chronic illness, like World War II, binds people closely in a common cause. Statistics show otherwise. In wartime, it was possible to hope for a victorious end to the fighting; but the protracted strain and uncertainty of living with multiple sclerosis is more than most marriages can endure. Grief does not necessarily bring people together; it can tear them apart. Few wives, and even fewer husbands, remain with a spouse when the dynamics of their relationship have been irreversibly skewed.

Officially, Jacqueline's marriage would survive. In practice, it would eventually become a source of deep conflict and guilt for Daniel, and humiliation for her. Her growing vulnerability, her guilt at being a burden, her shame – the greatest of which was sexual – about being a deficient partner, and her fear of abandonment all contributed to a desperate need for reassurance. Barenboim, overwhelmed by feelings of powerlessness and filled with regret for past transgressions, was torn between his very real affection for his wife and pursuing his first love: his career.

In 1974, when Georg Solti resigned as artistic director of the Orchestre de Paris, Barenboim was offered the job. He had reached the point where he needed a regular orchestra, rather than a succession of guest-conducting engagements. It would mean spending a minimum of twenty weeks a year in Paris, which was close – but not too close – to London. He would be able to visit Jacqueline fortnightly, and could otherwise have as much independence as he wished. It seemed a reasonable compromise and, with Jacqueline supporting his decision, he accepted the offer.

The marriage had not been as idyllic as the press had loved to portray it, but Jacqueline's happiest days had been spent within it. Before her illness became apparent, the relationship had withstood the strains of her immaturity, his self-absorption, their mismatched backgrounds and their pressurised lives. Jacqueline had few illusions about her husband, but she adored him. His visits and phone calls were the highlights of her life – but she could not spend the rest of her life waiting for them. Gradually, her need to retreat into herself gave way to her need to reach out to others, and she began to encourage company. Christopher Nupen's wife, Diana, was her closest friend and most frequent visitor. Liza Wilson went to Rutland Gardens twice a week to talk, read poetry and sometimes play the cello to her, which she said she enjoyed. On an informal, irregular basis, she gave informal cello lessons to Kate Beare and to another friend, Joanna Milholland, a member of the English Chamber. When Barenboim was in London, Olga's culinary skill made it possible for them to entertain the cream of the music world, whose presence simultaneously cheered Jacqueline and heightened her feelings of alienation.

Adjustment to chronic illness is a lifelong process, and Jacqueline's decision to live was a choice that would confront her over and over again, with each change in her physical condition. She may never have fully recovered from the initial shock of her illness, and her depression lingered until the end of her life – but if her body was paralysed, her mind was not; it remained active and curious, and the subject of her illness began, inevitably, to bore her. Although the illness limited her range of choices, it did not deprive her of free will; she could still control her attitude, and her opinions. She could still make some choices: to love, to forgive, to accept or reject; to continue to hide, or to show herself in public. The illness could never be completely forgotten, but it would shrink in importance as she moved first out of her bedroom and then, tentatively and with justifiable fears, into a strange and treacherous place – the land of the able-bodied, as seen from a wheelchair.

The occupant of a wheelchair is a living *memento mori* – a visible, unwelcome reminder of the chaos that can at any moment shatter our illusion of a fair and orderly universe. In that padded prison, one is the object of stares, avoidance, fawning, condescension, and the combined ignorance, insensitivity and outright cruelty that prompts total strangers to volunteer details of the worst possible cases of whatever one's illness happens to be. If one happens to be a celebrity, all those reactions intensify. To prepare for her re-emergence, Jacqueline had to mobilise resources unsuspected even by herself, at a price unimaginable except to those who have paid it.

In October 1975, Dame Margot Fonteyn wheeled a smiling Jacqueline into a party given in Fonteyn's honour at the Crush Bar, Covent Garden. From then until only weeks before her death, Jacqueline appeared in public whenever her health permitted, demonstrating a degree of dignity and courage for which she would deserve to be remembered even if she had never played a note. Whatever had happened to her body, something indestructible and rare sat, smiling, in that chair.

24

I n January 1976, the Duke of Edinburgh presented the OBE to a
beaming Jacqueline at Buckingham Palace. The honour and the
recognition restored her morale to the extent that after having
refused interviews for three years, she agreed to speak publicly
about her illness for the first time. On the BBC's *Tonight* television
programme, she told of her fears of the future, and of her struggle
to come to terms with her illness and to regain some degree of
confidence. With a mixture of common sense and bravado she said,
"I eventually realised that it's my own bum. I had to get out of bed.
One is still alive. One can still enjoy. There are things to do."

The following month she appeared at the Festival Hall, where,
surrounded by echoes of her triumphs on that stage, she achieved a
different kind of triumph. The occasion was the launch of a young
people's movement within the Multiple Sclerosis Society. "CRACK"
– the name signified the optimistic hope that MS would be "cracked"
within the near future – was the conception of another young woman
who suffered from MS. Nicole Davoud's experience with the disease
had been similar to Jacqueline's, with erratic early symptoms that
had caused her to question her sanity. CRACK was her attempt to
dispel the shadows of hopelessness and gloom that surrounded MS,
which many people confused with muscular dystrophy, and "to
show people that MS is not the kiss of death . . . to be positive about
it, to stress that one can still lead a fruitful life".

At the launch, Jacqueline, who had until then never met anyone
else with MS, addressed an audience of MS sufferers, many of them
in wheelchairs, and a battery of reporters. "I had my life totally
fulfilled before," she philosophically told the press, "so nothing was
left unachieved. I was loved to the full, I had lived to the full. I'm
sad not to be able to play. But I can still teach. And my marriage is
even closer than it was before." She spoke of rethinking her life,
of finding new activities: teaching the cello, making necklaces of
semiprecious stones and beads, going to concerts and "writing down
what one goes through. Life can start from a wheelchair. It has to.
It can. Sometimes, when I hear a pupil play, I might say to myself,

188

'Dash it, I wish I could do that.' But I also know and live with a rather privileged feeling that my talent expressed itself very young, and I led a very fulfilled musical life." She said she still tried to play "because I think it's good exercise, but the sound is atrocious. I can't feel the strings, so I don't know what notes I am playing. It could come back, but I don't hang onto that as a desperate last hope. The disease is a mystery. I'm still young. Maybe some day, with all the research going on, something will be found."

Although there is nothing remotely glamorous about illness, it is, ironically, glamour that draws public attention to the need for research and relief. Jacqueline personified glamour, and touched people's hearts, as well. Without ever intending it, or perhaps ever even fully realising it, her open acknowledgment and discussion of her illness gave a human image to a disease which until then had been either invisible or misunderstood. With that single act at the Festival Hall, she became a heroine to everyone who suffered from the ignorance that surrounded MS.

She was never entirely comfortable, however, in her unexpected new role. Although some people with MS can find support and encouragement in sharing experiences with one another, it had never been easy for Jacqueline to connect with people except through her music, and the rocky common ground of her illness was not sufficient to relieve her sense of isolation. She was, however, happy to feel that she was of use. In the ensuing months she received hundreds of letters, some written out of the depths of loneliness, others expressing appreciation and encouragement. She answered most of them conscientiously, using a typewriter when her fingers refused to obey her brain. Unanswered were disturbing letters from cranks; one predicted she would die by the age of thirty-four, another that she would become blind, deaf and mad.

Having emerged from her self-imposed seclusion, she accepted as many invitations as her energy allowed. In July, Barenboim wheeled her onto the stage of the Albert Hall for her first public musical appearance in a wheelchair: playing the side drum in a celebrity-studded performance of Leopold Mozart's Toy Symphony, in honour of the Harold Holt organisation's centenary. She seemed to find it great fun, and to relish the applause. That summer she also contributed to a forty-minute BBC radio documentary about her life. Its title, taken from a remark she made on the programme, was *I Really Am a Very Lucky Person* – a phrase she later greatly regretted having uttered. She had used it in the specific context of how much she had been able to accomplish during her performing career, but it was widely misinterpreted to mean that she had achieved some sort of saintly acceptance of her fate.

The programme borrowed from Christopher Nupen's *Jacqueline*, and added some recent quotes about her illness and her reactions to it. For someone who had never found words a congenial medium, she was remarkably articulate. She said, "You try to analyse each symptom and watch its progress as though under a microscope. I managed very poorly. It is difficult to face up to what one sees as oneself in bed, and one must also deal with the guilt of what this does to people close to you, however willingly they accept the situation. It's a horrid thing to have to be dependent. It can make one feel furious at times." She said she hoped that the most frightening times, and the sense of uselessness and hopelessness, were behind her. "There are obviously times when one feels low. But it's not the general rule, as it was. The norm can be a pleasant if not a very happy day. I'm not so frightened any more. I feel that what I've done in quite bad times I shall be able to do again. I also know I shall have round me people who are totally steadfast and caring. I will not be left alone."

Of her continued attempts to play, she said she had little control of her bowing and fingering: "What comes out offends my professional ear, but I still love to hold the cello." William Pleeth, who sometimes played with her, was struck by a curious spiritual quality, "a depth of mood and purpose that almost, *almost* had nothing to do with what you were hearing. It was as if you were in the room with a very powerful actor and he wasn't on the stage, he had a hoarse throat and he would tell you something or read you something and you would feel that quality . . . that intensity."

Her condition was relatively stable, and although there was no predicting how long it would remain so, she took advantage of the respite and kept her diary filled with engagements. She had guests every afternoon and evening. If she went out to a concert or opera or the theatre, she liked to invite people back to Rutland Gardens afterwards for a meal. Perlman, Zukerman and other friends sometimes stayed at the house when they were in town, and Olga reckoned that she served an average of fifty-five meals every week. "I was exhausted. I told Daniel, 'I can't cope, it's too much!' He said, 'You are right, you can't do this. I will tell her.' And he told her. So for one week, we had less people."

The problems of people with disabilities are compounded by the common misconception – possibly a result of sexual anxieties in the minds of the beholders – that they are asexual. To demonstrate that her sexuality was very much alive, Jacqueline dressed to emphasise her femininity. She had always enjoyed shopping, particularly at Harrods, and now took advantage of her proximity to "the corner drugstore" to indulge her passion for clothes. Olga says, "She was spending £500 a week only for dresses and shoes. Aida used to ask me, 'Why is she buying all those shoes if she can't walk?' I said, 'She thinks maybe one day she will.'"

It seemed to photographer Clive Barda that "When Jackie was first incapacitated, I suppose everybody, including herself, felt that in the circumstances she deserved any physical comforts that money could buy. So for a period of time, she was a tremendous shopper. She would go out to all the great shops and she dressed very glamorously and luxuriously. She always had beautiful bags and wonderful boots. We'd quite often go out for meals, invited by Daniel, to Mr. Chow's, or Gaylord's. There would be quite jolly, glamorous evenings out."

Rosie Barda says, "If you suggested a trip out, she'd always say yes. We went to concerts with her. She always looked stunning, everybody would look at her. We took her to a recital by Fischer-Dieskau, and when we got back to Rutland Gardens Mews, the telephone was ringing. It was Fischer-Dieskau – he hadn't been able to see Jackie in the green room, and he wanted to tell her how thrilled he was that she'd been to his concert. *She just was so beloved.*"

In November 1976, the Bardas drove Jacqueline and Olga to a concert Barenboim was conducting at the Fairfield Hall, in Croydon. After the concert, Rosie drove out of the car park with Jackie sitting beside her in the front seat; Daniel and Clive and Olga were crowded into the back. As she did so a car came speeding out of nowhere, with no warning, and hit them with such force that their car overturned. Jacqueline hung upside down in her seat belt, unhurt but terribly frightened. The folded wheelchair fell on Olga, who broke her collar-bone and five ribs and ended up in hospital – where Jacqueline sent her a roomful of flowers, and spare ribs from Mr. Chow's. The next time the two couples went out together, Barenboim suggested, "Why don't we just go directly to St. John's Hospital, and not bother to stop at the restaurant first?"

During the first three years of Jacqueline's illness, nurses came and went at the rate of about two a year. Some were tender, gentle and fun; others simply did their job. Some were unable to cope with the emotional overtones of Jacqueline's situation; one had a nervous breakdown. All of them had a hard time keeping up with their patient's daily activities and peregrinations around London, which required many transfers to and from the wheelchair. They also had difficulty getting her into and out of the tiny lift in the Rutland Gardens house. As she gradually became less able to help herself, lifting her became trickier, and more risky. The number of wheelchair-accessible theatres, concert-halls and cinemas in London is negligible, and there were occasions when friends attempted to carry her, in the chair, up or down a flight of stairs, and she unceremoniously ended up on the floor. There were accidents at home, as well: the unfortunate Olga once sustained a hernia when attempting to pick her up from the bathroom floor.

Five mornings a week, Jacqueline was driven to Dr. Limentani's consulting room in Upper Wimpole Street. The analyst felt a tremendous responsibility. "When I went on holiday for any length of time she would develop little symptoms or have a relapse, so I would come back to find that she couldn't see from one eye or something. Finally I said, 'If you relapse again, I'm not coming back.' She was very cross – but she *didn't* do it again."

Limentani believes that his treatment merely slowed the progress of Jacqueline's illness, and counts as one of his few successes her eventual ability, a long time coming, to get angry with her doctors – himself, her GP and her neurologist – for their failure to help her. "She finally admitted that we had been a dead loss to her. She had to accept that we are not so wonderful." Jacqueline's was a dry-eyed, quiet anger; after all the years of smiling regardless of how she felt, her attempts to scream were, he says, pathetic.

Limentani understood why she went to such lengths to surround herself with people, day and night. "Music was there in her head all the time. She would go days and days with one piece in her mind. Over and over and over. Again and again – she could not be free from it. She could only have got rid of it by picking up her cello and playing it. She said she felt she was being persecuted by the music – but she always said it in a loving way. I didn't know whether that was good or bad. That was at the bottom of her thirst for people to be with her, to take her mind away from the music.

"She kept reviewing her interpretations. She was extremely critical of her music, wondering how she would do the pieces again. She'd been so young when she recorded them. In all the years I knew her, the only piece she ever insisted I listen to with her was Dvořák's *Klid*, which means 'silent woods' [originally a duet for piano and cello, the work was later arranged by the composer for cello and orchestra]. When she moved to Knightsbridge I once had to go there to see her;

she asked me to put it on and listen with her. I always kept myself out of her music, only letting her use it in the treatment as she wished. She would talk about a certain passage that was going through her mind over and over again, how it made her feel. Talking about it led to her understanding of her frustration at being deprived of her art.

"As it happened, I like music, and was familiar with it. Once I made the usual analyst noise, a slight hm-mmm; that was fatal. She said, 'That is F, B. That's nasty.' I went home and looked it up in my music dictionary. *Diabolus in musica* – the devil in music." (The Latin expression refers to two notes which are very difficult to sing and are usually avoided in vocal music; in the Middle Ages they were associated with the devil, and expressly forbidden.)

During the first three years of her illness, Jacqueline rarely mentioned her cello and her music-making to her friends, and found it unbearably painful to listen to her own records. Rosie Barda recalls that when she once ill-advisedly played one of Jacqueline's records in her presence, she had asked her not to "because I'm not playing very well at the moment, and it makes me a bit sad. I'll be all right when I'm better, but I can't listen at the moment." But in 1976, EMI released two of her recordings for the first time: the Beethoven sonatas with Barenboim, recorded live at the Edinburgh Festival; and the Elgar, also live and with Barenboim, recorded at Carnegie Hall. Both had been recorded in 1970, and in neither performance can one hear a hint of her impending illness. The inescapable implication was that EMI saw no point in waiting for a better version – one recorded, perhaps, under optimum studio conditions – because they did not expect her to play again. The release of the records, combined with the lack of improvement in her physical condition, made the possibility that she might not recover a probability, and told her that the cello was irrevocably gone.

The realisation provoked a crisis that she eventually dealt with in two ways. Once she realised that her records were and would remain the only evidence of her music, she longed to hear them, and only them, all of the time. Despite her obsession with how she might wish to play them differently, they gave her a vicarious sense of performing, and reassured her that what she had done could not be undone. The other effect of her new awareness was her decision that if she could not play, she could teach. At least it could be a connection, albeit a secondhand one, with making music. At best, it would occupy some space in the empty centre of her life.

25

Jacqueline's first students were three of her good friends: Kate Beare, Joanna Milholland and Diana Nupen. Kate Beare says, "Jackie wanted to give what she could, but when she was first really sick, she was too shy to teach anyone she didn't already know. She gave me lots of lessons, but not on a regular basis. In Hampstead, she'd be lying in bed flat out, but when I'd take my cello out and start playing, she'd sit up and wave her arms around; it really got the adrenalin going. The only way she could play *anything* on the cello herself was if I played the right hand and she played the left. She found it frustrating, but she also seemed to find it quite funny.

"When you're studying with someone, the whole point is to try someone else's ideas. As long as Jackie was there, putting her own character into her ideas, they would work for me. Later I would sort through and know which ones I could use and could give to my own students. Normally, if you disagreed with a teacher, you would say why – but when I didn't agree with Jackie's interpretations, I never discussed it with her. Maybe she would have preferred that. But it was so unfair that I was playing at all, and she wasn't – I wasn't going to argue with her over any of her ideas.

"*Projection* was an important part of Jackie's character and her playing and her teaching. To project, you have to exaggerate. If you play only to yourself, you won't get the idea across to the audience. Very few teachers can convey that to students as well as Jackie did.

"I learned an awful lot from her. She could find fantastic fingerings for you, just as though she were still playing. Not fingerings that she had necessarily used herself, either – she was still able to think as clearly about playing the cello as if she was playing it, which was quite remarkable.

"The most helpful thing she taught me was about the takeoff note. It's applicable to all string instruments. You play each note to the full, especially if it's followed by a shift. Also, her slides – getting from one note to another – were very special. They were almost a trademark for her. She made it clear how terribly important it is when you're sliding up not to start the shift until you've changed the bow stroke. Nobody had ever told me that. And she told me that when you get to a note that has to be long, you *play it forever*. She used that word quite often: *forever*. You can certainly hear it in her playing. She could put more colour change and character into one long note than any ordinary person could. 'Forever' sums up the whole way she played – the sound, and the way she put her whole self into each performance. It stays with you forever. I don't think you could play like that if your whole personality wasn't absolutely pure and natural.

"Just the fact that Jackie was willing to give me lessons gave me the courage to want to play more. And when she saw that she helped me, and made me play better, it gave her the confidence to teach other people. I took some of my students to her; whoever was playing, she would really throw herself into it and *concentrate*, just as if she was playing herself. She always had something helpful and caring to say. She had obviously thought a lot about the music and developed her ideas about it after she'd ceased to play. She'd been so busy hurtling around from one place to another – if she'd had time to think about the music, I think she would have played a lot of things quite differently, and she would have improved."

In 1976, Jacqueline accepted her first and only child student. Dawn Goodwin had written from the north of Scotland of how her ten-year-old daughter, Jane, had been inspired by Jacqueline's records to learn the cello. Jacqueline invited Jane to play to her, was delighted with the cheerful, curly-headed child, and thought enough of her talent to take her on as a student. During the next three years, Jane and her mother, and sometimes her father as well, made the long journey from Perth every fortnight, sometimes staying overnight at Rutland Gardens. Jane Goodwin, now a professional cellist, remembers a "bubbly and warm" Jacqueline. "She always greeted us with a smile. I can see the doors of the lift opening, and there she'd be in her wheelchair. 'Hello my love,' she'd beam. In the first years we knew her, she never stopped smiling.

"She loved to play jokes. She had a battery-operated flashing red heart; she would put it inside her dress and then clutch her chest and say, 'Oh, my heart!' and start it flashing.

"As a teacher, she could make you feel what she felt, through the force of her personality. You felt that she knew *exactly* what the composer wanted, even if the piece wasn't familiar to her. She'd say 'Let's try something crazy' and suggest unorthodox fingerings – or she'd say, 'Be a devil, end on an up bow!'"

Jacqueline called Jane "Poppet" and named her cello Amadeo,

telling her that the name meant 'gift of god', but not that it belonged
to her analyst. She gave her little presents and sent her affectionate
cards and letters, thanking her "for playing so courageously and
beautifully", but also gently reproving her if her dedication faltered.
"Unfortunately," read one letter, "learning a musical instrument is
not only fun and games. It is seasoned with some hard mechanical
work, so that one's fingers may dance as merrily as your notes in the
end." When she became too ill to give regular lessons, she passed the
child along to William Pleeth, saying, "I hope you will love him as
I always did."

By 1976, the need for a live-in nurse with the ability to lift Jacqueline
and the willingness to make a long-term commitment had become
acute. The woman who believed she was born to do that job assumed
her enigmatic role in Jacqueline's life that summer, on the steps of
St. Paul's Cathedral.

Clive Barda had escorted Jacqueline and her mother-in-law to St.
Paul's to see Barenboim conduct Beethoven's "Choral" Symphony
on the cathedral steps, as a part of the annual City of London Festival.
The photographer was shooting some photos of the Barenboims
when Aida said, "Daniel, isn't that Ruth Ann, who was so sweet to
Jackie at St. Mary's?" When Barenboim confirmed that the black
woman at the edge of the crowd was indeed one of the nurses who
had looked after Jacqueline in hospital, Aida pursued the woman to
the bus stop and offered her a job on the spot.

Ruth Ann Canning and Jacqueline were the same age and sex, but
had little else in common. Ruth Ann was born in Guyana, had
emigrated with her family to the United States, and then moved on
to London for her nurse's training. A born-again evangelical Christian, she believed that it was her divinely-ordained vocation to nurse
Jacqueline du Pré.

To say that the subject of Ruth Ann is controversial is like saying
that Mozart wrote some pretty tunes – for although no one would
deny that her single-minded dedication lengthened Jacqueline's life,
there is deep disagreement about her effect on the emotional quality
of that life. Jacqueline's friends are divided between those who believe
Ruth Ann to be a saint and those who believe that her insensitivity
added greatly to the frustration and misery of Jacqueline's last years.
Although Jacqueline herself declared repeatedly and unequivocally
that she hated Ruth Ann, Dr. Limentani contends that it was her
own helplessness that she hated, and that the nurse was merely a
convenient target. That Jacqueline's complaints were undoubtedly

exaggerated by Ruth Ann's increasing control over her environment, movements and most intimate necessities does not necessarily, however, make them invalid.

As the ongoing power struggle between patient and nurse moved towards its foregone conclusion and the nurse's control became virtually absolute, Jacqueline's professed hatred for Ruth Ann would become obsessive. During their first years together, however, while Jacqueline was still relatively active and Olga was in residence, a precarious balance was maintained.

Barenboim now had a flat in Paris; he gave about fifty concerts a year with the Orchestre de Paris, and another fifty elsewhere, and he phoned Jacqueline nearly every night, from wherever he was. On his fortnightly weekends in London, he was tender, affectionate and protective with her. He encouraged her to visit him in Paris, and she did so once, for ten days, staying in a hotel with Olga and a nurse Aida had found in Tel Aviv. The trip was not a success; Jacqueline felt alienated and insecure away from home, and subsequently limited her travelling to brief holidays in Brighton, in the English countryside, or with Barenboim in Edinburgh (when he appeared at the Festival). With Jacqueline unable to move and Daniel unable or unwilling to stop moving, it is less surprising that they grew apart than that they grew apart so slowly.

Barenboim made some efforts to build new bridges between them. Liza Wilson recalls his suggesting that Jacqueline fill in the gaps in her musical education. "Jackie didn't really know very much music except what she had actually played, or listened to because Daniel had played it. He said, 'Why don't you learn about harmony? Why don't you study the Beethoven Quartets? Here are the scores and here are the records. You listen, and I'll come back and practise and you can tell me about them.' But her music was so instinctive that she found it difficult to read a score. And she could be quite obstinate, she didn't like to be told what to do. I think he was very disappointed that she wasn't interested in these little projects he had for her. Maybe it was a kind of little rebellion on her part – or maybe she was genuinely not that interested."

Jacqueline did in fact listen to the Beethoven Quartets, with a man for whom she developed a serious, though platonic, attachment in the late Seventies. Throughout her life she had given love with an open-hearted profligacy, and craved it as a flower craves light. In 1977, when she met William Ingrey, she was loved by many people in many ways, but none of them could begin to satisfy her voracious desire for intense and exclusive affection, tenderness, reassurance and sex. Denied the ideal, she sought fragmentary substitutes – one of whom was the charming and *simpatico* young man who initially came to the Knightsbridge house for the purpose of cleaning it.

Ingrey, now a theatrical stage manager, became a part-time major-domo in the household; his tasks included taking Jacqueline for walks in Hyde Park, and he spent a good deal of time with her. A former dancer, he was artistic and witty, and well-informed about a great many subjects. He had never played an instrument but knew a lot about music – much more than Jacqueline, who, he says, knew virtually nothing about music except her own repertoire. "When we listened together to Beethoven's late quartets, she would always pick up on the cello line. We used to follow them in the score; neither of us were very good at it, but her eyes may have been going, she could really only take in broad things by then. Once we realised we were both on the wrong page!"

Ingrey was, he says, her clown. "I liked to see her laugh. People thought she was intellectual and she tried to respond, but what she really wanted to do was laugh." She showed him the notebooks in which she wrote down her thoughts – "no great philosophical truths, nothing at all pretentious; she was sort of a simple man's William Blake. She had so much love to give, and no real outlet for it. She wasn't at all careful with her love. She came to know, though, who the people were who came only so they could drop her name at other dinner tables.

"She still used to toy with the cello, pick it up and play a few notes, maybe a scale. It was never any good, but the feeling was still there, and she enjoyed it. I don't think it mattered to her whether the notes were right or wrong. I once heard her play 'The Swan' with Daniel; it was heartrending."

The indomitable Aida Barenboim still lived and taught piano in Tel Aviv, but she visited Jacqueline at every opportunity, and always arrived speedily if a crisis needed sorting out. Ingrey found her "terrifying to everyone, but everyone loved her, as well, and she was very kind to Jacqueline. One just *submitted* to Aida. She seemed to be in charge of every aspect of everyone's life, to know exactly what everyone should be doing. She wasn't always right, but she had such a *strong* will and personality and intellect, she usually got what she wanted. Jacqueline realised that Aida was running her life, but she couldn't run it herself, and probably Aida was the best person to do it."

Reprising a theme from Jacqueline's childhood, when Joan Clwyd had tried to introduce her to a world wider than her cello, Aida asked

Ingrey to help develop another dimension to her daughter-in-law's life. "She asked me to take her a book of poems, or suggest that she listen to some different music, not just her own records. I read her 'Kubla Khan', just because it's musical, and short sections of Gray's 'Elegy' – because her attention span was short – and we talked about it a lot. I played Schubert and Schumann songs for her – short pieces, for the same reason. But she never could bear to be by herself. She wanted people and fun every night. When she had to have dinner alone, she was miserable."

In the summer of 1977, Jacqueline accepted an invitation to give two consecutive days of public master classes on the Elgar Cello Concerto at the Brighton Music Festival. She was apprehensive about making the commitment; she knew that an attack could confine her to bed at any time, and she was nervous about teaching publicly without being able to demonstrate on the cello. But when Barenboim wheeled her onto the platform and 250 people applauded wildly, the performer in her rose magnificently to the occasion. She quickly put students and audience at ease with encouraging comments and jokes. She sang or whistled where she would have played, and offered alternative solutions to phrasing and technical problems. Although she no longer had any sensation in her hands, she was able to control their large movements with her eyes, and her gestures were animated and expressive. She kept her left hand in cello position and suggested fingerings and interpretations, but took pains to avoid the dogmatism she had disliked in Casals and Tortelier. The one thing she demanded was that students be willing to experiment, and that they perform with as much conviction in class as they would in front of an orchestra.

Jacqueline would never have an analytical mind like her husband's – but although she explained apologetically, "I'm not used to thinking this way," it was clear that after all the years of speaking through her cello, she had discovered a new medium of communication: language. Before her illness, she had never discussed her playing, but had simply played – and listening to her records with Ingrey, she had been unable to answer his questions about how she had played certain works, or passages. But the more she taught, the more articulate she became about what she had previously known only intuitively. She expressed herself with the same quirky originality that had characterised her music, telling one student to "pamper" an F sharp, another to "Play without vibrato; it gives more feeling of agony and hollow desolation," another to try something different because "You don't pour the same sauce on every plate of food you prepare."

As a teacher, her greatest weakness was not her inability to play, but the fact that, as Guilhermina Suggia once wrote, "Only those who have had the greatest struggle to become good players will make the finest teachers." Playing had come so naturally to her that she had never had to solve many of the problems that confronted her students. Her great gift to them, says William Pleeth, "was just her enthusiasm in making someone live at a higher plane, which is very important. She could make somebody feel they could be better than they were – and consequently, of course, they *would* be."

Between 1977 and 1980, Jacqueline gave master classes at Dartington, the Aldeburgh Cello School, the Malvern Festival, the Walsall Festival and, in London, at the Purcell Room, the Guildhall School and the South Bank Festival. On Saturday and Sunday afternoons she gave mini-master classes at Rutland Gardens for students who came from Europe, Canada, the US and Australia. At those sessions she was intensely serious about the music, but not about anything else; there was a great deal of joking and giggling, and her students treasure their memories of those bittersweet afternoons.

She also gave private lessons, which were slotted into a carefully orchestrated schedule that included visits to doctors and analyst, shopping excursions and outings to Hyde Park, physiotherapy, "medical siestas", visitors for dinner and tea and sometimes lunch, and attending the concerts of students and friends. There were moments during which she still found life delicious, when she was more alive than most people ever are. She had a great capacity for enjoying small pleasures: strong coffee, fine chocolate, good food. Most of all, she enjoyed the company of musicians who spoke her language.

Her health was uneven; intermittent exacerbations confined her to bed, making it impossible for her to teach for weeks at a time. Attacks were sudden, and entailed the loss of some function – on one terrifying occasion, her ability to speak and swallow – with no way of predicting the duration of the loss. She recovered from each attack, but never completely regained the ground she had occupied before it.

She still hoped for a cure. At a time when she was temporarily unable to write, she sent Dawn Goodwin a typed note, saying, "Your friendship and the love you express are such a gift that it makes me more determined than ever to get better so that I can greet you with a very welcoming heart." In January 1978 – the beginning of her thirty-fourth year – she and Barenboim formed the Jacqueline du Pré Research Fund, to which Itzhak Perlman, Pinchas Zukerman, Zubin

Mehta, Artur Rubinstein, Sir Clifford Curzon, Dietrich Fischer-Dieskau and other musical luminaries promised to donate the entire proceeds of four concerts a year. Interviewed about the fund, Jacqueline said, "We still can't be sure that I will never play again. Nobody knows if I'll ever regain mobility. It could be that next week I'll find myself walking down the road. I believe in realistic optimism but not wishful thinking."

In August 1978, Jacqueline herself performed at a benefit for the fund, reading the narration to Prokofiev's "Peter and the Wolf" with the English Chamber Orchestra for a small, select audience at the Piccadilly Hotel. "All my friends were there," she said, "and my husband conducted. Suddenly there wasn't an instrument between my legs, there were words." It was her second public reading. The previous year, at a special service for the Multiple Sclerosis Society at Westminster Cathedral, she had read a passage from Ecclesiastes – because, she said, as a Jewish convert, she wanted something from the Old Testament. She had been pleasantly surprised by the beauty and musicality of the words, and said that the psychological emphasis, the structure and the *timing* of reading aloud was "a little like playing an instrument".

Jacqueline narrated "Peter" with a fresh, natural spontaneity, as though sharing her delight in a story she had just heard for the first time with the audience. She relished the suspense, the changing moods, the colourful sounds of the consonants; her "s's" hissed like snakes, her "r's" rolled merrily to the back of the room. Even without her cello, she loved to perform: an audience nourished her in a way that nothing else could do. When Peter vanquished the wolf, the greater victory was her own.

In October she repeated the performance at the Queen Elizabeth Hall, and recorded it for EMI. By then she was beginning to have difficulty forming words clearly, and had to overemphasise them to be understood. The exaggeration was appropriate for a children's story, however, and even added to the performance. The following summer she read, with even greater difficulty, Ogden Nash's nonsense verses written to accompany Saint-Saëns' *The Carnival of the Animals*. Barenboim once again conducted the ECO, and the performance was broadcast on the radio. The poignancy of her reading of "The Swan" section of the work, and the ECO's principal cellist's rendition of the music which Jacqueline had played so often and so memorably, drenched the warmly supportive studio audience in emotion.

In 1979, BBC Television filmed two consecutive days of her

master classes, in which eight students participated. Throughout the exhausting six-hour filming sessions, Jacqueline was radiant. She was still puffed up from the cortisone injections she received every other day, but was making a great effort to lose weight; she told a reporter, "One gets the sitting syndrome. I've put myself on a diet and since I've been eating less, there should be less of my vast ass."

Jacqueline had some unquestionably talented students, including Alexander Baillie and Raphael Wallfisch, but she never found one who possessed what she considered to be the magic combination of talent, commitment and technique. She faithfully attended their recitals and was always encouraging; privately, however, she was a cruel critic, for she could not help applying the same stringent standards to her students that she had applied to herself. Teaching was frustrating for her, but it fed her shaky self-esteem, and gave her a sense of usefulness, a connection with music, and a small income. But in 1980, as her health grew more unstable, classes often had to be cancelled, and it became impossible to schedule lessons in advance. There would be no more master classes, and no more public readings. Mercifully, she could not foresee the seven years of relentlessly diminishing returns that lay ahead.

26

The physical pressures of Olga's job had lightened somewhat by 1980, for two reasons: Barenboim's visits were shorter and farther apart, so there was less entertaining; and as it became difficult for Jacqueline to feed herself, fewer people came for meals with her alone. Olga felt heavier emotional pressures, however, as Jacqueline's condition declined. Two new and disastrous symptoms – severely blurred vision, and tremors, or involuntary movements, of her head – made it impossible for her to read, or even to watch television.

Olga remembers the six years she spent in Rutland Gardens as "the *best* time I had in England. I met musicians, people I liked . . . everything was special. I was really happy in that house." But her responsibilities there, compounded by the effort of coexisting in the same house with Ruth Ann, depleted her energy. She needed a life of her own, but rarely had a day off; she felt she was losing all her friends. Her departure, in April, saddened and angered Jacqueline, and left a vacuum into which Ruth Ann quite naturally moved. After Olga, there would be a succession of cleaners and cooks, but none of them would live in the house.

Ruth Ann cannot be blamed for the fact that during her eleven years with Jacqueline her authority grew to exceed her competence. The problem was not Ruth Ann, but the fact that except for occasional relief nurses, there was *only* Ruth Ann – for although she gave Jacqueline a high quality of physical care, her wavelength – by virtue of her limited experience, intelligence and sensibility – was unalterably distant from Jacqueline's.

In the substantial and revelatory body of writings by paralytics, a recurring theme is that one survives the indignity of being lifted, rolled, pushed, pulled, and twisted, as well as the violations of every corner of one's privacy, by emotionally detaching oneself from one's perfidious body. This, Jacqueline was able to do. She could not, however, remove herself from Ruth Ann's voice. Her principal objection to Ruth Ann, whom she surreptitiously called Purity, was what she called her "tiny mind". Ruth Ann claimed that she never tried to impose her passionately held religious convictions on Jacqueline, but they were implicit in her very presence, and in the frequent presence of fellow members of her church, and she had no compunction about stating them with sanctimonious certainty. And although she denied ever telling Jacqueline that her disease was a punishment for having abandoned Christianity to become a Jew, that was the message that Jacqueline received. (When she repeated it to her GP, he said, "Wonderful! For two thousand years medical science has tried to find the cause of multiple sclerosis, and Ruth Ann has discovered it for us!")

On the subject of what was and was not acceptable behaviour, Ruth Ann's opinions were puritanical and dogmatic. Their effect was to inhibit, if not *pro*hibit, Jacqueline from being her natural self – from indulging, for example, her penchant for the four-letter words that were an outlet for her rage at what she called multiple fuckosis. Too "bolshie" to meekly feign agreement with Ruth Ann's views, she knew that open defiance would only invite a lecture, or series of lectures, at which she would be a literally captive audience. Nor did she wish to incur the serious displeasure of the person without whom she could do little more than breathe. Her dependence was so complete that when Ruth Ann left her alone with a visitor while she ran an errand or attended a church service, her relief was offset by anxiety. When Ruth Ann took an infrequent holiday, the relief and the anxiety escalated.

Jacqueline's complaints about the nurse greatly distressed some of her friends, who had no means of alleviating the situation. Other friends shrugged off the complaints as childish rhetoric. Zamira Menuhin believes that "Underneath it all, Jackie *adored* Ruth Ann. I could just feel it," and adds, with unintentional irony, "As far as I can see, nobody gave her more love."

Some people chose to believe that the illness affected Jacqueline's mind, rather than that she was as miserable with Ruth Ann as she claimed to be. Dr. Limentani maintains, however, that her mental processes were virtually unimpaired, and that even her most outrageous statements contained some truth. Although madness was one of her greatest fears, she remained, to the end of her life, excruciatingly sane.

Christopher Nupen, a close friend of Jacqueline's throughout her adult life, points out that "Her loneliness, her need for affection, and her terrible need for people made her more vulnerable, but her perceptions about music and people had always been deeper than most people gave her credit for. After her illness, they became even more profound. If she had gone stark, raving mad under the pressures she was struggling with, nobody would have been surprised. One would have expected her to collapse under the weight of the unbearable. But things are unbearable just until you have to bear them. You have to carry on or die, and she certainly didn't want to die – not even two weeks before she died."

It would not be surprising if Jacqueline exaggerated some of the more improbable stories she told, if only to stir up the sea of boredom on which she was becalmed. She had always had a great sense of drama, which added dimension to her playing and to her offstage life, as well, and she had never allowed mundane facts to get in the way of a good story. Now, she seemed unwilling or unable to remember happy times, which would perhaps have been unendurable. The tales she told were often tragic, even bizarre – of her mother locking her in a room to practise, for example, and other instances of shocking mistreatment by her parents. If she darkened the truth for dramatic effect, or simply as an attempt to invent a more interesting history for herself, the pain in her stories was real – particularly with regard to her family.

Whatever problems Jacqueline had had with her family in the past, they were the only family she had, and during the first years of her illness, they saw her regularly; Iris was in the audience at her daughter's televised master class, white-haired, looking ten years older than her age. But to William Ingrey, who observed many family visits, "It often seemed as though her parents weren't related to her at all – as though they were perfect strangers. Distant. Remote. One day Iris arrived and said, 'How are you, William . . . and how is my daughter?' Like, How is my garden, or my horse? I thought, You don't really care! It was just duty. There was no warmth, just a show of affection. They were all good at performing.

"Jackie talked a lot about her unhappy childhood, her isolation. Even animals play – it trains them for life. That was never there for her. She seemed to be grateful to her mother, for helping her to develop her talent – but she *loathed* her father."

Appearances were important to Iris and perhaps even more so, by virtue of his upbringing, to her husband. Derek du Pré was a product of the provincial middle class – a businessman who wore a monocle, belonged to a suitable club, and had one lifelong passion: collecting and polishing rocks. He had always been a rather shadowy figure in Jacqueline's life, neither interested in nor appreciative of her gift. During her years as an invalid, he developed Parkinson's disease;

their illnesses progressed together, hers at a much faster pace, and he was present and alert at his daughter's funeral.

Jacqueline particularly looked forward to her brother's visits; Piers and Hilary and their children, and even their pets, were very much a part of her life, and Hilary even filled in when Ruth Ann went on holiday. Gradually, however, her family moved to the periphery, and then, for all practical purposes, out of sight. Jacqueline attributed Hilary's withdrawal to her enduring jealousy (which would have been incredible under the circumstances, if jealousy were rational). Her parents and brother, she said, rejected her for having rejected Christianity.

The subject of anti-Semitism is a minefield, but the number of people who, when contacted for this book, expressed shock and sadness about Jacqueline's conversion to Judaism – some even asked hopefully whether she had, at the end, renounced it – makes it impossible to avoid. Iris and Derek du Pré only became ardent churchgoers late in their lives, after they and their son had been "born again", but their values and attitudes had always been piously Christian. They could not forgive Jacqueline for what they saw as her defection to the Jewish faith – nor could they resist connecting that perceived defection to her illness. In that sentiment, they were not alone. Liza Wilson recalls an afternoon at Rutland Gardens with Rostropovich and his wife, Galina: "Slava was very upset because Jackie couldn't play. He brought her the score of the Lutosławski Concerto and he said, 'I'm sure you will be able to play again, so have a look at this. It is such a wonderful concerto, it's just been published. You can learn it with your eyes, and at least you'll still be involved with the cello, and keep your interest up.' And Galina had to say, 'This illness has come about because you changed your faith.' She was one of the first people to tell her that. Slava had a bit more tact, and I think was feeling that Galina shouldn't have said it. Obviously, Jackie didn't like being told it. But a lot of people said it, including her parents."

Jacqueline's friends tended to dismiss her conversion as merely rebellion, or a romantic gesture – both of which were assuredly factors, but not the only ones. She took it quite seriously indeed. Although never in any sense a religious Jew, she cherished the connection with people she loved and admired, and sometimes attended services at Rabbi Albert Friedlander's Westminster Synagogue, which was practically next door to Rutland Gardens. Rabbi Friedlander says, "It meant a lot to Jacqueline to be part of the family of Israeli musicians. Christianity had been spoiled for her by fanatics and bigots – the most derogatory word she knew. She recognised that there were fanatics in Israel, but she liked my calm, rational approach to life that recognised the reality of suffering.

"When I first knew her, she was very vibrant and aware. I would bring friends to see her. Donald Swann, twice; Dannie Abse twice, because she liked poetry, and he's a doctor. Fritz Perls, with whom she flirted. I brought [Rabbi] Lionel Blue, and told him his brief was to make her laugh.

"I saw her every week, for years. She wanted reassurance that one could have a simple faith in God. She wanted belief in human goodness. She needed a lot of shoring up. I would bring word of her records being broadcast, of the Harrods sale when her records sold out. We would joke that she had more doctorates than I had; it was very important to her that she was not forgotten.

"She wanted to know why this had happened to her. I told her it wasn't that she had been particularly selected for it – it was like a traffic accident, or booking a ride on the Titanic. The only comfort I could give her was that of a friend; we would embrace and kiss a lot. I think it gave her an extra sense of freedom that she could use profanity with a rabbi. She talked at length about her sexual frustration."

Jacqueline continued to teach a handful of remaining students, who accommodated her by showing up at short notice whenever she rang to say she felt well enough to give a lesson. When the American cellist Gerard Leclerc arrived nervously for his first lesson and took out his cello, Jacqueline said solemnly, "Put down your cello, I have something to tell you. I have a really terrible illness, you know. It is very severe. I've been to doctors all over the world, and no one can cure it. It completely destroys a person – death is the only answer, there is no way out. Do you know what the name of it is?" Struck dumb, Leclerc shook his head. "It's called," said Jacqueline with devilish glee, "*glissanditis!*"

Leclerc says, "When I made the mistake of playing to her like a student, she said, 'You play like a little boy.' If I was playing a concerto, it had to really *be* a concerto, as if the orchestra was there. Once I thought I had exactly what she wanted, and I did a huge slide. She just looked at me and said, 'That's the most horrible thing I've ever heard!' I was really embarrassed, because I had applied a Jackie technique to mediocre ends. She said, 'You have to just be a musician. Let the music speak, but don't do anything to *make* it speak.'

"Another time, when she wasn't well enough to get up, I went into her bedroom. She said, 'I really want to hear Chopin. Go and get my cello and play me the slow movement of the Chopin sonata.' So I played that for her, by her bedside, on her cello. Then she asked me to play it again, and she made suggestions, with a very few words – like a great painter would change a mediocre painting into a masterpiece with just one or two brush strokes.

"When she grew tired, she would ask, 'Would you like to hear *me* play that?' and I would put her record on. To me, her playing conveys colours and temperatures – hot, cold, wet, dry. Hers was the most textured cello playing I've come across. People always said she played the slow movement *so* slowly. And it *was* very much slower than anyone else played it. But what she had to say was so important and intense and ultimate that it needed time to be said, and to be absorbed. She put so much into every note – and *between* every note, too. She was right to take the time. When I hear other cellists play it faster, I feel like I've eaten something that was made out of inferior ingredients, and I'm still slightly hungry."

Jacqueline often asked her students to take her Peresson out and play it for her. Leclerc says, "I told her that if I played even well enough for her to bear to listen, it was because it was her cello. In a way, she participated by her cello being played. The Peresson was her baby, she loved it very much. At one of my last lessons [in 1986], she said, 'My cello is mad at me because I haven't played it for years now.' I said, 'Why don't we play it now?' I took it out and leaned it up against her, and I guided her hand up and down the fingerboard. I held her hand and the bow in my other hand, and just played some open strings. She didn't say much, but it was important. It goes too deep to say in simple words. I'm quite sure that was the last time she ever touched it."

27

In 1983 Barenboim bought a flat in west London, near Notting Hill Gate, and in August, Jacqueline and Ruth Ann moved in.

The flat in 36/38 Chepstow Villas was on the second floor of a four-storey brick building. It was all on one level, so that Jacqueline could easily be wheeled from room to room, and it had two small balconies; but it was new and sterile, and Jacqueline missed the charm of Rutland Gardens – its sunny courtyard, and its proximity to Hyde Park.

Barenboim's friends sympathised with his dilemma. Clive Barda believes "Daniel was heroically loyal . . . but when Jackie was unable to provide the domestic pleasures that a wife would be expected to provide . . . things changed. In the fullness of time, it was inevitable that other relationships would occur. He came every fortnight to see her until he started his family in Paris; then it was more difficult. She expected so much from him. How she craved love. In the end, I think they became strangers."

Alexander Goehr says, "Daniel certainly agonised about what was right to do. I know that he took Jackie and her mental well-being into account in rejecting some extremely good jobs, which would have taken him either too close or too far from her and would have led to some change in her perception of him. And ultimately it resolved itself the way it did. But in my opinion, the gilded cage in which they locked her up was a form of torture which was largely unnecessary. If they hadn't got so much money . . . if she'd been a more modest musician, she would have gone to a place where there were other people like herself. She might have had some sort of normality there, talking to people and making friends. But Daniel had the conventional middle-class Jewish reaction: anything that money could buy, let her have it. The purely human angle, like her being bored out of her wits, wasn't taken into account.

"The problem for Jackie wasn't the lack of the cello, it was the lack of everything else. When she first got ill, people used to say, If someone as brilliant as you can't play the cello any more, you must develop some *new* thing. She said, 'God, the bloody fools! Don't they realise that's the only thing I can do, to play that damned instrument! *I know nothing else!*' And yet, in a normal human environment in an institution, with people who had been educated, some of them young, she could have found much more satisfaction than in this navel-gazing, listening to her own recordings. Someone should have taken them all away and smashed them. She should have had another life. But that was beyond their comprehension. She was simply too famous for that."

Goehr is not alone in believing that Jacqueline would have been happier in the company of people "like herself". There are peer groups for people with MS, and the people who run and participate in them find them to be a kind of surrogate family, in which they can feel "normal" and share their common concerns. But multiple sclerosis has been called "the great exaggerator"; it exaggerates one's strengths and one's weaknesses, and Jacqueline's predicament was compounded by the fact that she had never in her life felt "normal". Alienation is prevalent amongst prodigies and an occupational hazard for superstars, and Jacqueline had always found it difficult to believe that *anyone* was "like herself", except in the context of music.

What friends discreetly referred to as Daniel's other life (with pianist Helena Bachkirev and, eventually, their two children) was an open secret in the music world – but although Jacqueline must have had her suspicions, she never mentioned it directly. She did, however, explicitly ask every male visitor for affection – appeals that Dr. Limentani interprets as her way of saying, "You must not discount me, I'm still a woman, I have not lost my sexuality." Language was her only weapon; she loved to tell sexual and scatological jokes, the cruder the better – the naughty little girl, repressed in childhood, coming out to play, and thoroughly enjoying her visitors', and even her husband's, embarrassment.

If some people sank into the depths of embarrassment, others, such as the friend who tried to help her translate "fuck" into every language, rose to the occasion and defused the tension with laughter. Jacqueline was fascinated by words and their definitions, which she took with perfect literalness. Although her attention span was brief and her short-term memory unreliable, she could still recite long poems from memory, her phrasing as singular as it had been on her cello. She liked poems that were funny, or wry, or satirical – John Betjeman, D. J. Enright, R. D. Laing and D. H. Lawrence. She remained most fascinated, however, by her own records. Her musical memory and sense of pitch remained intact – "C sharp," she would say when the phone rang – and she listened to the brilliant ghosts of her past with intense concentration and an unforgiving ear. "I still want to play for people," she told a friend. "That's what I always did for them. But I can't, so the records are all I've got to give."

She gave more than she knew, and far more than anyone was able to give her. Heartbreaking as it was to be with her, particularly for those who had known the young Jackie, contact was immediate and direct, and there was something rare and nourishing in her company. "There was always the element of apprehension when one went to see her," Rosie Barda recalls. "She went on plateaux. Then she'd tumble down a bit and you'd get used to the next plateau – and then she'd go down again. You actually had to stop, to remove yourself from your life, to go and see her. You had to completely absorb yourself in her world for the evening. Sometimes I'd be incredibly tired and think, I don't know if I can get all the concentration I need to be with Jackie. But what was amazing was that usually I'd come out feeling immeasurably better. She had that extraordinary effect on everybody!

"I think there were many sides to Jackie, many rooms that she moved through. One's relationship with her went through stages, from tremendous awe to tremendous pity, when she became so terribly vulnerable. I was always aware of the amazing dichotomy – on the one hand there was this lovely, gay, carefree girl who had every reason to cry continuously but was always loving and warm and giggly – while all the care of the world must have been going on inside. Only in the last couple of years did I see her depressed. She used to say, 'Why have I got it?' At first you'd say, 'Oh God, isn't it dreadful' – but latterly you realised there was nothing you could say."

As the illness tightened its grip, Jacqueline went out less and less. When she did, her low stature and immobility made her the defence-less recipient of the artificial cheerfulness of gushing strangers. Her blurred vision made her oblivious of the stares that followed her, but she heard the whispers: "Is that Jacqueline du Pré? I thought she was dead!" Her sessions with Dr. Limentani continued; the formal analysis had gone as far as it would go, but she could not give him up. He reduced the number of weekly sessions from five to three, using his advancing age as an excuse, and when the journey to Wimpole Street became too much for her, he went to Chepstow Villas.

From time to time there were public tributes, at which Jacqueline appeared when she could. She always wore beautiful clothes and jewellery – usually pearls, or the long thick gold necklace that Artur and Aniela Rubinstein had given her. Her long hair, too silky for clips to hold, always shone, and her smile was still luminous. A half-dozen universities awarded her honorary degrees. Christopher Nupen updated his *Jacqueline* documentary with a brief prologue; it was televised, and afterwards she loved to invite friends to private screenings of the film at Nupen's studio. An international women's music festival was dedicated to her, and the BBC commemorated her fortieth birthday with a radio documentary. She feared that she and her music would be forgotten, and was overjoyed whenever a tape of some long-forgotten concert arrived unexpectedly from some distant country or continent. She was elated when EMI released a recording of the Tchaikovsky Piano Trio in A minor, which she had performed with Barenboim and Pinchas Zukerman in 1972.

In her last years, there was one significant gain: the small, energetic Frenchwoman who prepared and served meals for Jacqueline and her guests. Anne-Marie Morin was the same age as Jacqueline; she had a keen intuition, a tender heart, and a native buoyancy that lifted everyone's morale. With Anne-Marie, Jacqueline even dredged up the French with which she had struggled so in school, and found it to be quite serviceable, and a welcome means of conducting "private" conversations. Anne-Marie's friendship brightened Jacqueline's life for four years, until circumstances required that she return to France. Her departure was one of a series of doors closing. Between 1982 and 1986, three significant people in Jacqueline's life died of cancer: first her great friend, Diana Nupen; then her mother; and finally her mother-in-law, Aida. Loss followed loss followed loss; speaking became increasingly difficult, but communication was vital to her, and she patiently repeated her words, or even spelt them out, until the visitor either got the message or, in despair, changed the subject. Her most understandable comment was, as always, a vociferous raspberry. At the end of 1986, she astonished her doctors by surviving a bout of pneumonia. After that, successive infections attacked and weakened her, and even breathing was an effort – but the deaths she had already experienced had not prepared her for the final one, and letting go was not an option.

During the week of the Yom Kippur holiday in October 1987, Jacqueline, visibly fading, asked each visitor to play her *Kol Nidrei* recording for her. "*Kol Nidrei*," she had once told Jane Goodwin, "was written for the Day of Atonement. The person is hopeless at the beginning . . . at the end you hear the ray of light – hope – coming in."

On October 19th, she again had pneumonia; this time, there were no options. Barenboim was summoned from Paris. Dr. Limentani, Rabbi Friedlander, William and Anthony Pleeth and other old friends came to say goodbye. At midday she lost consciousness. Late in the long, grey afternoon, Tony Pleeth, aware that comatose patients often retain their sense of hearing, put Jacqueline's recording of the Schumann Cello Concerto on the gramophone in her bedroom.

Schumann was a romantic and passionate dreamer; when he wrote his Cello Concerto, in a burst of feverish activity, he was already on the road to madness. By the time it was published, four years later, he was in an asylum, and there is no record of its having been performed in his lifetime.

Jacqueline loved her recording of the Schumann Concerto; her interpretation, dark and melancholic, expressed the inexpressible. The concerto's three linked movements are pure, distilled emotion: Zola called it "the voluptuousness of despair". The first movement is full of longing, the second tender and poetic. Near the end, there is a transition, and then the orchestra and cello begin together, softly nostalgic, as though Schumann could see his life receding. The ending is a powerful, bombastic, final farewell that makes us weep – and comforts us.

The music remains.

Index

Du Pré, Iris – *cont.*
  reluctant visits to J., 176–7, 205
  compared with Aida Barenboim,
    177
  dies of cancer, 212
Du Pré, Jacqueline Mary
  attitude to cello, 11, 26, 28, 39, 47,
    64, 75, 183, 208
  early symptoms of multiple
    sclerosis, 11, 77, 152, 159
  media myth, 12, 58–9
  relationship with parents, 12, 32, 34
  reaction of others to her illness,
    12–13, 16
  appearance, 13, 29, 32, 36, 49, 51,
    58, 61, 65, 66, 67, 76, 78–9, 84,
    93, 97, 109, 111, 112, 119, 120,
    125, 135, 137, 147, 161, 191
  as teacher, 13–14, 194–5, 199–200,
    202, 207–8
  and Judaism, 14, 15, 126, 127, 130,
    131, 206
  accepts OBE, 14, 188
  personality, 15, 16–17, 29, 31, 37,
    39, 43, 48, 49, 64, 75, 77–82, 97,
    102, 108, 109, 112, 123–4, 147,
    151, 154, 197, 198
  birth, 25
  early musical ability, 26
  first lessons, 27–8, 29
  schooling, 31, 36–8, 43–4, 46
  and Suggia Gift, 32, 34, 35–6
  relationship with Pleeth, 34, 44
  isolation, 38, 43, 65–6, 75, 103, 111,
    112, 152–3, 174, 180, 189, 205
  moves to London, 42
  musical memory, 44, 48
  Pleeth on, 44, 45, 46
  regrets at being "under-educated",
    47, 64
  friendship with Peter Thomas, 47–8
  at Zermatt, 50, 51–2
  on Casals, 52
  Wigmore Hall début, 52, 53–5
  wins Guildhall School's Gold Medal
    and Queen's Prize, 53
  acquires first Stradivarius, 53, 54, 58
  Festival Hall début, 56, 57–8
  love of concert process, 58
  adolescence, 59, 73
  coached by Lady Clwyd, 60

  first TV recital, 64
  first Promenade concert, 64–5
  at Dartington, 66–7, 82
  studies with Tortelier, 67, 68, 69
  first recording for EMI, 68
  Edinburgh Festival début, 68
  doubts about career, 69, 73–5
  taught mathematics by Debenham,
    74, 75
  shares flat with Alison Brown, 76–9
  and critics, 77
  Bishop accompanies, 84–7
  relationship with Bishop, 85, 99, 101
  records Elgar Concerto, 92
  first tour of USA (1965), 93–4
  love of chamber music, 95–6
  admirers, 97–8
  auditioned by Rostropovich, 99–100
  at Moscow Conservatory, 103–6
  infatuation with Rostropovich, 107
  glandular fever, 109–11, 112
  meets D.B., 112–13, 117
  tour of Eastern Europe, 118, 119
  tour of North America, 119–23
  engaged to D.B., 121, 125, 126, 127
  plays in Israel, 128–30, 139
  wedding, 131–3
  making of *Jacqueline*, 134–6
  hectic schedule, 140–41, 143
  first years of marriage, 144
  and Goehr's *Romanza*, 145–6
  midwestern début, 149
  at South Bank Summer Music
    Festival, 150
  tired during world tour, 151–2
  nature of marriage, 153–4
  and *The Trout*, 155
  records Beethoven with D.B., 155–6
  in Australia (1970), 157
  records Elgar again, 158, 159
  health breaking, 159–61
  cancels US and Israeli concerts, 162
  starts psychiatric treatment, 163
  last recordings, 164
  London "come-back", 164–5
  last public performance with D.B.,
    165
  last public performance, 166–7
  misinterpretation of her symptoms,
    171–2
  MS diagnosed, 172